M000306243

"I've had the privilege of reading Dr. Ortigara Crego's book, Release Your Obsession with Food; Heal from the Inside Out, and I was impressed with her findings and advice from word one. This profound piece of self-help guidance contains stories about people, their suffering and recovery, that I will never forget, and that I'm sure readers who are in trouble in their own lives will grab onto as they would a life preserver at sea. And, in fact, this is information that can save them from an endless round of misery--or worse. I'll be very happy to see people find this simple yet effective path to inner peace and health."
--G. Miki Hayden, author of The Naked Writer, a writing style guide

"Dr. Lisa Ortigara Crego enlightens us to become free from our obsessions with food and let go of diet mentality. Sharing her own journey from food addiction to spiritual recovery, she teaches us how to heal from the inside out, with practical advice, encouragement, and understanding.
Once I understood the physiological connection between certain trigger foods and food addiction, everything else made sense. Making a lifestyle choice and choosing real, not processed foods, is key to achieving the goal. With a focus on three fundamentals of healing, spiritual, emotional, and physical, this is not just another diet book."
--Margie Miklas, author of Critical Cover-up

"This lovely and gentle book is extremely powerful. Dr. Lisa shares her own journey, and her intelligence, wisdom, and spirituality shine throughout the book. She guides the food-addicted person to look at painful past issues, to become physically healthier, and to find his or her spiritual link, whatever that means for each individual. A hopeful, kind and simply wonderful book. Her kindness, brightness, and love almost jump off the page."
--Dr. Aleta Edwards, Psy.D., Author of Fear of the Abyss: Healing the Wounds of Shame and Perfectionism

Release Your Obsession with Food

Heal from the Inside Out

Dr. Lisa M. Ortigara Crego

Release Your Obsession with Food: Heal from the Inside Out
Copyright © 2017 Dr. Lisa Ortigara Crego
ISBN: 978-0-9993025-0-7
Library of Congress Control Number: 2017913477

All rights reserved. No part of this book may be reproduced, stored in a retrieval system, or transmitted in any form or by any means without the prior written permission of the publishers, except by a reviewer who may quote brief passages in a review printed in a newspaper, magazine, or journal.

The author of this book does not dispense medical advice or prescribe the use of any technique as a form of treatment for physical, emotional, or medical problems without the advice of a physician, either directly or indirectly. The intent of the author is only to offer information of a general nature to help you in your quest for emotional, spiritual, and physical well-being. In the event you use any of the information in this book for yourself, which is your constitutional right, the author and the publisher assume no responsibility for your actions.

Madeira Publishing
Hollywood, Florida
Madeirapublishing.com

Dedication

This work is dedicated to all who suffer from the disease of food addiction, those in spiritual recovery, and my patients who always believed and believe in my work. May all who are in a spiritual recovery from food addiction continue to light the flame for those who remain in the dark.

Introduction

Often, we can achieve an even better result
When we stumble yet are willing to start over,
When we don't give up after a mistake,
When something doesn't come easily but we throw ourselves into trying,
When we're not afraid to appear less than perfectly polished.
~Sharon Salzberg~

Release Your Obsession with Food: Heal from the Inside Out is a book for anyone trying to end the vicious cycle of compulsive eating. It is not a primer for quick weight loss, a fad diet of the month, or an attempt to sell another weight-loss book. Instead, I have tried to present a rich and provocative understanding of chemical imbalance, psychology, and spirituality—a bio-psycho-spiritual point of view—as it relates to compulsive eating. Along with an attempt to show how I have come to see the situation, I also endeavor to help readers meet this difficult challenge through practical, structured, step-by-step, synthesized information and advice, including anecdotes designed to demonstrate how individuals may obtain relief and resolution of never-ending issues with food.

This book is the end product of my lifelong journey of self-discovery, research, contemplation, and application of a means of ending compulsive eating—to help free you from the obsession with food. My goal is to share my journey from active food addiction to spiritual recovery—and lead you away from compulsive eating.

As I've explored and researched to bring this book into being, perhaps the most surprising revelation for me has been how starved we are for information as to why we can't seem to stop eating out of control. Diet books explaining *what* to eat line the shelves of book stores and fill pages at Amazon, but few explain *why* we binge eat. I recognize that to look toward chemical imbalances and spiritual depletion may be to tread dangerously on long-held sacred myths, but ignoring this nugget of enlightenment would do readers a disservice, as these factors absolutely do connect to the *why* of the *what* we eat.

Combining an understanding of spiritual awakening with knowledge of the chemical imbalance that foods may give rise to can unlock the hidden treasures of actual change and *release you from the obsession with food* so you can *heal from the inside out.*

I'd like to think that everyone has a personal take on his or her own *Divine Source*, whether from Judaism, for instance, or through Buddhism, Sikhism, Christianity, or whatever, perhaps combined with that or another particular spiritual training. Regardless of *your* Source, you can tap into your own heart and soul using the approach that fits your belief system best, to find an authentic foundation and open the door to a much deeper, more soulful experience of life. Spirit doesn't lead to a particular communion but rather all real communions are born of spirit.

The end result I've tried to produce in *Release Your Obsession with Food: Heal from the Inside Out* is a mix of a spiritual slant on the food addiction dilemma, together with practical, down-to-earth advice. I want to help readers learn how to live more fully day to day in order to break free from compulsive eating (or any addiction for that matter).

Release Your Obsession with Food: Heal from the Inside Out is the *elixir vitae* for food addiction—an alchemic preparation capable of prolonging life on an emotional, physical, and spiritual level. I have set this book up to take you through a series of explorations, just as I would if you came to me as a private patient, sharing positive and negative experiences from others who walked this path prior to, during, and post recovery. If you will examine your personal inventory as questions appear in the book following each chapter, by the time you've finished, you will have begun to change your life.

My immediate goal is to help compulsive eaters get under control in 21 days or less, thanks to:

- The book's groundbreaking identification of 13 patterns condensed into 6 themes
- Personal Inventory Questions designed to unleash any food addict's unique natural/spiritual path to recovery
- A step-by-step, customizable "Outpatient Plan."

My suggestion is that you first read through the book once to orient yourself to this approach. Then slowly read the book again; only this time work through the questions following the end of each chapter.

As you read, you'll also note that each chapter opens with an inspirational quote from spiritual leaders, authors, or the Bible. Don't skip these as they are nuggets designed to get you thinking at a deeper level.

To help the reader best use *Release Your Obsession with Food,* the book is organized into three basic parts.

The first section (*The Whirlwind*) explores the life of a food junkie prior to the awakening to a healing path—followed by a passionate and clear explanation of and glimpse into spiritual recovery. A partial solution to compulsive eating is revealed as the initial awareness of the reality of food addiction is uncovered. Then, the goal is to analyze the effect and impact of active binge eating while unmasking the end result of spiritual depletion blocked by active bingeing.

The second section (*Realignment*) takes the reader from the whirlwind of out-of-control eating and encourages journal writing, meditation, and prayer as a foundational part of daily healing. This section also introduces self-hypnosis as it connects to an individual's spiritual alignment, while exploring the impact of the ever-presence of a higher consciousness. Realignment takes hold as phenomena, miracles, and medical healings are unveiled—relying on enlightenment—light delivered—from a Higher Source.

And finally, the third section (***Turn the Corner***) teaches readers how to embrace and combine the spiritual connection with a higher-level energy, the power of positive thinking, and a healthy relationship with food by establishing a constant communication with the Source while learning how food fits into spiritual recovery. And last, this section explores some final, additional thoughts and commonly asked questions.

The Dissertation

Often I'm asked how this book ever came into being, and of course many reasons pop into my head long before my pencil ever hit the paper. The passing of my mother ignited my burning desire to help anyone who would listen, and soon after her funeral, I started the process of earning a PhD in addiction psychology. I knew, without a shadow of a doubt, I wanted to address compulsive eating and spiritual recovery as my dissertation topic.

So I began a doctoral inquiry into the spiritual journey of food addiction healing as experienced by eight individuals working a Twelve Step program, who had achieved long-term abstinence.

Once I published my dissertation and graduated with my doctorate degree, I began revising my dissertation—and it morphed into *Release Your Obsession with Food: Heal from the Inside Out*. I thought adding patient experiences to those of the original eight participants would then enhance and drive home points I'd made in the first form of my thesis and contribute a far richer texture.

The patients and people discussed in *Release Your Obsession with Food...* range from individuals in their mid-teens to someone more than 70 years of age. All those mentioned in the book have been associated with; either Twelve Step groups, psychotherapy, or both. In accordance with Twelve Step protocol and patient confidentiality, names have been changed and at times genders switched to keep each person anonymous, while the name of the exact group has been omitted. In addition, establishments, towns and storylines has been changed and/or embellished to prevent identification.

Although a great amount of weight was lost by most individuals discussed in this book as a result of "clean eating"—and many were at one point extremely overweight—some of the people I mention never had any weight issue at all. In either case, all binge-ate to their detriment in some area of health and/or life. And regardless of whether overweight or not, each experienced a subsequent shift from lethargy and fuzzy thinking to clear thinking, energy, and improved moods when they changed *what* they ate.

For participants in the study I describe, and I included myself as a secondary research subject, physical recovery from food addiction began immediately as a result of our changing the types of food we took in. Afterward, those of us who were overweight or underweight returned in relatively short order to normal weights for our body sizes and bone structures. In time, after abstaining from trigger foods (processed foods such as sugar, flour, and wheat), our recoveries took precedence over the focus on our bodies and weight, and instead our attentions turned toward prayer, meditation, and working a Twelve Step program and/or therapy of some sort.

In time, we all reached a spiritual place of peace and serenity, not at every moment of our lives, certainly, but for a preponderance of our waking hours. Those emotional imbalances that did arise would dissipate reasonably quickly, as for those normally mentally and emotionally robust.

The initial purpose of my study was to explore the internal spiritual experience of food addicts actively implementing a Twelve Step program. As time wore on, I realized that the tones and shadings from actual patients' experiences I'd learned in over 20 years of private practice added a dimension that reinforced and complemented the data I'd gained from the original study. My mission was to have a better understanding of food addiction and to identify the essential themes and meanings of the participants' tribulations, hoping for the advancement of treatment and prevention.

My investigation aimed to uncover some of the ways food addiction impacts the spiritual, emotional, and physical realities shared by me, and others, as explored through our reflection, examination, sifting through, and clarification of the phenomena.

I think of recovery as it relates to a three-legged stool. Each leg represents one of the fundamentals of healing: spiritual, emotional, and physical. An individual who ignores a single leg of this foundation is at risk of weakening the support of the whole healing process.

Our stories of food addiction shared in this book are just the tip of an iceberg of stories that need to be told, souls who need to be healed, and bodies that must be restored to optimal health as our Divine Source intended. As a result of my compulsive eating, it was inevitable I'd be at risk of severe obesity, which put me at a greater risk of obesity-related problems such as heart disease, diabetes, liver disease, and even possible colon cancer—with the enormous amounts of foods passing through my digestive tract, not intended to process foods at such a drastic rate. As I neared 235 pounds on my five-foot, six-inch frame, I knew I was in deep trouble in every respect.

My quest led to an understanding about human existence and behavior. I had a personal opportunity to explain the lived process of spiritual recovery and added the most insight possible into comprehending phenomena related to the disease of food addiction.

Of course, this is only a brief synopsis of the actual dissertation; a full discussion but not the actual dissertation can be found at the end of the book as a sidebar for those of you who are curious.

My Story

Ruth Stark Blodgett Risetter was blessed with stunning beauty that well matched her muscular, toned physique from years of swimming professionally. She had the world by the tail. Ruth came from a well-to-do family of newspaper entrepreneurs and rubbed elbows with the town's elite. Ruth's grandfather, Charles G. Starks, pioneer newspaper editor and founder in 1870 of *The Berlin Journal*, which came to be known as the "biggest little daily in the United States," was loved by all, not only for his business sense but for his unshakable faith. He allied with Christian Science in 1903 and resisted catering to public opinion, whether regarding news or personal actions or his belief system—all of which were intertwined. He was known around town as a "force for civic good and community."

Ruth, unlike her self-made grandfather who barely scraped past fifth grade, was well educated at the University of Wisconsin in the late 1920s, a time during which women rarely attended college. She was beautiful, wealthy, and smart, and in love. She married Arnold Blodgett, her prince—a love short lived. Arnold, at 40, died of a massive heart attack, leaving behind his young wife and two teenage daughters.

Although Ruth appeared to have it all, she had a dark side to her life, which became visible after the loss of her husband. Her relationship with food and at times alcohol was Ruth's downfall. Unlike those in her family heritage, Ruth was estranged from any spiritual underpinning. She wasn't a particularly kind woman, and her nasty, angry side magnified as she began to gain weight uncontrollably. When Ruth was in her forties, her body proceeded to show the physical effects of carrying massive amounts of weight. With aching joints and a wobbly gait, and often favoring one knee or the other, she was easily out of breath climbing up a flight of stairs.

Ruth dieted constantly, only to regain her weight as she prepared for the next diet. From her late thirties to her early eighties, she maintained her miserable personality and went up and down with her weight—both brought on by a chemical imbalance—her nemesis. It was when Ruth moved into a nursing home run by the White Habit nuns, who served only natural foods, love, and spiritual nourishment; she morphed into the sweetest, loveliest woman until the age of eighty-six, when she passed away.

It wasn't her fault…

Ruth was my grandmother. She didn't particularly like me nor I her until her later years when I began to understand why she was an angry, bitter woman. The real tragedy is that if she had known what I know now, she (and my mother who showed a similar pattern of food abuse) could have been saved years of pain, out-of-control rage, and a lifetime of obesity. Early on in my childhood, I saw the glint in her pale-blue, watery eyes, a slight mischievous grin every time she talked about sweets and alcohol—a crazed-lust look—vicious and giddy rolled into one. She frightened me.

What I saw in Ruth, I saw in myself—a disconnect—unlike the personality of my great, great-grandfather Charles, who was always chatting and interested in anyone and everyone. He radiated true kindness. Love. He didn't seem to have the chemical imbalance my grandmother and I had. Unlike Charles, we were chemically, emotionally, and spiritually bankrupt. Perhaps you are too.

My mom and grandma Ruth were not so fortunate as to find relief, and both died never to know the freedom of spiritual recovery or that their defeat in the battle to lose weight wasn't their fault.

My story compares two adjacent worlds: food addiction and spiritual recovery. My hope is that this book helps you to recognize, deal with, and resolve compulsive eating—and transition to living in a more spiritually oriented realm. If my journey lifts you from the pure hell of obsessive eating, I will, indeed, have accomplished my goal. I write for my mom, I write for Ruth, and I write for you.

By 22 years of age, my mother (Ruth's daughter) had given birth to six children. When Mom was 17, my sister Christy was born, followed by the twins Michael and Michelle eight months later; one year after that, she had another set of twins, Daniel and Debborah; and 19 months later (with a miscarriage in between), I was born.

It was told several of us were Southern Comfort Liqueur babies…

My mother was knee deep in diapers for what must have seemed like an eternity while she was only a kid. I learned early on to comfort myself with a bottle and food.

Although I was a scrawny child who was on iron drops for anemia, my dysfunctional eating behaviors were already developed. I remember climbing up on the kitchen counter to retrieve chocolate syrup and pouring it down my throat until I felt the sense of "ahhhhhhhhhhh" that food addicts are so familiar with. I was barely five. I hid in the dark hall closet and stole change from my parents' coat pockets to buy stashes of candy.

Once, I was so desperate I stole my father's pouch of parking lot change from the third drawer of the china cabinet—hundreds of dollars—and took it to Pennies to buy candy. I was seven and the bag was awkward and heavy to carry. I dropped the bag, coins flew all over, and the storeowner turned me in to my parents. It was the first and only time my dad ever spanked me.

In third grade, I gave up candy for Lent only to sneak sweets during my 40 days and 40 nights of abstinence—certain God would punish me.

By the age of 10, I was adept at stealing money to purchase sugary foods, filled with guilt. Sneak-eating caught up to me as I turned 13 and my hormones raged out of control. My body began to grow, and I found myself a full-breasted woman with a little kid tucked inside of her. My diet days began.

My craziest diet at 17 was nothing but Ritz crackers and cream cheese, hot tea with skim milk, and Sweet 'N Low. I dropped 50 pounds in six weeks—and began to lose my hair in patches, along with my short-term memory. My face took on the texture and color of a pasty, soggy cracker while my eyes sunk inward—framed by dark circles. My moods vacillated from deliriously happy to utterly miserable. When I broke down from food deprivation and resumed eating, the pounds returned—*and then some.*

I went on to diet pills and any wacky diet I could find. In this way, I gained and lost 50 to 100 pounds at a time for years—losing weight temporarily and regaining more than was lost. Each diet failure left me a little more bruised mentally and emotionally: and larger physically. I felt worthless and fat.

Fortunately, in my late teenage years I found my way to Weight Watchers and began to lose weight and build confidence, and my mood swings were less volatile. The original Weight Watchers' program back in the mid-1970s, under the guidance of Jean Nidetch, the founder of the organization, followed a "natural" food program adopted from the hospital diabetic diet. *I instantly felt relief.* Little did I know back then that I was sensitive to "processed" foods, which led to binge eating.

I reached my "healthy" goal weight for the first time at the age of 19, and I stayed there and basked in my glory for a whole five minutes, only to gain most of the pounds back again when I reintroduced sugary foods as I entered into the maintenance program. I went on to reach my goal weight three more times, and in my thirties, I finally was able to maintain a 100-pound loss for 10 years by following each new and improved Weight Watchers' diet—armed with willpower and a clenched jaw.

With my false sense of success, I went to work for Weight Watchers, thinking I had finally found my solution. But once the novelty of shedding weight had lost its punch, periodic binges, mood swings, terrible fatigue, low self-worth and low-grade depression again resurfaced. Through diet and exercise, I managed to keep my weight down but not without a terrific battle with binge eating and a string of typical food-addict head games. I ate according to Weight Watchers' food plan (which after the 1970s Diabetic Hospital Plan introduced boxed desserts and pasta delights!) for several weeks then binged on large amounts of sweets and starches over short periods of time while telling myself I deserved to eat—promising to begin my diet the following day.

Out-of-control eating gradually allowed my weight to creep back on, a pound here and a pound there. Before I knew it, 35 pounds had found their way back, and none of my old promises worked. I was petrified that I was headed for a return to daily binges and on my way up to 235 pounds. Even worse, I was in graduate school studying to become a clinical psychotherapist with a focus on eating disorders and mental illness. I was the expert, yet I drowned myself in food. I sought education and information and used a blind trial-and-error approach, while I strove to find answers with individuals who had the same issues I had.

Eventually, I became conscious of a change in my behavior and moods with certain foods, as well as constant fatigue with specific foods. Some foods were so powerful they compelled me to eat enormous amounts, leaving me high, while others simply knocked me out. In either case, I lacked control. These foods induced anger, anxiety, and low self-esteem. This was a tremendous breakthrough. My predicament wasn't my fault. I wasn't weak. I had a definite reaction to certain foods.

Still working for Weight Watchers while studying for my Master's degree in mental health, I noticed I wasn't the only one going up and down the roller coaster of how I ate—so were many of the Weight Watchers' members as well as the staff. I knew they were trying to "diet" the weight off, and like me, were running through the revolving door of Weight Watchers to find the answer to their weight-loss impasse. I knew intuitively the answer wasn't just in following the plan, because as wonderful as the program was (and still is); it wasn't equipped with an educated, licensed psychotherapist. A psychotherapist could have walked the members through the *why* you're eating as well as *what* you're eating, though most wouldn't understand the situation if the member had a food sensitivity.

I knew I had to do something about this terrible problem for both myself and for others, so with great trepidation, I left the fold that had initially showed me the way. I was scared! It was like leaving the mother's womb as I stumbled off into the dark alone. I took along with me little guidance except knowing that certain foods were causing me to react with extreme highs and lows, and that my spirituality, which I had been brought up to respect, was squashed because I couldn't see past the next binge.

With awareness, I developed a list of the foods that profoundly increased my cravings, mood swings, and a serious case of fatigue. After I'd worked with hundreds of patients and weight-loss participants and attended a regular Twelve Step meeting to fill my spiritual deficit, I found unambiguous answers and knew I was on the right path at last. I learned, too, that I wasn't alone.

I isolated three specific ingredients that gave me the most egregious side effects: sugar, flour, and wheat. I found when I ate a balanced breakfast, lunch, dinner, and snack, and avoided sugar, flour, and wheat, while at the same time I moved toward my Spiritual Source, my moods stabilized, my weight dropped, and I stopped bingeing. My cravings disappeared, my energy soared, and my depression lifted.

My weight and my relationship with food were a constant struggle for me until I began to understand my chemical reaction to certain foods. After years of trial and error, research, clinical knowledge, weight loss, and stability of weight, I became calm. These days, I follow a simple formula, breaking down each meal with structure and commitment rather than eating randomly. I also include daily exercise such as walking or biking along the ocean and try and live my life as a prayer.

No, I am certainly not perfect (and realize I sound as if this is so easy), and my life isn't always bliss. I would love to eat any food I want, but I understand the consequences aren't worth the indulgence. I do get angry when I'm tired and work too many hours, or when I have to turn down an invitation to an event because the atmosphere won't be conducive to my food needs and bringing my own foods is inappropriate, or when everyone will be eating a delectable piece of chocolate cake and I'll be stuck eating a piece of fruit with yogurt. But no matter what life struggles present themselves, I know that binge eating simply is no longer an option for me. Nor are sugars, flour, or wheat on my food list, because I understand that the sleeping giant within (addiction) will wake, and chaos will return with a vengeance if I ingest any of these. I compare my situation to that of a heroin addict who can't have just a smidgeon of heroin; he must abstain completely to stay clean.

When I began to follow these specific guidelines—even when I didn't want to—my negative mind chatter quieted, and for the first time in many years, I could become still and hear the infinite spirit's whispers. I connected to my inner strengths, and a pure understanding emerged in me. I found inner peace, transcendence, and love. Love for myself, others, and the universe evolved inside me.

Not only was I calmer, kinder, and less self-centered, but I began to see a bigger picture. I saw food as real and not real: nature's food and man's food. I chose food of the earth, sea, and air rather than processed and boxed. I turned to my Mystical Source so that the "noise" in my head ceased, and the addiction flattened. These days, I eat to live rather than live to eat. Healthful foods and a refreshed belief are now my fuel to optimal health and weight.

Table of Contents

Part I

The Whirlwind

Chapter 1

A Food Junkie

*Do not spoil what you have
by desiring what you have not;
But remember that what you now have
was once among the things only hoped for.*
~Epicurus

WHEN LIFE IS CHALLENGING, IS YOUR FIRST
INCLINATION TO EAT?

Have you ever wondered why you start every Monday
with a promise to yourself to eat healthfully, only to end up
making several rounds of fast-food and grocery-store stops—
the displays beckoning you to indulge in succulent sweets and
crunchy or salty delights—and with you devouring the entire
container almost trance-like? Do you feel you're doing
everything right, but your weight keeps increasing, and your
night-before promise to yourself to start clean eating
disappears by the end of the following day?

Do you find yourself eating when you're not hungry at
all? Does the mere picture of a succulent chocolate cake

cause you to obsess over the urgency to get a piece—or perhaps eat the entire cake? Do you experience a drug-like stupor after eating certain foods? Do you feel high at the thought of eating chocolate, followed by a deep depression soon after its consumption?

Is food your lover?

Is food your worst nightmare?

Do you panic at the thought of not eating cookies, candy, and bread?

If the answer to any of these questions is yes, then you may be a food addict.

Food addiction is real. *It's not your fault.*

You may feel you have no way out of this hell you're experiencing day in and day out but you do. There is hope and there is help. ...*Do not spoil what you have by desiring what you have not...*

His legs were like tree trunks—necrotic, and oozing sap-like dribbles one drip at a time as crusts formed that often became infected, leaving a foul odor. Doctors speculated the symptoms were caused by an interruption of the blood supply to his legs.

His massive weight enveloped him and buried the little boy within. A simple, natural body function like urinating became impossible without help because his penis was plunged deep in the thick folds of his excess flesh.

Imprisoned in his body, incarcerated in his room (bars covered his windows permitting no food to enter or exit), Jonathan continued to gain weight, nearing a thousand pounds when he conned delivery persons and siblings into bringing meals. His addiction led to his sneaking food even if he had to steal, lie, bribe, or coerce someone into helping him do it. The impossible became possible. Jonathan, who once had thick black hair, eyes that sparkled like green emeralds, a magical smile that lit the room, now harbored shame in his gray-slatted eyes, eyes washed of all color. The lights were out inside. No warmth, no hope—only helplessness and fear.

The insanity of thinking just one more bite wouldn't turn into a million is one of the luring deceptions of this chronic, progressive, and fatal disease.

He slept in a chair, fearing asphyxiation as food reached to the brim of his throat. He wore weight as a banner of his truth, and in time that weight strangled his heart. The food was never enough, yet always too much. He took his last breath at 25 years old. Free at last—in the hands of his Maker.

Yes, Jonathan's story is bleak and sad but this doesn't have to be your story. Take petite Sarah, for instance, a high-strung high-achiever who binged and purged through intense, excessive exercise for years, all while attending medical school and working through residency. Today, she runs a medical practice and raises three active pre-school-aged children with her high school sweetheart, managing to maintain a healthy weight, free of cravings, bingeing, and destructive thinking and behavior.

Then there's Marcie, a lean, active drop-dead gorgeous girl, who runs a mega-million-dollar company and is married to the love of her life while bringing up four tweens just about to launch into high school. Life wasn't always so great when Marcie drank alcohol in excess, stumbling to bed night after night and carrying an extra 40 pounds. Marcie was spiritually depleted, swinging from volume eating when not drinking, to using Valium to relax and cocaine to fire up. Today, Marcie is drug, alcohol, and binge-eating free. Yes, another success story.

And I can't forget Sinclair, who once weighed more than 500 pounds, and who devoured anything and everything, if it was edible—paying zero attention to the egregious consequences his actions took on his body. Sinclair was totally at the mercy of food and had no higher source to turn to. Today, he weighs 185 and is spiritually centered and financially free of all debt, living his best life.

You can be a success story, too, by learning from Jonathan and everyone featured in this book—happy stories and not so happy stories—all lessons, for sure. The seven original participants in the dissertation and I turned this darkness around; nearly anyone can do the same, through the way, the truth, and the light...

This book is designed for all those trying to end the cycle of compulsive eating. In this and the following chapters, you'll learn how to obtain relief and resolution of lifelong issues with food and body image. I will lead you to do this through understanding, and through creating new experiences with eating as you step off the food junkie plank onto spiritual consciousness, moving past compulsive eating. You will soon start to realize, first of all, that healing begins with the awareness of food-addiction-blocked spirituality caused by active bingeing.

An increased connection to your Source of being and other people can release your continuing obsession with food. When you isolate yourself, suffering in the trenches of your food addiction as evidenced by the stains on your shirt and crumbs that hang from your lips, you are detached— alone. You need something or someone to believe in and hold onto in hope of change, or you'll merely exist and jump from one diet to another, one binge to another, weight up and weight down. This is no way to live.

As a child, I felt as though God had abandoned me. I struggled with food and weight every day. What was wrong with me that I was forgotten? Why did others eat what they wanted and remain thin? How could they stop at one cookie when I needed the whole box? Where was *my* Source of being? I felt worthless—God probably didn't want me because I was a disappointment to Him.

Losing Control

I used to binge daily on cakes, cookies, ice cream, and baked potato chips. But soon after taking my first bite of a "sugary/salty treat," I fluctuated between a hair-raising, euphoric "sugar high" and a dark, negative wretchedness. To make matters worse, I swelled to 100 pounds over my ideal weight. From the sugar, I experienced depression, anxiety, and irritability, only to return to such sweets to fend off my melancholy, tranquilize my sense of being ill at ease, and lessen my agony—my intense physical and mental suffering. I experienced a violent struggle between outbursts of excitement and despair. A vicious cycle indeed! I didn't realize these quickly metabolized carbohydrates briefly made me feel wonderful but then took me from that deceptive, blissful high to a tumultuous low.

Hi, my name is Lisa—I'm a food junkie.

A food junkie thinks about food every waking moment: She is an addict. I was physiologically dependent on simple carbohydrates such as chocolate, pretzels, and cake. I developed a physical dependence from chronic use of all these foods, which produced in me a high tolerance to them. The chemical dependence was related to changes in my brain chemistry. Those changes involved the "pleasure circuit," where certain neurotransmitters and receptors created pleasurable feelings after being stimulated by simple carbohydrates because of my sensitivity to these substances.

With an abrupt deprivation of cookies and breads, I experienced withdrawal symptoms, including severe headaches and body aches. I broke out in a cold sweat and was irritable and fatigued. I found comfort in nothing except returning to sweets and starches.

I first developed a chemical dependence after consuming simple carbohydrates in large quantities every day for months, to the point of being well beyond full. The negative symptoms of withdrawal were the result of abrupt discontinuation or cutting back on the amounts I consumed.

The higher the dose of sugar and starches typically the worse the physical dependence, and thus—the worse the withdrawal symptoms. Withdrawal symptoms can last days, weeks, or months, or on occasion even longer, and will vary from individual to individual.

My dependence began in early childhood, though I wasn't aware of it. Initially, I needed a single doughnut to feel calm, and then the number I needed progressed to two, three, and four—and before I realized, the baker's dozen wasn't cutting it.

My first job at age 13 was at the local bakery in town. Getting that job, I thought I'd won the lotto. When the baker left, I began building the most incredible doughnuts and filled them with white cream beyond their capacity—so that they weighed triple the normal amount. I proceeded to eat and eat until my shift was over and my belly bulged. My starting weight there was 115, and it ended three years later near 200 pounds. I marvel that Mr. Newman, the bakery owner, never commented on my weight gain or understood that I was eating into his profits, or that I was out of control with food.

For many years I thought I was the only one who lost control with food. But I'm not. The world is heavily sprinkled with people who regularly lose control over food. These people take on diets, weight-loss programs, pills, and purging as a way of life in the hope of gaining power over their lack of control—or they eat themselves to death like Jonathan. I see this, every day when I go to work. I see it in the Twelve Step rooms. I see it when I walk in the malls and grocery stores.

Many who are overweight engage in pointless and endless struggles to achieve a certain weight, only to find that the excess weight resurfaces when normal eating resumes. Most then try to resolve their food issues through an ongoing "diet" mentality rather than coming to understand what caused the problem in the first place. In many cases, the origin of added pounds lies in sensitivity to particular foods—more specifically, a chemical imbalance.

I, too, once resolved my weight and food issues through countless commercial diets, fad diets, and diets I created myself, none of which worked. A diet approach to weight loss is something like trying to lasso a bucking bull with a thin thread of string—eventually, the thread will snap. At 16 years old, out of my desperation to be thin, I drove to the town doctor across the street from Wautoma High School to purchase diet pills—a blast of amphetamines—without parental supervision. The dark blue pills jazzed up my energy to the point of my cleaning the house like an overwrought maniac, speed-talking like an auctioneer, and having my thoughts race in five different directions.

Without an appetite, I stopped eating and for months lived on hot tea with skim milk and artificial sweetener. My moods, once again, swung from depression to elation, to rage, while my face sprouted acne, and my eyes darted about in extreme paranoia. Although miserable from lack of sleep and the jitters, I was proud my frayed blue jeans scraped the floor as they fell off my newly found hips after the rapid weight loss. Of course, this was another one-minute success story that turned into failure. When I started eating again, the pounds returned—and the diet cycle continued.

Research indicates more than half of Americans are overweight and at least a quarter near obesity. Weight-loss products and services cost consumers over 50 billion dollars annually and the numbers are climbing. More than 325,000 annual deaths are attributable to obesity-related causes.

My mother and grandmother were included in these statistics; their lives were shortened through a series of strokes and finally pneumonia as a consequence of their obesity.

Although more than a quarter-of-a-million yearly deaths as a result of extreme overweight is startling, and that I lost precious time with my mom when she died at 67 years old is sad, neither of these facts was behind my joining the millions who hop on and off the diet merry-go-round to lose and gain weight.

The simple truth was that I had a fat phobia. I didn't want to lug around extra weight and have clothes that didn't fit me. I didn't think about how I overworked my digestive system with enormous amounts of foods eaten in a short period of time or that my heart was taxed, or that I could develop diabetes, or that my bones were being crushed with so much extra weight, not to mention my sore, swollen feet.

I wanted to be skinny, and I tried every way imaginable to accomplish this goal—with no long-term success. It was when I began to *heal from the inside out*, turning to a Source greater than me, I was able to let go of simple carbohydrates, and I began to melt down to a "normal" size. ...*but remember that what you now have was once among the things only hoped for...*

This isn't to say losing the weight, stepping off the food junkie plank onto spiritual consciousness, was an easy task without three steps forward and two back. But weight loss through dependence on my Source was a process I leaned into, and in time the miracles began to unfold. Moreover, this isn't a recommendation offered to change your opinion of *your* Divine Source relationship, but rather that you see yourself as so strongly connected to *your* Source of Being that you know and trust you're a piece of it.

Be aware that normal weight can be misconstrued to mean being skinny, which is definitely not the intent of this book. I want you to learn about how an increased connection to a Higher Source and other people, and abstaining from certain foods, can release the obsession with food. I intend to explain how to get off the merry-go-round and stop the insanity to reach a weight impossible to obtain by compulsive dieting.

The idea of normal weight isn't to be identified with Americans' fixation on reaching a size zero, *which is no number at all*. Talk about insanity! I use the words "ideal weight" in the context of weight ranges according to a chart provided by the Metropolitan Life Insurance Company, which pioneered the widely used weight-by-height tables.

I began nearly 100 pounds over my *normal* weight. While obesity was a key issue for me and for most food addicts, it isn't uncommon to meet individuals who are underweight and normal weight, who also binge eat. Some people featured in this book began their journey underweight, some were normal weight, and some happened to be overweight, as I was. The heartfelt experiences shared in this book are those of individuals who all have chemical imbalance and sensitivity to certain foods.

My goal in writing this was to explore the lives of ordinary people who compulsive ate and who found solutions through adopting a physical, emotional, and spiritual recovery from addictive foods—not to set forth how or why people lose weight. In my experience, turning to our spiritual foundation, as well as developing self-awareness, form the optimal basis of a successful weight-loss plan that leads to truly long-lasting results.

Food addiction is defined as an uncontrollable urge for excess food, particularly refined carbohydrates such as sugar and flour substances, which are quick to metabolize. The disease—for food addiction truly constitutes a disease—is biochemical in nature because the body of the food addict reacts differently to some foods than the bodies of other people. A common link between food addicts is sensitivity to sugars and certain carbohydrates. More specifically, the reaction of deep craving begins with just one chocolate bar, a slice of cake, a bowl of pasta, or similar carbohydrates: *all normal foods for most individuals.*

I recognize food addiction as an addiction that, when addressed through abstaining from specific foods, causes cravings to cease. Refraining from eating these foods then allows the person to live a "normal" life tapped into a higher wisdom connected to spiritual recovery.

After I struggled with my addiction for well over thirty years, I found if I let go of my trigger foods, the monster within quieted. I began my personal journey by adopting a manner of eating in order to get "sober" and avoid relapse. I learned quickly that if I plugged into the universal life force and omitted processed foods, the demon was tamed, and I was relieved of the disease—yet I remained keenly aware that the consumption of sugar would open the mouth to the devil and ignite the addictive phase.

Compulsion is defined as a strong, usually irresistible, impulse to perform an act, especially one that is irrational or contrary to a person's ordinary state—and that leads one to become a sort of Dr. Jekyll and Mr. Hyde, living a double life. When he or she eats the *strange potion*, otherwise known as simple carbohydrates, the food addict is transformed into a devilish creature who moves from being a rational person to behaving as a raging, obnoxious fool—a tainted soul. Food addiction involves engaging, despite adverse consequences—in a continuous and compulsive use of food in an endless and incessant pursuit of a mood change.

Compulsion is always present in the disease of addiction, whether the addiction is to cocaine, vodka, or chocolate bars. Researchers contend the food addict has a metabolic, biochemical imbalance that results in the characteristic symptoms of addiction. The foodaholic is obsessed with food, particularly sugary, high fat, and starchy foods, and consumes kinds or quantities of these foods to destructive physical, emotional, mental, and relational consequences.

I recall in the heat of my food addicted phase, as I sat in the big, fancy, hunter-green leather chair in my office, a patient in front of me told me her deepest fears, while all I thought about that session was the fast foods I would hunt for on my way home. And I was giddy with excitement. I knew for sure I'd hit Kentucky Fried Chicken for their barbeque chicken wings, potato slices, coleslaw, and two side orders of biscuits and butter, all washed down with a thick chocolate milkshake.

The addict has no way of knowing if or when the food frenzy will activate. To think I'm listening to a patient depending on me to help move her through her guilt, and I'm all the while thinking about my food fix on the way home. How horrific! Once this cycle is initiated, the food-disordered individual has no way to know if or when the urgency will strike—an addict is at the mercy of the disease. The pressure to eat cannot be controlled; once in motion it can't be held in check by force of will, a decision to indulge or not to indulge, to use or not use, to taste or not to taste—the disease makes the decision for the person afflicted.

With the addiction set in motion, I sat in the parking lot alone and inhaled the food, then found a trash can to get rid of the evidence, not mindful of the drips and dribbles left on my face and clothes.

Typically, then, I'd unload the garbage before heading to the grocery store for a re-stash of goodies I planned to hide in the bedroom closet for later on. Of course, I couldn't make it all the way home without ripping into the box of Little Debbie's chocolate rolls filled with white cream and tearing into a package of potato chips and shoveling them in my mouth—all while I shifted my car and drove through traffic. I never thought about the accident I could and would cause one day.

As soon as the episode was over, remorse set in. I sank. *I am worthless.*

An episode consisted of hours of nonstop eating that often led to days. I could be sucked into the dark hole with one simple thought of chocolate, just one piece melting on my tongue. I romanced the idea. I promised myself one bite only, but one piece turned to two—to a pound of chocolates, opening Pandora's Box, from creamy sweets to salty foods. I *needed* to get as much food in as possible because: I won't eat them again. *I promise.*

Afterward, the guilt set in since I couldn't just eat a bite or a few pieces. I ate until I could eat no more—until it hurt. Pain pierced my stomach, resembling the turn of a cold, sharp knife. I deserved the pain. I suffered a deep and agonizing regret for letting my eating run out of control. The pain removed the remorse, and penitence set in, which led to the promise I would never do this again. I regretted my wrongdoing and vowed to restore my disciplined food restriction; hence, a vicious sequence of diet and binge ensued.

I was 22. It was a slate-gray Chicago day in the thick of winter. On my daily commute to DePaul University from the suburbs, I stopped at McDonald's for biscuits, eggs, sausage, potatoes, an extra side dish of fried potatoes, and a few orders of pancakes with thick, sugary maple syrup and extra butter melted and drizzled over the sweet cakes. To add to this symphonious concoction, I had a special, humungous flat-bottom cup I filled to the brim with dark coffee laced with cream and *diet sugar*, which I balanced on the front dash.

That day, in my haste to shovel the food into my mouth, I was oblivious to any activity around me. I dug into the food, drove, shifted gears, and smoked a cigarette in the thick of traffic on the Stevenson Expressway in morning rush hour—numb. It was only when I reached for my hot coffee to wash down my food that I realized my cup was on the roof of my car! In a panic, I stretched my arm out into the cold air to feel around blindly for the cup, still eating, and then BANG—CRUNCH—KABOOM. I hit the car in front of me and the car behind hit me. In alarm, all I could think about was cramming the half-eaten food under my seat to hide the evidence, ashamed of what I'd done. In all this chaos, my cup of coffee hadn't budged from the roof of the car and was still piping hot—a special cup indeed.

It is evident that as a foodaholic, who binge ate, I was obsessed with food, particularly sugary, high-fat food, and could and did consume large quantities of these foods to physical, emotional, mental, and relational destructive consequences every single time. I never thought about who I might hurt, including myself. *I only I worried about how fat I'd get.*

For sugar-sensitive people, certain foods can be as enslaving as cocaine, alcohol, or any of the other substances that are addictive to some. A number of clinicians say alcoholism is an allergic addiction. Many, however, who suffer from food addiction aren't recognized and treated as addicts as well, although they share numerous patterns similar to those with (other) chemical dependencies. Yet scientists such as Haddock and Dill (2000) have concluded certain food can be considered psychoactive, supporting the validity of the food addiction model. Moreover, the food addiction model is widely accepted by a portion of the general public—because it works when other understandings fail.

Researchers have also found high rates of substance use and substance use disorders in patients with eating disorders. Repeated studies indicate some similarity between drug and alcohol abuse and food abuse. People who binge eat as well as those who abuse additional substances report cravings to consume certain foods. More importantly, binge eating is associated with other eating disorders that are often linked with addictive disorders. In fact, it was not uncommon for the binge eaters I talked with to participate in Alcoholics Anonymous and/or Narcotics Anonymous, while attending some type of food anonymous program.

In nearly every person I studied (patients and participants who were binge eaters), I found unexpectedly high rates of substance use and substance use disorders for the person and/or the individual's family of origin. I commonly heard about a father or a mother suffering from alcoholism and a sibling or several siblings suffering from food addiction and/or substance abuse of some kind. These multi-addicted binge eaters told me that food addiction held the black belt of all their addictions—was the hardest to kick.

Evidence from biology, psychology, and spirituality with reference to the possible psychoactive effects of eating suggests the addictive potential of a piece of chocolate cake, chocolate bar, or cookies and points to a significant effect of these foods on the mind and mental processes including mood and behavior. And let's not ignore the fact that chocolate, too, includes caffeine, which is itself a mood-altering substance and often needs to be abstained from along with sugar, flour, and wheat.

Evidence from neuroscience including positron emission tomography (PET), functional magnetic resonance imaging (fMRI) data, and clinical experience indicates important similarities between overeating highly palatable and hedonic foods and the cause-effect of the classic addictions.

Other commonalities between binge eating and drug use include mood effects, external cue-control of appetites, and reinforcement, such as reinforcement that comes from the triggering of pleasurable sensations. The sight of a chocolate cake cues the "I gotta have it NOW to feel better" thought.

We chronic binge eaters suffer from depression. We sit with the veil of darkness pulled over us and assume we are grumpy and irritable because of something we did wrong. We don't realize we have an addiction to certain foods that creates these very uncomfortable feelings as a rebound result of having indulged repeatedly in those foods we actually don't process well.

Food addicts have a severe and ongoing disturbance in how they handle food. The depiction of addiction to food resembles the hallmarks of any addiction. The food addict is caught in the grip of a compulsive, habitual behavior that *can't* be controlled. The binge eater begins eating when she didn't plan to and can't stop eating when she wants to.

Addiction is the persistent and repetitive enactment of a behavioral pattern the person recurrently fails to resist and that consequently leads to significant physical, psychological, social, legal, or other major life problems. Loss of control over eating and obesity produce changes in the brain similar to those produced by drugs of abuse. Food addiction shows up as a loss of control over eating, coupled with the physiological tolerance and psychological dependence that occurs when a particular food is ingested. Typically, this addiction can result in negative consequences for basic life functions as well as relationships with family and intimate relationships; in social situations; the sufferer's relationship with Higher Wisdom and his spiritual development; and/or in relation to the law, health, and work life.

Binge eaters and drug abusers commonly report an undeniable yearning to consume the substance *no matter what* the cost. Binge eating is a prominent feature of many eating disorders and shares many diagnostics with substance abuse. Binge eaters, similar to excessive drinkers, prefer privacy and isolation and an element of secrecy prior to and during a binge.

Considerable research evidence supports a genetic component to the development of eating disorders. As is seen in many other types of disturbances of normal functioning, eating disorders cluster in families. Twin studies consistently furnish evidence that eating disorders may be inherited. Recent research suggests that biological relatives of those with eating disorders run a five- to 12-fold times the normal risk of also developing an eating disorder.

It Is Not Your Fault!

Food addiction (and other addictions) and eating issues can be traced in my family as far back as my family-based knowledge is able to take me. My food addiction is not their fault. It is not my fault, either, nor is your food addiction *your* fault. You aren't uncontrollably consuming large quantities of foods in a short period of time because you have no willpower, but rather because you were born with a chemical imbalance and perhaps a blocked connection to that power that is higher than you.

It wasn't uncommon for my weight to go from 134 pounds to 234 pounds. I binged my way up to a high weight and dieted my way down to a considerably lower weight. I ate bags of chips, cartons of cookies, packages of Little Debbie's (my ultimate drug of choice), and tubs of ice cream until the food filled me up to my eyeballs. A monster took over my head and I could do nothing about it. I stole, lied, hid, and connived just to get my food—not to mention fogged out during psychotherapy sessions with a patient.

One time I even thought about leaving my sleeping baby in his crib *for just a few minutes* to run to the store and get my "fix." I thank God I had the sense not to, but I seriously entertained the thought! I have no doubt in my mind I behaved as an active addict. I didn't think about what a large amount of food might do to me physically, with the exception of a tremendous dread of getting fat. I was paralyzed with the fear of becoming really obese—*yet I could not control the periodic binges.*

Webster defines addiction as the state of being enslaved to a habit or practice or to something that is psychologically or physically habit-forming, as narcotics, to such an extent that its cessation causes severe trauma.

An individual who binge eats deals with an eating disorder. According to the American Psychiatric Association (2000), an episode of binge eating consists of the following characteristics:

(1) Eating in a discrete period of time, an amount of food that is larger than most people would consume in the same period of time under the same conditions and (2) A sense of lack of control over eating during the episode; it is a feeling that one cannot stop eating or control the amount of food that is eaten and (3) The episodes are associated with three (or more) of the following: eating more rapidly than normal, eating until feeling uncomfortably full, eating large amounts of food when not feeling physically hungry, eating alone, and feeling disgusted, depressed, or very guilty. (p.787)

Transition from food junkie to the spiritual side of food addiction is accomplished with an increased connection to a spiritual foundation and to people. Spiritual fortitude is what heals your body and your mind, *your release from the obsession with food* in order to *heal from the inside out.* Grab on to your Source of being that you know and trust—something or someone to believe in—and hold on, and transcend.

17

You can read an ample supply of diet books and stay on the roller coaster with a diet mentality, or you can explore a spiritual recovery from food addiction through abstinence from processed foods. Remaining abstinent, you can move forward, embracing the power of a higher essence that influences your everyday life. Functioning is optimal when we are in harmony with this spiritual life force.

Personal Inventory Questions

1. In what ways are your eating patterns similar to those shown in the chapter? When did you first notice you couldn't stop after just one cookie or potato chip, or whatever your addictive food was/is?

2. Would you say you isolated yourself from your Source of being and other people to continue your obsession with food? Did you feel that God abandoned you?

3. Do you fluctuate between hair-raising, euphoric "sugar highs" and a dark, negative wretchedness? Even more telling, does your weight swell to excessive pounds gained or sometimes spin to the side of significant weight loss?

4. Do you experience withdrawal symptoms—including severe headaches and body aches—or break out in a cold sweat and become irritable and fatigued—when you deprive yourself of sugar, flour, and/or wheat—only to find psychological and physical comfort when returning to sweets and starches?

5. Do you attempt to resolve your weight and food issues through countless commercial diets, fad diets, and diets you create yourself? Have you ever stopped eating altogether, thinking drastic restriction might be the answer?

6. Would you say you're a person who has wanted to be skinny to the point of physical harm or wanted to achieve a weight impossible to obtain even through restriction or compulsive dieting?

7. While at work or in class have you ever obsessed about the foods you would hunt down on your way home, and then become flush with excitement, stopping at store after store and drive-through after drive-through, driving and eating afterward only to discard the evidence in some dumpster or trash bin on your way home? Did you feel remorse as a result?

8. How close have you come to a car accident due to eating and driving? How many accidents actually occurred? Have you ever thought of leaving your sleeping baby in the middle of the night to get your fix?

9. Do you, yourself, have substance-use disorders in your medical history, or does anyone in your family of origin? How does this connect to your compulsive eating?

10. Do you fit the criteria listed in the American Psychiatric Association's Diagnostic and Statistical Manual of Mental Disorders (DSM-IV-TR: 4th ed.) itemizing the characteristics of binge eating?

Chapter 2

The Awakening

Awakening is not a thing.
It is not a goal, not a concept.
It is not something to be attained.
It is a metamorphosis.
If the caterpillar thinks about the butterfly it is to become,
Saying, 'And then I shall have wings and antennae,'
there will never be a butterfly.
The caterpillar must accept its own disappearance in its transformation.
When the marvelous butterfly takes wing, nothing of the caterpillar
remains.
~Alejandro Jodorowsky

No one really knows for sure how spirituality is related to health, but no doubt the body, mind, and spirit are connected. The wellbeing that arises in any one of these elements seems to affect the wholeness of the others.

Moving from food addiction to spiritual awakening is an individual process that goes through many continuous winding roads, leaving behind the old and creating the new. The awakening comes about by way of spiritual fortitude, a mental and emotional strength that guides you through addictive temptations, dispensing the courage to find your truth—and your truth is the spiritual path. Denial is the backbone of addiction.

"The body, full of faults, has yet one great quality: Whatever it encounters in this temporal life depends upon one's actions." Siddha Nagarjuna.

What actions does one take to reach an awakening—the transformation? Perhaps, no action is needed but rather a metamorphosis.

Research demonstrates positive beliefs, comfort and strength gained from a religion, spiritual connection, meditation, and prayer can contribute to healing and a sense of wellbeing. Improving your spiritual health may not "cure" food addiction, but it may help you feel better in many ways, lending strength in preventing binge eating and preventing some health problems such as diabetes and obesity, and/or help you cope with illness, stress, or premature death like my mother's.

What or who is your Source of Being that you can grab on to—that Life Force that you know and trust—that something or someone to believe in and hold on to, and transcend? Sit quietly and your source will appear to you in a way you can recognize. The manifestation may be a blend of your formal religious training combined with a spiritual awakening, or it may a simple spirituality, and not a mix or a choice of one or the other. As Froma Walsh, PhD, says in *Spiritual Resources in Family Therapy*, spirituality experienced outside formal religious structures can be both broader and more personal.

Should we explore a spiritual recovery from food addiction, and abstain from processed foods, and move toward the Enlightened Source that influences our everyday life? In heading in this direction, we can hope to find an optimal functioning when we're in harmony with this spiritual life force. Taking this route is about acceptance, *letting go in order to transcend*. Everyone is looking for peace; most of us just don't know how to get there.

Peace is our natural state, but we let life stressors get in our way, leading often to negative conditions in our body, or in this case, compulsive eating. All stress has an emotional charge connected to it, and this frazzled feeling comes from the external world, rocking our internal natural state of peace. This disruption of peace doesn't feel good, and change is imperative if we don't want to be dragged down into that dark place. *It's not your fault…*

As a clinical psychotherapist, I have a mission to help my patients find *their* peace on whatever path that's right for them. By the time they reach me, they're most often desperate after trying everything to quiet the addiction and not finding answers in the current treatments they're receiving. Perhaps this is your story too, which is why you picked up this book. My job isn't to find a religion or spiritual path that is right for you but to open the awareness that another way to sanity and health exists. The universe *wants* you to be healthy.

Our belief systems, the internal statements that I'm fat, I'm ugly, and I'm a failure, etcetera keep us sick. My goal is to help you *release your obsession with food* so that you can *heal from the inside out*—to remove the obstacles and to tap into attracting a better way. It's not about the weight, but it *is* about *what* you eat and more specifically *why* you eat certain foods. The answers are always within, but you don't have the access yet.

Resistance to change keeps us in the same insanity. Steven Pressfield in *The War of Art* notes that resistance is that negative force that arises when we're trying to go from our lower force to our higher force. The more important the activity is to you, the more fear and resistance you will experience. And of course the pain of not moving out of an addictive phase is worse than holding on to the addictive foods and the weight that often accompanies the bingeing. The dream of eating healthily naturally, not by clenched teeth, often is extinguished by doubt, fear, and blame. But the solution is to have a desire stronger than the illness. *It's not your fault…*

The challenge lies in finding the right fit for each person's understanding of this *awakening*, as not all of us relate in the same way. Kahlil Gibran in *The Prophet* writes, "No man can reveal to you aught but that which already lies half asleep in the dawning of your knowledge." In other words, there's an un-tapped nudge within just waiting for the push. As the old saying goes, you can lead the horse to water but you can't make it drink. Sit still—wait—and it will be revealed to you, all in God's time.

Trust in the Wisdom that created you.

And as Kahlil Gibran elaborates, "Say not, `I have found the truth,' but rather, `I have found a truth.' Say not, `I have found the path of the soul.' Say rather, `I have met the soul walking upon my path,' for the soul walks upon all paths."

Ask; are my actions congruent with my spiritual belief? The answer is truth. Your truth! If you don't like a particular person, or you rage in the line waiting at the concession stand, or you flip the bird to another driver in a fit of anger because he isn't driving fast enough, *stop*—reflect. It's about self-esteem, self-worth—what you don't like in that situation is what you don't like in YOU! Go to your truth—your inner knowing—the place your Source of Love resides.

Dr. Pam Peeke, M.D., author of *The Hunger Fix*, has combined her medical practice and scientific training to become a nationally recognized expert who supports the fact that food addiction exists, using the latest neuroscience to explain how repeated exposure to life stressors combined with food can ensnare you in a vicious cycle of food obsession, overeating, and addiction. While Dr. Wayne W. Dyer, author of *Change Your Thoughts—Change Your Life: Living the Wisdom of the Tao*, reports on someone who overcame life-threatening addictive behaviors by reading and rereading the 81 verses of the *Tao Te Ching—The Way*—authored by Lao-tzu, who had the reputation of being a man of wisdom.

Food addiction is a chemical dependence caused by changes in the brain in reaction to the biochemistry of a specific food, several foods, or a volume of food. Dopamine is one of the neurotransmitters—a chemical messenger in the brain—that is linked to the reward system, hence the tingle from a particular food sends a reward message to the body, leading to a compulsive, out-of-control rampage with food. It's not easy to reach the Source of Love within when you are on a rampage. And where is your frenzy stemming from? Look inside. This is your truth. How do you get out of this quagmire? What about a combination of letting go of these so-called trigger foods, exploring your inner truth, and turning to your Higher Source of understanding simultaneously. When you go through the withdrawal—and you will—your Source can carry you, lighten your burden so you can transcend.

You *the caterpillar* must accept your own disappearance in your transformation. *When the marvelous butterfly takes wing, nothing of the caterpillar remains...*

As Dr. Brian Weis, M.D., eloquently notes in *Miracles Happen*, those habits and patterns that bring us to such transcendent moments may work well for one person and not as well for another. Mystical or spiritual phenomena open the floodgates of the "real" world though many means such as meditation, prayer, time spent in churches or temples, near-death experiences, hypnosis, dreams, comas, or in many other ways. In other words, find the path that works for you; everyone's path may be different.

We live in a time when we want a name attached to this Higher Source, but what should that name be? Can we agree to call it one name only? When we get caught up in what to call this *Great Being* we miss the *awakening*. Stop thinking about the butterfly that you are to become but rather let the wind cascade beneath your wings and trust that you will fly when you're ready.

Dr. Wayne W. Dyer suggests in *Change Your Thoughts—Change Your Life* that we practice letting go of always naming and labeling and let things be—trusting, permitting, and allowing. In the *Tao Te Ching* opening verse, Lao-tzu tells us that the "Tao is both named and nameless," and yet we try to name to no avail. Dr. Dyer advises to let the world unfold without always attempting to figure it all out.

The book you are reading now is not a book on religion but rather designed for anyone trying to end the cycle of compulsive eating—a guide on how to jump off the food junky plank onto spiritual consciousness, emotional wellbeing, and psychological *healing from the inside out*. People not only are often confused about the difference between religion and spirituality but bring to the table their personal experiences and "conditioning," making it difficult to know where the Higher Force fits.

Religion isn't necessarily a context for the spiritual. Religion can be defined as a (mental) belief in and reference to a supernatural power or powers regarded as creator and governor of the universe. It's an institutionalized or even personal system grounded in such (mental) belief and, ideally, worship—which consists of a mental/emotional turning to that supernatural reference point.

Religion generally includes a set of credos, values, and practices based on the teachings of a spiritual leader. It is a cause, principle, or activity pursued with zeal or conscientious devotion and/or mental allegiance. Religion, hopefully, encompasses an increasing experience of the *spiritual* reality of one's relationship with God. Your daily life is your temple and your religion; wherever you go it's right there with you, awake or asleep, in work or in play—there is no separation—no divide.

I struggled in the beginning process of writing *Release Your Obsession with Food, Heal from the Inside Out* as to what to call this Higher Entity that I know as *God, my Higher Source*. But that's not to say you have the same understanding that I do, and it's not for me to try and figure out what name, or path for that matter, is right for you. Only you know and can find *the way*, and I can possibly point you in the right direction by sharing my experience, expertise, and stories and you will carve out your spiritual awakening wherever it seems fit.

Dr. Dyer writes in *Real Magic*, "Without exception, all of our greatest teachers and those who have made the greatest impact on humanity, have been spiritual beings. All of the great teachers and doctrines, including Christianity, Buddhism, Judaism, Islam, Sufism, and Confucianism, have left us with a similar message. Go within and discover your invisible higher self, know God as the love that is within you."

So, what *is* this entity known as spirituality? It's an intermittent companion of Spiritual Presence through trials and tribulations. It answers questions—often not posed—when everything seems dark and foreboding. Spirituality is the hug from the *life force* when you feel alone. It is union with the eternal strength when you feel weak. True, this "thing" called spirituality isn't tangible, but it is ever present when you're able to open your heart and receive its influence. It holds no bias and no preference as to persons and is available to anyone who seeks.

Not being in spiritual alignment, you feel that the sun no longer shines and the birds are silent—you drown in despair, *so alone, gasping for relief—any relief to stop the pain*—an innate, gnawing sense that something isn't right within. To not be in Spiritual Presence has as powerful an effect as to be in that light—but on an insane track, hiding food in your purse, closet, or drawers and filling up to your eyeballs with food—stomach distended—dying within and without.

Spirituality is a term impossible to define because each individual acts his or her spiritual-self differently. Spiritual sacredness is a personal, internal vision—a part of the self that refers to faith in something greater and more profound than self. Faith isn't necessarily in the framework of organized religion, but rather shows up as how one perceives his own connection with a force higher than himself. In the context of this book, spirituality fits an internal exploration rather than objective reasoning.

Psychologist Phyllis Ericson in *Journey of the Soul...The Emerging Self...from Dis-ease to Discovery* (1996) may perhaps say it best:

Although I am well versed in the "techniques" and "tools" of psychology and psychotherapy, I believe that these are merely "tools." The real healing takes place with these tools and the willingness and openness to allow that "power greater than self" to intervene. I believe that to use these tools without a healthy respect and inclusion of the spiritual process is like trying to run a race with one leg. (pp.104-105)

As a clinical psychotherapist, I have all the tools and techniques coupled with my doctoral training in addictions, and certifications as an eating disorder specialist and addiction professional; yet, without my deferring to a source greater than myself, these credentials didn't prepare me to lead patients to recovery. But when therapy connects with the spiritual process, patients link to *their* source—hence recovery. To this end, the role of spiritual and religious influence in recovery from food addiction is now being increasingly recognized in the medical and psychological professions, and the results are promising.

Combining science, spirituality, and food addiction is at the core of explaining the *what* and *why* you eat. *What* you eat refers to specific foods that send you into a tailspin of out-of-control eating—which leads to the *why*—the chemical imbalance that causes the spiral. Going the spiritual intervention route is a way of "taking the edge off" so you can move forward in recovery—though it can ultimately become much more for the individual.

Dopamine isn't the only hormone that plays a role in compulsive eating; so does serotonin. The neurotransmitter serotonin, a naturally occurring chemical in the brain, makes us feel good. For the compulsive eater, the ingestion of trigger foods causes release of this luring chemical—pulling us in. Judith Wurtman, Ph.D., author of the book, *Serotonin Solution*, reports the good news: Contrary to every eating plan you've ever tried or read about, the cure for emotional overeating is not expensive therapy or superhuman will power. It's food.

The quest for serotonin could be another neurobiological factor contributing to the addictive process. Stop eating the "trigger" food, and voila the withdrawal comes on with a vengeance in those with eating disorders, only prompting the sufferer to eat more of the trigger food to get relief.

Furthermore, you may have an increased degree of depression and anxiety due to decreased amounts of serotonin in your system. Where do you turn? Who do you turn to? Change what you're eating, and *look up*—the rest is easy. We can actually raise serotonin simply by ingesting the right kinds of foods. Wurtman suggests the reason you feel an uncontrollable urge to eat is because your brain is crying for relief; it's desperately seeking serotonin. The good news is when you eat the right foods, serotonin is replenished and *you release the obsession with food*. Now add a dose of your Source and voila...you *heal from the inside out*. The *what* and *why* solved.

In Chapter 3, the eight participants in my study discuss tapping into their personal connections—a glimpse into spiritual recovery. Although we are a mix of Catholics, Jews, Spiritualists, Free Floaters, all naming our Source with a different twist, you'll soon learn we are all madly in love with the same God, regardless of what we call Him or Her...

Personal Inventory Questions

1. What or Who is your Source of Being that you can grab onto—that Life Force that you know and trust—that something or someone to believe in and hold on to, and transcend?

2. Peace is our natural state, but we let our life stressors get in our way, leading often to negative conditions in our bodies, or in our case, compulsive eating. What stressors are you confronting, and how are they impacting your health?

3. By the time patients reach me, they're generally desperate after trying everything to quiet the addiction—they aren't finding answers in the current treatments they're receiving. Perhaps this is your story too, which is why you picked up this book. What have you tried thus far to quiet your binge eating and why wasn't it effective?

4. My job is to help you release your obsession with food so that you can heal from the inside out—to remove the

obstacles and to tap into attracting a better way. The path I suggest is not about the weight, but it is about what you eat and more specifically why you eat. The answers are always within, but you don't have the right access yet. What do you find to be the what and why you eat?

5. We live in a time when we want a name attached to this Higher Source but what should that name be? Can we agree to call it one name only? When we get caught up in what to call this Great Being, we miss the awakening. What name do you call this higher source and how does it work for you?

6. People not only are often confused about the difference between religion and spirituality but bring to the table their personal experiences and "conditioning." This makes it difficult to know where the Higher Force fits. What are your personal experiences with a Higher Source?

7. What is spirituality to you? From where did this understanding come from? Does it fit and work for you in your everyday life, or is your relationship with it strained?

8. What trials and tribulations have you thus far experienced in regard to binge eating and reaching out to a Higher Source? How does a Higher Entity fit in with your effort to control your urge to eat immense amounts of food?

9. Are you currently in spiritual alignment? What does that mean to you?

10. Is it possible to binge eat and be in a spiritual place simultaneously?

Chapter 3

A Glimpse into Our Spiritual Recovery

*Not only do you become what you think about
but the world also becomes what you think about.
Those who think that the world is a dark place
are blind to the light that might illuminate their lives.
Those who see the light of the world
view the dark spots as merely potential light.*
~Dr. Wayne W. Dyer

Night after night I lay awake to the sounds of my sister Debbie breathing. The room, pitch black, my eyes saw nothing, except an imagined" something. I wriggled close to Debbie's body, feeling her skin against mine for as long as I could, before she pushed me away, mumbling annoyed, "Move! Why are you so close?" Debbie required lots of space and claimed to be hot all the time. Her beautiful face often beaded up with little sweat balls as dark bangs clung wetly to her forehead in saturated ringlets. We were bedmates and roommates. Not noticing I rarely slept, little did she know I was riddled with fear and felt alone. I was eight years old.

We lived a block away from the railroad tracks—where trains passed several times an hour. One Saturday, late in the day, as the sun began to disappear, I walked alone to the neighborhood store, Oltoff's, a half-block from the tracks, to buy candy, when I heard the train screech and squeal as it fought to stop. A blood curdling scream followed, then a loud thump, then total silence. Terry Potts had been hit by the train, and pieces of his body splattered all over the tracks, grass, and sidewalks. I froze in sheer panic.

Each morning thereafter as I crossed those very tracks on my way to school, I feared I'd come upon a finger of his along the way. My siblings taunted me, finding my terror somewhat amusing.

Terry loved to play baseball, and I watched—as girls were not included. I didn't know him well and already I had a crush on him.

I feared the dark, trains, and death, and was daily gripped by apprehension. At night, when blackness engulfed any signs of light, I felt completely alone. The sound of my heart beating loud inside my chest and Debbie's soft, gentle breath went on for hours. For years, no sleep ensued during those dreadful, bleak and lonely times. I feared closing my eyes because I replayed the event of Terry's death over and over in my mind's eye, *scream: scream—screech—crash*—his body in a pile, immobilized *forever*. He was alone, as I, too, was alone. I prayed the rosary, counted sheep, imagined riding a beautiful white Arabian horse through a field of flowers—but nothing stopped the fear that seized me in the dead of night. And trains continued to whistle and swoosh on the hour every hour throughout the dark, slow passage until morning.

Today, darkness no longer takes hold of me this way, arousing fear, nor do I feel ever alone. I sense a higher consciousness that surrounds me.

But I didn't suddenly wake up one morning, and presto God lit my lamp and brightened the blackness encircling me. No, not quite. Finding that comforting, brilliant light was a lengthy process; though, the start of my awakened spiritual recovery began long before I came to terms with my food addiction. It began with slow trickles of illumination that led to my desire to step into change and become a thin, whole, and healthy me. Often during my most out-of-control binges, I heard God's whisper—*everything will be okay*. I had the desire and the discipline to make a change, if only I knew just where to begin.

Diet after diet, binge after binge, brought me to my knees—I prayed for a way out of my dark hole into the light of surrender. I prayed to give my little mind to a feeling of oneness with all that is, of an energy that connects everything and allow a life-transforming recognition of this essence to flow through me. I applied discipline, training, diet mentality to start my journey and feed my intellect, and to get up and exercise. I ate whole, natural foods at intervals of four to five hours apart, which helped me catch my breath long enough to glimpse a brief view of what life is like surrendered in peace and tranquility—long enough to let go of fear, knowing an essence higher than I could carry me through.

The start was difficult as I made my personal reality my focus. The internal dialogue repeated the same theme time and time again: *I am fat, ugly, dumb, a failure, and I will never ever be accepted or loved, not by family, friends, boyfriends, or even this Higher Entity.* This was *my* reality. What I focused on and repeated over and over in my mind came into fruition. I became what I planted in my mind—I couldn't beat this thing. The more I pushed against it, the more resistance I created. And then one day, when I was at a weekend training to become a certified hypnotist, I felt a *slight* shift.

The hypnotist pointed out that the mind in an altered state didn't know the difference between real and pretend. Click. A turn in a new direction of thought began to emerge. If I could pretend I could move from trigger foods to healthful foods, and if when I was stuck, a Higher Presence would carry me although I couldn't carry myself, I could be okay. My new thought was to change the reality I focused on to: *As you think so shall ye be. I am thin, strong, healthy, and spiritually revived.*

A slow but steady change began to take hold. Love and light replaced my doubt and darkness.

My addiction made me so desperate that I fell to my knees in hopelessness, and then I began to carve out a God. God can be a gentle breeze, the sun, or light. What you call this great love energy doesn't matter. You could call it God, Love, Lesley, Sam, or Toto—a name is simply that, a name. This higher entity is bigger than what you call Him/Her/It. He is consciousness—a higher self of me. He was in me all along. Sort of like the situation of Dorothy in the Wizard of Oz. She had everything she needed within herself, and it only took the wizard to point her in the right direction. Tap deep into your own desires and you'll find what it is you're looking for.

The Divine Energy may show up for you while you pray, sleep, dance, swim, or when you're in a compulsive *eat-frenzy* and can't stop. You'll find heaven through *your* understanding of what paradise is.

Right now, heaven to me is the morning dew and freshly cut grass, the smell of earth after an afternoon shower, the feel of a baby's lips to my skin, the soft feel of Oliver's feather's against the palm of my hand, the smell of my husband's hair, the sparkle in a student's eyes when grasping a concept, the aha when a patient understands the way out of the hell after a bout of binge eating.

Over the years, my own spiritual practice evolved into honest conversations with God, meditations, rides along the ocean, silence, and letting go of my silly mind chatter. From these efforts and spontaneous arisings, I felt an inner transformation and an overall improved sense of well-being emerge. This process of frequently turning to the greater power in all sincerity brought me closer to a spiritual connection I couldn't find with my religion alone. Thus, I have come to see a difference between religion itself and the spirituality it may or may not foster.

A participant in my study whom I'll call Marilyn had her own understanding of a power greater than herself. Although raised in a Jewish home, Marilyn's concept of God wasn't a traditional one. She searched for God in many venues such as Quaker meetings, Buddhist retreats, and Chinese philosophy, and boiled it down to "doing good and reaching out" for help from a higher source. Her God wasn't serious or morose but rather had a sense of humor and wanted the best for her and for mankind in general. Her understanding was that there is no definitive or fixed and final form to ascribe to God, and that much isn't understood about the Divine Intelligence in human terms because *when you define God you limit God*. This *Higher Consciousness* is a guideline for good living that Marilyn aspired to—not a set of rules but rather something she could see in other people and feel sometimes in herself.

Transformation

How many times have you tried to let go of your excess weight and obsession with food? I bet you can't even count. If you picked up this book, I'm guessing you had an urgent need. Did you ever think to pray and insist and demand the remedy directly from the enlightened source? Or were you raised not to ask for things *from* this higher entity but rather to serve—taught that it's selfish to think of yourself and ask for yourself rather than think of others first?

Ask *The Source* for what you want, and expect to get it. Persistence with a strongly held purpose for what you desire is a genuine path to your healing. If you want to be thin and free from obsession over your weight or certain foods—then ask for it. As surely as the sun will rise and set, I'm certain you'll begin to release your obsession with food and weight: *if you ask and expect.* Don't just whine and cry about your misfortune in this life, how you're saddled with obesity or binge eating. *Poor me* isn't going to cut it with the Divine. Rise above and turn it over to your *Source*, regardless of what you name it, and you will begin step by step, inch by inch to lift from your misery.

We're surrounded by magazines, billboards, depictions of movie stars, television pushing thin is in. That everything will be okay if you are skinny. Will it though? Take my former patient Julia, a beautiful Jewish girl who easily resembled Julia Roberts—with a movie star quality. She had the body, looks, and intelligence to have any life she wanted. She also thought she was fat, and she obsessed over food and her weight. She restricted her eating for the most part, but then binged and purged sporadically. Every waking moment, she thought about the foods she couldn't allow herself. Sometimes she gave in, but mostly she starved herself. She abused laxatives daily, in the hope of losing weight. Although she looked thin and beautiful, she, herself, didn't see it. Why? Because she couldn't see herself as she was, but only as she thought she was. And to her, she was fat, frumpy, and dumb—*think and so ye shall be.*

Few of us have been trained to tap into the power of our minds.

Many who struggle with the obsession over food and weight are like Julia, suffocating at their own hands *and thoughts*. She didn't believe in her beauty—nor that the *Divine* could or would lift her burdens. She white-knuckled her way to being thin—to a permanent physical disability that has perplexed every doctor she has seen from the Cleveland Clinic, the Mayo Clinic, and everything in between. She drove herself mad to the point of mental and physical depletion— *all because she wanted to be thin*. Like Julia, many of us strived and struggled to be thin, fighting our cravings and ignoring our hunger, and frequently gave up because of ignorance of our powers, ignorance to know to go within to discover our invisible higher self and acquaint with the magnificent Source as the love that is within us.

Julia's eating disorder history was one of either too thin or too heavy and rarely in the middle. She didn't trust the natural foods the universe provided to fuel her and give her energy. She feared foods. She feared eating. In her mind food represented fat. And she feared if she started eating she wouldn't be able to stop. She and I discussed eating healthful meals every four to five hours and staying away from foods that triggered her negative thinking and prompted her cravings. We talked about the power of her mind when connected with the Divine Source. Somewhere in adulthood she stopped believing in a source greater than herself. She felt He wasn't real, but just *something* people turned to in a make-believe kind of way. Like a magical talisman.

I recall one of our sessions when Julia bounced around in the room pacing from one end to the other and catching glimpses of herself in the mirror that makes up the east wall in my office. Pinching a handful of skin on her hip, she'd look at me, disgusted, and say, "Am I fat?" And of course I'd assure her she wasn't fat and looked beautiful. She talked fast—and skipped over what I said—only to repeat how fat she was and how she couldn't understand why, when she barely ate and tried to exercise every single day. She didn't understand her situation resulted from her lack of trust in herself; in a Higher Energy; and in the healthful, unprocessed foods provided to fuel her.

I don't mean to simplify the answer to a lifetime of difficulties. To release the obsession with food and cease compulsive eating takes work, and often a dance of three steps forward, and two back. Where should we put our trust to begin with: The Enlightened source, self, and then good food? Or is it good food, The Source, and then the self? What is good food? No doubt if you eat *real* foods, free of sugar and flour it is a positive starting place. Simple carbohydrates may trigger obsessive thoughts about food. Should you remove these foods first or call upon *The Enlightened One* first? Can you reach the Higher Source while in the throes of active binge eating? The answer is whichever works for you—just start somewhere. If you choose to turn to the Tao first, let Him carry you while you lean into more healthful food choices, then you'll not walk alone. Think of the *Foot-prints in the sand,* written by Mary Stevenson—when she was in her early teens in 1936:

A man asked, "Lord, you said that once I decided to follow You, You'd walk with me all the way. But I have noticed that during the most troublesome times in my life, there is only one set of footprints."

The Lord replied, "My precious, precious child, I love you and would never leave you. During your times of trial and suffering, when you see only one set of footprints, it was then that I carried you."

Julia didn't believe *Love Energy* walked with her all the way. She believed she was alone and had to find her own path, unable to reach a higher source for help. She didn't trust her doctors (including me); she didn't trust her food; and, she certainly didn't trust our Enlightened Source. She believed in the little voice in her head that told her that if she wanted to be thin, she couldn't eat—*and that try as she might, she was fat.* She couldn't hear anything or anyone.

Today, she lies naked in bed unable to bear anything touching her skin and has a nurse 24/7 and can't rise and walk because her mind has shut down, and she no longer even believes in her own voice—as *off the mark as it was.*

Turning back to you, I ask, how many times have you tried to let go of your excess weight and obsessions with food? Although most likely your case isn't as drastic as Julia's, perhaps you hear a piece of your story in her story. You picked this book up for a reason. You're searching for the answer to what feels like a lifelong problem with no solution. You have an urgent need that remains unresolved. Try and pray and insist and demand Adonai give you the remedy. The Divine Source is a gift for you. He loves you. You are His child, and He will be there with you every step of the way. And if you can't walk along with Him, just let Him carry you. He is strong and tireless, loving and kind. You are worthy of His love. Give Him a try—*what do you have to lose?* (No pun intended). You can ask from the Super Natural Being for things that affect your well-being. It's okay to serve yourself in such a way. It's not selfish to love yourself and to let The Enlightened love you. Break free from your obsession with food and step into a life of peace and tranquility.

After a series of observations and conversations with patients as well as food addicts outside of my practice, I compiled six themes breaking them into 13 patterns, which I share with you next in the hope of bringing you answers and direction concerning your issues with food, compulsive eating, and addictions—and leading you to a closer connection with the Source of all.

Chapter 4 looks at all six themes and 13 patterns through a few excerpts from my personal journal along with Charisma and John's personal journals—each kept prior to our conversation.

Personal Inventory Questions

1. Do you recall walking to a grocery store or gas station on your own when you were young in pursuit of sugary or starchy treats? Would you go to any lengths to obtain these, such as stealing or sneaking?

2. Did you experience any trauma as a child that might have triggered fear? Where did you turn for relief from this fear? Can you recall turning to a Higher Source to alleviate your discomfort and spark a spiritual recovery?

3. Have you ever become quiet, enough to hear God's whisper that everything will be okay? Have you prayed for a way out of your dark hole into the light of surrender?

4. What internal dialogue repeats the same theme(s) time and time again? The continuous tape in my own head suggested: I am fat, ugly, dumb, a failure, and I will never ever be accepted or loved, not by family, friends, boyfriends, or even God. What's your lie?

5. Can you decipher what is real and what is imaginary in your thought process? As the hypnotist I studied under pointed out, in an altered state the mind doesn't know the difference between real and pretend. What new positive verbiage can you program into your subconscious? Remember—what you think, so shall ye be.

6. When does God (or your understanding of a Higher Power) show up for you? He can show up while you pray, sleep, dance, swim, or when you're in a compulsive eat frenzy and can't stop. You can find Him through your understanding of what He is.

7. How has your own spiritual practice evolved over the years? What changes or adjustments do you need to make? What is your understanding of spirituality? Religion? Do you combine the two? Remember Marilyn's concept of God was "doing good and reaching out" for help from a Higher Source. Her understanding was that we can't ascribe any definitive or fixed and final form to God. Much isn't understood about the Higher Intelligence in human terms because when we define God, we limit God. What do you think about that?

8. How many times have you tried to let go of your excess weight and obsession with food? Did you ever try to pray and insist and demand the remedy directly from your Higher Source?

9. Have you ever asked your higher consciousness for what you want and expected to get it? If not, what would you ask for now if you expected to receive it through this energy of love?

10. Think about Julia, who so resembled the actress Julia Roberts. She had the body, looks, and intelligence of the film star who has her same first name, yet the Julia here thought she was fat, and obsessed over her food and weight. Do you do this? Or do you see yourself thinner than you actually are? The Julia in this chapter abused laxatives. Have you ever purged through laxatives, throwing up, or excessive exercise?

Chapter 4

A Partial Solution for Compulsive Eating

*Practical wisdom is only to be learned
in the school of experience.
Precepts and instruction are useful so far as they go,
but without the discipline of real life,
they remain of the nature of theory only.*
~Samuel Smiles

No doubt practical wisdom is only to be learned in the school of experience. It's real life that teaches valuable lessons. The road of life runs in countless directions leaving us a myriad of choices. At times we take the new path—other times the old—not certain which will keep us steady on our feet. The answer may drowse all along in our hearts—ignored.

Perhaps you're at the crossroad in your life trying to determine which route is best for you. You can continue on as you are, swinging from diet to diet, and lose and gain the same 20 pounds over and over, or, you can release the obsession with food and your diet mentality and get what you wanted in the first place—weight loss. Ask, and listen where the good way is, and then walk that path, and you will find respite along with peace in your soul. A partial solution for compulsive eating and a closer connection to God is in the ancient path—your ancestors' way.

To help you find practical wisdom through life experiences and reach resolution and relief from food addiction and a spiritual connection to your source, I will set forth countless experiences here that reveal themes and patterns, and that unveil insight, direction, and answers, some of which might ring true for you.

Everyone discussed in this book as part of my study (which included me as a subject) binge ate and wanted to stop. Weight itself wasn't an issue for all, though all used Twelve Step programs, some used commercial weight loss programs, and treatment centers to lose weight. A few engaged in previous and current psychotherapies to deal with compulsive binge eating issues and, in a couple of instances, weight loss as well. Some of us had multiple, ongoing addictions, while others were recovering alcoholics and/or drug addicts. Some of those discussed experienced uninterrupted relief from compulsive eating—up to 20 years—and never abused any substances other than food before or after their recoveries. Those in the group studied varied greatly in age and background.

I conducted the conversations I report on in interview settings as well as during therapy sessions. I spoke to both men and women ranging in age from adolescence to those who were in their seventies. The participants came from many different vocational backgrounds and included psychotherapists, psychologists, social workers, nursing home administrators, business administrators, business consultants, business managers, accountants, writers/editors, physicians, pharmacists, retirees, and students. Our outside interests and activities encompassed music, dancing, spiritual retreats, education, psychology, political lobbying, gardening, reading, writing, walking, meditation, praying, and running.

Some of us found our spiritual paths as we exchanged binge eating for connections with the universe, while others still search. Those you will hear from were Catholic, Jewish, Christians, or had no religion at all. Some were widowed, some divorced, some single, and some married. Divorces and new relationships took place prior to and during recovery. Those participating were mothers, fathers, daughters, sons, sisters, and brothers—tall and short, heavy and thin, black and white, and in between.

As our discussions ensued, definite patterns began to emerge. Mapping and charting experiences soon led to a collection of meaningful information, which unfolded 13 primary patterns of occurrence, eight during the active illness state:

1. An early awareness that something was wrong with our relationship with food.

2. A preoccupation with food and/or body weight.

3. The use of food as a drug.

4. Habitual sneaking and hiding of food.

5. Shame over the inability to stop eating.

6. An inhibition in spirituality during periods of active bingeing.

7. The experience of being out of control with compulsive and binge eating.

8. The bargaining for one last binge before the start of yet another diet.

Then, at the point of actual recovery, five further patterns indicating a transformation could be seen:

9. The perception of a spiritual connection intertwined in all our life situations and events.

10. Recovery finally taking precedence over mere weight loss.

11. The eventual feeling of peace and serenity.

12. The Source (God, Higher Power, the Universe, etc.) seen as a power for good.

13. The acceptance that chemical imbalances have led to food sensitivity.

These 13 patterns capture and portray essential meanings, although the patterns often times overlap and intermingle. These 13 primary patterns can be condensed into:

1. An initial awareness of food addiction.

2. The effects of active binge eating.

3. The blocking of spirituality by active bingeing.

4. A recourse to prayers and meditation as part of daily healing.

5. The healing impact of the ever-presence of a strong spirituality.

6. The demonstrations of phenomena, miracles, and medical healings as our connections to God increased.

We all had an initial awareness that something was wrong with our relationship with food and the inability to stop eating whether we were full or hungry. Early in childhood we were obsessed with the fear of not having enough to eat, particularly not enough sweet and starchy foods, regardless of whether we came from affluent families where food was abundant, or not.

As I pored through years of my old journals, the same 13 patterns that were evident with patients and interviewees came to light in my writing. My personal diaries revealed something very deeply wrong in my relationship with food. I'd recorded hours of plotting and planning how to get food and hide it in a safe, snug spot to pounce on when I was completely alone.

Then, I didn't stop eating until the food was gone, no matter how much remained or how full I was. And the cycle soon repeated—while at the same time I was preoccupied with my body and my weight. Reading this during the time I was involved with my research, I clearly saw my pattern of wanting sweet and salty foods and guilt for consuming so much of them. Yet I never had enough of these special items. And beyond feeling full during and after bingeing, I felt ashamed for not being able to control how much I ate. Between my binges, I often bargained with myself and promised to only eat these foods one last time, and then quit for good.

Marilyn, an interviewee (and no stranger to 12-step programs for food addiction and binge eating), dropped her tone to a whisper as she described a shameful time when she resided in the heart of Maryland and drove four hours from where she lived just to get to the ocean. The beach represented an all-encompassing love to Marilyn. She *had* to get there to walk on the beach in order to *come home*. She was desperate to find an answer to her lifelong obsession with food and weight. "When I *really* need help or I need to think, I always end up at the ocean where my higher, higher, higher power hangs out."

Once she arrived, in deep despair and with her dogs in tow, she walked and walked, mind chatter filling her every moment—while she ate slices of pizza and piece after piece of salt-water taffy. On and on she walked and ate as the sun slipped down to nothingness—a farewell.

She stared out at the dark, vast sea, alone except for subtle whispers coming from God as wave after wave crashed on the shoreline. Looking out, she contemplated a walk into the sea: her farewell. And then the sun peeked up from beneath the horizon—crusts of burnt orange with pink hues against a cobalt blue backdrop, a spread of incredible beauty and hope that reached out, like the arms of God, to hold and embrace her. In that moment she made a decision to stop bingeing or it would take her life—one way or another. No more could she live in the state she was in. She then proceeded to etch out her plan in the sand with a broken sea shell:

1. I am not a victim.
2. I no longer need to eat sugar, flour, and wheat. I turn to prayer, not junk food.
3. I let go of binge eating.
4. I exchange sadness for happiness.
5. I am found, not lost.
6. My sick body is restored to a healthy body.
7. I let go of the old and begin anew.
8. I move in line with nature.
9. I choose life over death.

Marylyn wrote all the things she wanted to let go of in the sand and then watched the waves wash away her words, sending her intentions out into the universe.

What makes a person turn from compulsive eating to what they define as God? Marilyn had reached a very low point in her life—contemplating death over the pain she endured that was covered by her obsession with food and the struggle with her weight. I too had been at the same crossroad—and more than once. When I was 15 years old, I sat on the edge of the pier at Big Silver Lake in Wautoma, Wisconsin, and thought to slip into the water and sink to the bottom—relinquish myself to God—and let water fill my lungs—to be no more. What had led me to such despair? A binge that went on for weeks without interruption, during which I inhaled food like a starved sailor lost out at sea. No amount of food filled me. I was empty.

An active binge often blocked God from my view and left me hungry only for more food. Although I called to my higher consciousness for help, it was difficult to receive what was sent in the middle of my binge, which took precedence over everything. I ate. I ate as a fish out of water gasps for breath, as a starved person gobbles nourishment, as a person in a desert gulps water at an oasis—compulsively, secretly, in pain, terror stricken.

In desperation, I stood at the crossroads and looked to the universe for direction. I asked for the ancient path and where the good way was. Spurts of spiritual recovery began to take hold, seeking to permeate all of my life's events and situations—replacing negative thoughts of body image and weight. I pondered the thought that perhaps a power higher than me *could* help me find acceptance, peace, and serenity—rather than rage and irritability. Three steps forward and two back, I began to walk in God's direction to find rest for my weary soul.

I began to journal when I was thirteen years old, capturing my eating frenzies and emotional deficits. To help you better understand the life of a child food addict, I decided to share some of my entries. On January 1, 1973 at 16 years of age, I wrote:

It's New Year's Day! It's beautiful here [Madeira Beach, Florida] and a nice day to start another life diary on the start of a new year. I'm 16 years old. Life is good. I'm visiting my grandparents in Florida. We went to the bar last night. Ick! We've been eating so much. I love the coconut butter. Yum! I'm going to gain weight. I miss my friends, home...mom...all stuck in the cold.

As I look back, I remember that day as if it were yesterday. It was New Year's Day, and already at 16 years old,

I was quite familiar with bargaining for a fresh start after a binge—the motive behind my starting a new journal. This was my pattern for many years. I binged, and then promised to start clean eating on a Monday; the first day of the month; Lent; first day of the year; or *any* first. Always, I promised an end-binge date and a start clean-eating date—a way to calm my guilt and shame because I was going to fix my problem and never binge again. Yet in reality I was completely consumed with what I ate and out of control with food—unable to stop.

On the morning of that New Year's Day, I woke to a squawking and carrying on outside my window. Ah, the American Egret, the large white heron stalked slow and methodically past my bedroom window with its statuesque posture, and interrupted my morning slumber. While I lingered in bed a few minutes longer, I reflected on the eve before—an event similar to others I had witnessed on many occasions—my maternal grandparents drunk as they swung at each other and created a familiar, embarrassing scene filled with drama and crisis.

My grandfather Hale was an alcoholic and my grandmother Ma a food addict. Of course nobody discussed or acknowledged this family secret, which is so evident to me now. Moods changed drastically when she drank or ate certain foods and when Hale (and my grandmother for that matter) drank whiskey. Of course back then I didn't know or understand alcoholism or food addiction. I just thought my grandmother was an evil person who didn't care much for me. Little did I know she probably saw some of herself in me—*and perhaps I saw me in her.*

New Year's Eve found us in a smoke-filled bar, with the music deafening to the ear, the clinking of glasses, the smell of fermented liquor in the air, and Ma and Hale bickering. Hale crooned at the piano bar and winked at beautiful women, while Ma screeched and flailed her arms to get his attention. I slipped out unnoticed to sneak- smoke cigarettes I'd lifted from Hale's pack and to escape their all-too-familiar escapade. They squabbled, screamed, scratched, and hit, which brought the evening to a halt.

That next morning, my head pounded. My throat, raw and scratchy from the smoke-filled bar and the cigarettes I'd inhaled, brought me back to the present, and I kicked off the covers and bounced out of bed to record in my journal the idea for the new, upcoming year after my last binge. As I scribbled a plan, I knew something was wrong but wasn't sure what. That day, I ate countless pieces of toast smothered in coconut butter jam. I was preoccupied with two basic thoughts: How could I get more food? And how, later, when we went up and down the waterways in the boat could I wear my swimsuit when I felt so fat?

I was filled with shame and fear, yet giddy with the excitement only a binge can bring on. At the same time, I was lonely, empty, and homesick for my mom and my dear friend, Mary, and my job in the local bakery where I had free access to whatever sweets I wanted, a Willy Wonka reality for me. In hindsight, I blocked the painful events of my grandparents' rumpus, which mimicked some of the scenes I'd witnessed with my own parents growing up, as I stuffed down food.

June 2, 1974

I woke up at 11 o'clock, got dressed right away, and had a cup of coffee. I refuse to eat—although I wish for a chocolate something. I weigh 126 pounds. I gained two pounds from "senior week." I feel disgusted with myself and fat. Tomorrow I leave for the outskirts of New York to go to a dog show with Mom! I went to the drug store and bought a box of Ayds (a diet candy). I did my wash, went to Mary's house, and talked to various family members while Mary peeled potatoes in preparation for the usual family dinner (which is foreign to me as Mom is rarely home). Mary and I went for a long car ride. Later J.C. took me for a boat ride meeting up with Dave— my boy crush. I listened to Janis Joplin croon in the lower cottage for an hour as the water lapped up against the shoreline. I went for a long walk and danced my guts out to burn up calories. Bless me, Lord.

As a teenager I needed the charge of caffeine to wake up. I was always tired. Every morning I wakened with the same clenched-jaw promise: I WILL NOT EAT! To eat or not to eat was my daily question. Of course I gave in shortly after I bargained *just this once*, and then, afterward, I started a diet. I thought I was weak, a failure, as those *normal* kids didn't obsess over their bodies, weight, and what they were or weren't going to eat. Even at a healthy weight of 126 pounds, five feet, six inches tall, I saw myself as enormously fat. I was focused on my body and the numbers on the scale. I was conflicted over what I weighed and what I wanted to weigh. Shame consumed me. I promised God to never binge again even if it killed me. And when I did eat, I purged through exercise—long walks and dancing.

It was senior week, June, 1974, and high school was coming to an end. My class booked several quaint cottages on Big Silver Lake in Wautoma as our final farewell before launching into adulthood. At the get-together, my skin crawled with discomfort, and I was full of unease. I was out of control with food—I was consumed in shame. I felt fat and full of guilt because I was weak—*a disgusting nobody*.

While my classmates mingled, I was off bingeing in secret. I stuffed my face with chocolate, cookies, crackers, and cake. I ate beyond full in hiding, so much so that I decided I would walk out into the woods that were directly across the street from the cottages and I'd shove my fingers down my throat and puke up the junk I'd stuffed my face with. I walked into the woods, careful to pick each step to avoid the three-leaf plant (poison ivy) and proceeded to gag as I stuck my fingers down my throat to "fix" the binge.

I broke into a cold sweat while bent over the wet soil, pushing, coughing, and gagging. But nothing happened. My stomach came up dry. I believe a higher energy watched over me that day because I never graduated to purging my food through vomiting as a result of that one incident during senior week, out in the woods alone, gripped in fear, petrified of what was to become of me. *Scared.* I had no college plans, no plan whatsoever. I was nobody going nowhere.

One night during senior week, we tried a board game where the player had to drink x number of shots depending where a peg landed on the board. I hit the bull's-eye many times, one shot, two shots, three—and somewhere I lost count only to awaken draped over a lawn chair recliner outside where passersby commented and gawked. I was an eater not a drinker. But, because I was so insecure and uncomfortable, I ate *and drank* just to get through senior week. Unlike my classmates, I had no future plans to go on to college. I lived on the nearly 400-acre farm with Mom, who was always away at a dog show or visiting dog friends somewhere out of the state. I had no plans and looked forward to a dismal future, to say the least. I was alone.

I couldn't understand what was wrong with me. Why was my eating so out of control? Why couldn't I control my weight? Shoot, I didn't even have the simple ability to throw up to get rid of what I ate. I plotted and strategized ways to solve my food and weight issues and yet I didn't have the backbone to fix my obsession with food.

When I realized purging through vomiting was out of the question, I turned to excessive exercise and a diet candy called Ayds. They looked like caramels or chocolate caramels, and you were supposed to eat one with a hot cup of water.

The instructions warned the user to not eat more than one every four hours. *I ate the whole box in one sitting.* Not good! I ended up in the bathroom for hours with stomach cramps and a bad case of diarrhea—on many occasions.

Being boy crazy and self-conscious about my weight and looks rolled into one continuous ongoing theme in my head. I often stayed isolated with my bag of little cakes and cookies *alone* in our lower cottage at Silver Lake, where we had family cottages stemming from four generations back. I knew something was wrong in my hiding out with food while I could hear my brothers' and sisters' laughter and screams of delight as they splashed in the lake right outside my door. In the distance, boats with water skiers whizzed by on many warm and sunny, hazy, lazy summer days, but I was too ashamed to put a swim suit on and join in. I binged, smoked cigarettes, and napped alone in the cottage. How sad. Later I tried to fix the damage by dancing and walking just to burn the calories—another way to purge.

June 1, 1975
Today was also a drag, I slept till 12, and it was nice. I spent a couple of hours with Carol on the beach. Mike likes my car. I've been eating like a pig! Mom ate at Katie's so I went to bed early.

January 20, 1976
Well, today I weigh 135 pounds. Wish I could eat.

July, 8, 1976
Another day over so soon—and I'm so very unhappy. I overate today—bet I gained two pounds. I weighed 126 this morning. I'd like to weigh about 118. I think I'll start dieting Monday really seriously.

January 1, 1979

Today is Monday, January 1, 1979. I'm 22 years old and feeling like a loser; right now I live in Oak Forest, Illinois with Jasmine P., a hard core alcoholic, because I have nowhere else to live. I've been very ill for the past three weeks. I have continuous boils, and a very bad foot. The doctor says it may be diabetes judging from the boils, and my heel is probably a spur, which is a chipped bone. How awful! I didn't tell the doctor I've been eating nothing but junk foods for months. I'm still going to Weight Watchers as I'm really fat again. My weight has risen again to 175 pounds.

After graduating high school, out of desperation to fill my loneliness and have some kind of direction, I attached to the first guy who looked my way ignoring his shortcomings. The relationship was short lived. At the age of 21, leaving from the small resort town sunk in the heart of Wisconsin, I fled to the windy city, where I was born and lived my childhood years until I was 12. I returned an adult with three dollars in my pocket, a few items of clothing, and no car.

In Chicago, I overstayed my welcome with my eldest sister, Christy, and then stayed briefly with my brother Danny before I rented a room with a thirty-something-year-old, washed-out bartender will call Jasmine. Jasmine, drunk more often than not, lived in a huge, dark and dusty home with old furniture from a life that had once been filled with joy. Again, I was alone and lonely. Weekends, I spent locked inside, eating nothing of nutritional value. And the week days weren't much better. I became quite ill, as a result of a lack of proper nutrition and had a potassium deficit, both of which led to my boils.

July 16, 1980

A memory flooded over me that I must write about. I just read an article in *Weight Watchers* magazine on simple breakfasts. One breakfast in particular started off with half a grapefruit. While reading, I slipped into wonderland—overcome by the memory of my childhood during long hot summers at Baba's (my great-grandma's) on Silver Lake. My five siblings and I shared breakfasts at the long, deep-orange wooden table. Baba always set out grapefruit, blueberry pies, and of course burnt toast, all served on brightly colored dishes of turquoise, bright yellow, and deep orange (the popular Fiesta dinnerware from the early 1900s). She believed burnt toast made your teeth white. I can still smell that delicious aroma of perked coffee, fresh pie, and burnt toast. Life seemed easier then. I was thin.

February 26, 1987
I am very unhappy. This may sound weird, but sometimes I feel more alone now than when I lived alone. I'm sick of eating at fast food restaurants. I'm sick of eating with the television for company; I'm sick of struggling up and down with my weight.

On October 31, 1993
I took my son, Benjamin, who was five years old, trick or treating in the neighborhood. It brought back my Chicago childhood memories when my five brothers and sisters and I hobbled up and down the streets in our getups for both Halloween eve and Halloween night. I lived for these two nights *because I wanted candy* even though I was absolutely petrified of the ghosts and goblins. I filled two pillow cases with the goods until they bulged. Then I hid my bags and ate every sweet treat myself until they were gone.

This Halloween night, I sat on the floor with Benjamin to sort candy as I had done with my siblings when we were children. I felt the adrenalin rush and my heart started to race. I was eager for Benjamin to go to bed, so I could eat *his* candy. I told him some candy didn't look safe, so we put it to the side to throw out. *All my favorites went in that pile.* After he fell asleep, I ate the "bad" candy plus the candy we'd bought for the neighborhood trick or treaters, and whatever else I could find to eat. Later, I lied to my child when he inquired why his pile was so small. I felt sick and fat—and very bad about myself.

September 26, 2000
I think my struggle all along is to become "free," to not obsess over food! I just want to live healthfully every day. I want to exercise, eat right, take vitamins, drink tons of water, love my job and just "be." I'm tired of this fight. This craziness has gone on long enough. I'm 44 and I've fought this disease for 31 years! I have the right to feel tired and angry. No more scales. I will judge by the way my body fits into my clothes. No more counting or weighing—just clean eating when I'm hungry and I'll stop when I'm full.

March 20, 2003
I was anxious this morning for no apparent reason, and I alleviated my stress by courting an entire entrée of food rituals. I decided to go to the store and somehow ended up with brownies, chips, and a magazine with a story on how to lose 20 pounds easily. I ate the entire box of Entenmann's fat free fudge brownies along with the baked chips, followed by a long nap. After, I took a hot bath and pored through my magazine that promised rapid weight loss. I am disgusted with myself. I can't believe once again I went to a very sick place with my food because it was cushioned by the resolution that tomorrow I start my new diet—or so I told myself. But tomorrow never comes.

August 19, 2004— this entry was written the day before starting a Twelve Step program for compulsive eating. A Twelve Step Program is a set of guiding principles (accepted by members as 'spiritual principles,' based on the approved literature) outlining a course of action for recovery from addiction, compulsion, or other behavioral problems.

At the age of 13, I became aware of my issues with food. I thought I was alone. Through many diets—gaining and losing tremendous amounts of weight—I managed to let go of nearly 100 pounds. I thought I had arrived. I worked for 13 years with Weight Watchers—a popular and reputable weight loss company—and earned a Master's degree in mental health, practicing as a psychotherapist in the area of mood disorders and eating disorders.

It certainly sounds as though I have the world by the tail. I don't. I still have episodes of bingeing, although not as frequently as during my earlier years. I still gain and lose, but not huge amounts of weight (25 pounds). I guess you could say I'm still playing the diet game. I need to stop.

Two days ago, I wrote an anonymous e-mail to a Twelve Step group and admitted to myself and to others that I am a food addict and my life is unmanageable. I am today in my illness, eating sugary foods like a drunken sailor, but I turn my will over to God tomorrow after one last supper. On August 20, 2004, I begin my abstinence and promise to live my life without food obsessions and binges.

I attended my first meeting on a conference call at 9 p.m. I was scared. Tears rolled down my cheeks as listened to strangers tell a familiar tale on the other end—all the while stuffing a concoction made up of dark cocoa powder, sugar, and butter, into my mouth—for the last time—for real.

As I pressed the phone tightly against my ear and held on to every word as if each was a trinket of gold, I questioned why an educated psychotherapist in private practice, who helps those with eating disorders, needed to attend a Twelve Step meeting. While I humbly sank deeper onto the floor, locked in the bathroom knees up against my chest, cradling the phone with one hand and shoveling chocolate into my mouth with the other, the answer flashed before me like a neon sign. This disease has no bias. It infects everyone from all walks of life who has a chemical imbalance. I am no exception.

I binged my last binge tonight, stuffing myself while I listened in silence, in the dark. It's time. It's time to take the next step and become abstinent from sugar, flour, and wheat. The issue is more than weight loss—it's about the quiet voice within. Thank you, God, for these people on the other end of the phone line sharing their thoughts. I am grateful and no longer feel alone.

August 20, 2004

Oh my sweet God—I had no idea of what I was in for! It started last night and proceeded to get worse and worse—my head felt and feels as though it's falling off. I'm experiencing serious withdrawal—and "they" say food is not a substance we can have an addiction to. Wrong! I somehow managed to see six patients today, but not without serious consequences to myself (not to mention my inattention to them). I feel as if I'm dying—as though I'm experiencing a brain aneurysm— like someone is taking a door and slamming me in my head over and over. I had no idea what anyone said during the sessions today, or what I said to him or her.

Still, I managed to weigh and measure all my food today in spite of how awful I felt, and feel. I dedicate myself, my research, and my work to helping all those who are addicted to deleterious foods. Although most of my patients are overweight and have binge eating disorder, I separated myself from them because I thought I was different—after all, I kept off most of my 100-pound weight loss, and I'm the expert. I missed the most important key—it's more than weight—much more. It's about abandonment and rejection by the people who really mattered to me and who I needed for my survival, and about how food covered up my pain. I'm no different than the person weighing 700 pounds. We both have a deep pain within and perhaps the one who is morbidly obese, too, has a chemical imbalance triggered by sugar, flour, and wheat. It is just that simple. An addiction is an addiction. Pain is pain. It's not about the weight.

I surrender. My life has become unmanageable, and I need a higher source—my Source—who will save me from myself.

Charisma had 12 years free of sugar, flour, and wheat at the time of my interview with her. Prior to her recovery, she had a history of binge eating into a coma-state. It wasn't unusual for her to eat until she blacked out as she witnessed her alcoholic husband do daily. Her childhood was filled with fear and shame. Grandpa lured her with promises of money for candy as he abused her sexually. She soothed herself with sweets. She spent every penny she *earned* on candy. She passed Sundays in church close to a loving Divine Source, but hiding her dark secret. Later in life her heart opened spiritually when she turned to Twelve Step programs and learned self-love and self-preservation.

Charisma became someone who gave time and love selflessly, and she reached out to battered and abused women suffering with addictive eating used as a coping mechanism. She gave freely of herself lending hope and help. An excerpt below is one of many recorded in the journal she kept for a month prior to our interview, referencing a telephone conversation she'd had with a young woman who was contributing an article on meditations for a book Charisma helped put together. The names have been changed to protect anonymity.

April 19, 2006

My day was routine but you (God) sent a miracle again. I found an old phone message that I hadn't responded to regarding meditations. I emailed Patty and agreed to call her that night. Lo and behold this was her 2nd day of abstinence, and she was beside herself, very depressed (morbidly obese) and wanting to die. We talked for almost an hour. I believe I was able to help Patty get through this day. I reminded her that she is detoxing, which magnified her depression. We'll try to talk again soon. This was timing, as I hadn't responded when I first got the message. Normally, I would have just e-mailed the meditation format to her. Instead, I called Patty on her 2nd day and at a horrible bottom. How great is that!

John, a soft-spoken man with hazel green eyes and an instant smile, had five years of recovery from food addiction and 30 years of recovery from alcoholism. He shared many journal entries, with one in particular capturing early years and showing an awareness of his binge eating.

February 14 2003

I've used food as security when fearful—just as I did as a kid. Bingeing caused a cycle of relief, remorse, guilt, and then more bingeing, followed by shame and more guilt. A sugar binge lifted me high, so high, and then I crashed and felt depressed. Sugar caused my heart to palpitate and often led to a panic attack in the same way as the effect of many other stimulant drugs I ingested.

When I was in treatment for alcoholism, I hit some lows; I felt suicidal. I was made aware that the sugar caused the mood swings. My AA sponsor was doing the grey sheet (a food plan provided by Overeaters Anonymous) so I gained some awareness of chemical addiction early in my recovery. Although knowledge is necessary, it is never enough. What I must develop is a total change of perspective toward food.

I cannot participate in a very spiritual life without living by such principles as honesty. Denial and honesty are diametrically opposed to one another. When I'm in denial I rationalize my behavior as being acceptable, when I know that it is harmful. This creates a barrier to the flow of God's spirit within me and between me and others.

When I'm in the addiction, it clouds my thinking. My motives and behaviors are self-centered, and I become obsessed with satisfying my addiction. At such times, it makes it hard for me to love or be loved. I become sneaky and deceptive and unbearable. I'd eat normally at home, and then sneak food outside, gobbling and running. Compulsive eating isolated me from others and caused shame when I hid and sneaked food, especially when my motive was to not share.

I now recognize eating while driving was dangerous— especially on the highway. Trying to retrieve French fries from the floor brought me close to collisions on numerous occasions. Sugar binges caused me to be foggy headed, unable to concentrate and stay focused.

The next six chapters will take you through the experience of food addiction, beginning with the initial awareness and shame, and what I propose as at least a partial solution for the situation.

Personal Inventory Questions

1. Are you at a crossroad in your life trying to determine which route is best for you? Are you bouncing from diet to diet, losing and gaining the same 20 pounds over and over?

What steps can you take to release your obsession with food and redirect your diet mentality to healthy thinking?

2. Have you ever experienced uninterrupted relief from compulsive eating? How long did it last, and what steps did you put forth to accomplish this feat?

3. Do any of the 13 primary patterns ring true for you? Did you have an early awareness that something was wrong with your relationship with food? What about a preoccupation with food and/or your body weight? Can you describe what this experience was like?

4. Did you ever use food as a drug? What about habitual sneaking and hiding of food? Did you have shame over the inability to stop eating? Can you recall when exactly you had these experiences? Were you alone? Did such an event occur recently?

5. Have you had an inhibition in your spirituality during periods of active bingeing? Have you sometimes been out of control with compulsive and binge eating? Did you ever bargain for that one last binge before the start of yet another diet?

6. Have you had points of actual recovery indicating a transformation? Have you had the perception of a spiritual connection intertwined in some or all of your life's situations? What does that feel like?

7. Have you experienced recovery or the feeling of peace and serenity taking precedence over mere weight loss? Do you see your Source (God, Higher Power, the Universe, etc.) as a power for good? If not, why not?

8. What are your thoughts about accepting that chemical imbalances have led to food sensitivity? Have you ever tried a Twelve Step anonymous program for food addiction?

9. Do you have early recordings or journals marking your diet ups and downs along with the trials and tribulations of your life? If so, perhaps the same 13 patterns that were

evident with those in this chapter will come to light in your writings too.

10. Can you relate to Marilyn's experience when she walked the beach in deep despair, desperate to find answers to her lifelong obsession with food and weight, bingeing while she walked well into the night? Did you ever contemplate taking your life because the pain was so great?

Chapter 5

Initial Awareness of Food Addiction

In you, Lord, I take refuge;
Let me never be put to shame.
In your justice deliver me;
Incline your ear to me;
Make haste to rescue me!
You are my rock and my fortress;
For your name's sake lead and guide me.
~Psalms 31:1-4

Early in childhood I was fixated on sugar—never getting enough and going to great extremes to obtain it by stealing, hiding my "finds," and hoarding. Although I didn't have an awareness of food addiction as a concept, I knew something was wrong. In hindsight, I realize I ate out of control and bargained with myself and God to stop—*after this one last pastry.*

I felt shame if I got caught stealing food or money to buy food, yet I didn't have the mentality to understand I was compulsive eating until my adolescent years when the weight began to pile on. And even then I didn't know an actual eating disorder called binge eating disorder existed—*and I had it.* What I did know was my friends ate when they were hungry and stopped when they'd had enough and didn't hide or sneak their foods nor had shame.

I cried out to a higher source for help in my own childlike way but never felt heard or delivered from my obsessions with food until I finally took refuge in a spiritual presence without reservation many years later. And then, the universe did just as I pleaded for: rescued me.

I now take refuge in God's energy. He is my rock and my fortress. This higher entity led me easily and gently when I was pre-school age; however, as a child and adolescent and in early adulthood, I had lost that connection and turned only to my inner chatter and self-destruct in food.

When I was little, I chatted with my higher consciousness as a best friend would gab. According to Dad, I was a round, pink-cheeked, happy baby who would break into a beautiful smile from ear to ear upon eye contact with anyone and everyone. Hard to believe I was this happy, roly-poly baby with a toothless grin, often observed in the crib laughing and cooing—absolutely content and entertained by my fingers and toes—staring intently as if they weren't a part of my body, but rather a toy for my amusement. Life then was magical and full of daily surprises and diversions. When exactly my body image turned to disgust and my moods soured, I'm not certain.

I can't pinpoint when the magic ceased and the daily surprises were no longer fun, but I do know a feeling of relentless doom became evident to me near the age of eight after I'd witnessed the gruesome death of Terry Potts. Near this same time, I was self-conscious about my body, related to my posture. When I was that little girl, my brother Michael teased me mercilessly, imitating how I looked. I had a curvature in my lower back pushing out my butt one way and chest the other. Other children noticed my poor posture as well and chanted remarks as I would make my way to the chalk board at school. During those moments, I wanted the walls to suck me in or the floor to swallow me whole.

I missed the safe days, prior to age five, when I was home watching Mickey Mouse and Donald Duck cartoons, eating sweet treats, and having special alone time with Mom while my siblings were away at school.

Yes, my friendly chats with a spiritual presence stopped long before that and had turned to pleas for help—to be heard, led, and guided. Although I had an obsession with food as far back as I can remember, at 13 I was horrified by a rapid weight gain and continuous hunger, which led to my neurotic quest to be skinny. Food replaced God and became my total focus. I comforted myself with food to survive the chaos around me and my simultaneous panic.

Prior to age 13, I was a scrawny kid on iron drops for anemia. Early dysfunctional eating behaviors had presented themselves, but weren't yet evident to me. I always looked for any opportunity to obtain and eat sugar. I can still picture the can of chocolate Hershey's syrup with foil clumped over the top to cover the holes pierced by the can opener. It didn't matter to me if the syrup was old and rubbery; I scraped it up and ate it anyway. I was five years old.

I was on a continuous prowl for sugary treats. I slipped into the dark pantry, fumbled my way to the cabinet, and climbed up to retrieve the chocolate chips and dried fruits stored there. I wasn't concerned about the mealworms from the flour crawling around the shelves. My hunt for food to calm this unexplained yearning within continued as I made my way to the coat room and felt deep into pockets for old gum, hard candies, and loose change to take with me to the store several blocks from our home.

In a "drunken" stupor I walked block after block carrying several empty Coke packs, neglecting my blistered and bleeding hands, to cash in the bottles for extra money to purchase thick pretzel sticks, chocolate stars, and Flying Saucers. The Flying Saucers, also known as Satellite Wafers, had a communion-wafer-like texture, only these were filled with colorful pebbles that hurt your teeth when you crunched on them.

I never made it back home with any candy left because I consumed it all like a dry drunk pouring endless amounts of liquor down his throat to get some relief, *any relief from this unexplained uneasy suspense and painful anxiety within.*

There was no mountain too high or valley too low to prevent the quest for sweets, *and lots of them.* My desperation led to my stealing parking lot change (hundreds of dollars' worth) from the third drawer of the china cabinet to purchase candies from Pennies candy store. At seven, I couldn't quite handle the big, heavy bag, so I dropped the pouch, and coins flew all over the shop floor, which caused everyone, including the store owner to look across at me. I sensed deep trouble when he called my father.

Dad took me into the bathroom on the first floor of our home. While I balanced my body and clung to the antique white freestanding bathtub with ornate thick legs and held myself in place, Dad took the belt to my bare skin and hit me for the first and only time in my life. I waited for the familiar sting, as Mom was comfortable with the belt—*but it never came.* Dad barely touched me with the belt, though I would have welcomed the pain over the sadness and disappointment in his eyes. Dad yelled loud and scary, but he wasn't one to hit.

I felt low and full of shame at disappointing my father, but, neither the punishment nor my humiliation stopped my addiction. Each episode became a little worse than the previous one.

In third grade, I gave up candy for Lent. I lasted a few days before stealing money and buying confections, which Mom confiscated and hid in her bedroom drawer. Not long after I sniffed out the goods, I snuck in and ate small amounts of candy at a time—in the hope of not being noticed. The fear of God's wrath (or the belt whipping from Mom!) wasn't enough to quiet my addiction. Nothing stopped my cravings and my seeking to satisfy them.

One time when I was around six years old, I meandered into my parents' room in search of goodies on Dad's side of the dresser where he kept his Old Spice cologne, loose change, tooth picks individually wrapped in cellophane, Wrigley's Spearmint gum, and little teeny tiny squares of black Sen Sen breath mints contained in a beautiful, alluring foil package. I well recall these refreshing little black mints that melted and released a strong burst of licorice-like flavor on my tongue.

On this particular day, I was distracted from my usual finds because a glass bottle containing a red syrupy substance with a picture of a skull on the back alongside a big red X captured my attention. The label was creepy to look at but that didn't deter me from twisting open the bottle and emptying it down my throat. Immediately, in sheer ecstasy, I tasted sweet cherry rapture and experienced a rush. Almost at once, the room started spinning and I fell on the floor in a deep slumber.

My next recollection was of being in a hospital with people rushing around murmuring something I couldn't quite make out, as they hovered in blurred view in front of me. I didn't know at the time what codeine cough syrup was or that I was in critical condition.

By 13, my body had grown and grown. Overnight, I was a full-breasted woman with a little kid tucked inside. An underweight child soon became 100 pounds heavier, and the compulsion to eat Long John pastries filled with thick cream and covered in fudge frosting, along with hot rolls slathered in butter, flurried further out of control, especially with easy access at my job working for the local bakery in Wautoma, Wisconsin.

My fear of obesity led to the birth of many diets. The lime-green uniform I wore at work either dragged on the floor from a huge weight loss or rose above my ankles after a big gain. At my heaviest times, the elastic band cut into my protruding belly and the buttons popped open, exposing my cleavage—to my intense mortification.

Up and down my weight went, as I swung from one diet to the next, my mood vacillating from deliriously happy to utterly miserable. My emotional self was stripped of any self-assurance while I silently cried out for someone to understand and fix what was wrong with me.

My daily existence morphed into the isolation of mental warfare—an ongoing argument with myself over whether I should give in to eating without bounds or suffer starvation. Depression and low self-esteem became all too familiar. Living a life of normalcy seemed out of the question. I thought only about my next meal or fast. I had no answer as to how to proceed.

The closest glimpse of resolution was when I joined Weight Watchers at nineteen years old and was introduced to their program, which was built around whole foods. In those days processed foods weren't allowed on the meal plan. Meals were balanced, calories were counted, and food was weighed.

The early days of Weight Watchers was the first time I felt relief from my addiction—that is until I reached my goal weight and entered maintenance, which introduced processed foods back into my diet. Then, chatter in my head returned with a vengeance, and once again I overate or starved. This was my initial awareness that certain foods triggered out-of-control eating.

I discovered that chocolate, cakes, and bread compelled me to eat more of the same or other, similar foods. The power these substances held pulled me in like a vacuum sucks in dirt. They activated my lack of control.

I became aware that natural foods had less of a harmful impact on my struggle with weight and my relationship with food. Yet I still had unanswered questions, though a ray of hope had materialized. I observed my response to various foods and learned if I eliminated certain ones, a calmer self-emerged. A connection to my inner strength, and a new understanding of spirituality began to surface.

Early Memories Something Was Wrong

My process of spiritual recovery from food addiction involved examining early memories that something was extremely wrong regarding food. The way certain foods are handled by the addict is very different than the way the "normal" person deals with those foods. Below are portions of the study interviews that provide a peek into my early memories and those of others who participated and that show something was wrong in regard to our relationship with food.

I knew I had a problem when I was a little child but I didn't know exactly what it was. I loved candy. I mean I loooovvvvvvvved candy. Candy was everything. I didn't really know it was a problem until I turned into a voluptuous teenager and began to get fat. I was petrified. My mom was obese, and I didn't want to go there—ever. I dieted down to skinny and then went on an all-out binge—just like a drunk trying to quit. The progression from overweight to thin and back again was horrible.

I questioned why I had been punished with this horrible disease. I thought at first if I became thin, the problem would simply go away. It never did; it only got worse. Each diet became more difficult for me to stick to until I felt like walking in the lake—to end it all. I wished I were stronger. I wished I were normal. When I did have my skinny moments I found guys looked at me—really looked. I was well endowed. I hated that, and I loved that. I felt powerful. I felt vulnerable.

In my thin phase, I flirted until I got the attention—then I became frightened and returned to my little corner to eat. I didn't know what to do with guys and their interest. I didn't want to be easy, but I wanted the hugs and the kisses and their notice. I wanted the love that was absent in my life. I was very, very lonely when I was young. Mom traveled, my siblings moved out, and Dad came home only every other weekend. I was alone. ~Lisa

Arthur recalled one vacation at the age of 12 or 13 walking through town with newly made friends, kicking twigs and stones, while they ate bags of candy they'd purchased from the local store. His mind was busy with worry when he realized that the candy he'd bought and gobbled down in front of his friends wasn't enough. Having mostly finished it and knowing he was going to run out was quite concerning to him. This was a first awareness that something was wrong in his relationship with food–further realization came to him in stages.

Charisma only became aware her relationship with food had a name when she finally entered a Twelve Step program. Earlier, however, she knew something was wrong when she ate trigger foods and went on one binge after another. Intent on recovery many years later, she began to pore over a series of books that opened up a whole new explanation about eating issues. This, coupled with the Twelve Step program and its anecdotal information, expanded her understanding.

Hearing that other people had what she had and finding a place to share her fears and hopes was the start of her eventual transformation. She learned that "some people have a condition called food addiction," and that food addiction was her problem as well.

Recognition, however, may not come at an early age when food addiction isn't the predominant problem, as another study participant indicates:

I had been sober from alcohol and drugs for about eight years, and up until maybe the sixth year feeling a real nice progression of recovery coming, and then all of a sudden during years six, seven, and eight, I just felt like I was sort of backsliding in some way—but I wasn't drinking or taking drugs. I couldn't recognize the fact that my food was now inhibiting me from progressing. It was like trying to hold a handful of sand in your hands and it just slips through your fingers. Why am I not so calm anymore? Why am I not so serene and why am I so agitated—so irritable? You know all those things. That was when I recognized I had a problem with food. ~Damien

As far back as Charisma remembered, she always binged. The quantities and duration of the binges weren't the same in her earlier childhood, but the amount she ate later morphed into enough food to feed a small army. She recalled that if the food was only a small amount, she didn't want to be bothered. For her, eating was always about quantity.

John remembered that on numerous occasions in elementary school he stole money, then walked two blocks from his home, having to cross a big street filled with traffic, just to buy French fries and thick chocolate shakes.

Marilyn's eyes twinkled at the mere memory of the corner store where she often strolled alone—even as a young child. She recalled how she hit the jackpot when she purchased three bags of chocolate-covered pretzels for a dollar. She ate so many, she became really sick. She laughed as she remembered she never ate chocolate-covered pretzels after that "… but I sure ate pretzels and I ate chocolate."

The memories of her early eating habits remained vivid for Marilyn, especially how her mom kept the house so cold that Marilyn could secretly keep ice cream outside the window of her room in the winter. Late at night she'd lie awake wide eyed, waiting and thinking, *There's ice cream out there*. She plotted how she could get to it. And then when the house was dark and still, she'd crawl out on the ledge outside her window in the dead of night and eat the cold ice cream, recalling fondly how it melted on her tongue and drizzled down her throat while she shivered from the cold.

Another study participant said: I was aware many years ago that if I started eating something I couldn't stop eating it. I couldn't have just one brownie. If there was only one brownie or one candy bar, I wanted more and more and more and more. I was aware of that very early on. ~Adriana

I was fat child because I ate everything in sight. ~Lucy

I always had an eating problem because I always loved sweets. It was my weakness for many years— maybe for ten years the addiction was real bad— bingeing was real bad. ~Charisma

Out of Control
Like me, those I spoke with went through bouts of out-of-control eating, always hoping to make this the last binge, while experiencing intense highs and lows surrounding devouring, in a short amount of time, as much food as their

stomachs could hold. Although the binge brought each of us down and filled us with shame, we also enjoyed a giddy feeling preceding it.

When my kids were little, I had birthday parties, or my sister would have them. I would slowly eat everything that was left. My niece used to call me "Aunt Munchy" because she said I was always munching, and that was years and years ago when they were little kids. I would take a whole cake and I would start eating slice after slice (motions with her hands) until nothing was left. ~Lucy

Lucy would come home late at night from working in a local restaurant and began to eat upstairs while her son slept downstairs. She ate and ate, pushing in as much food as she could. At around three in the morning, her son would yell up the stairs, "Ma, don't you think you ought to go to bed and stop eating?" These were scary times that still haunt Lucy.

Adriana kept going back for more and more pecan pie until she'd eaten the whole pie. She did it in slivers and never forgot how it made her very, very depressed—*to the point that she didn't want to live.*

And Lucy said:

On the way home from work I stopped at three different supermarkets. I used to love the produce section because in that section were rows of these candies that you bought by the pound. I would eat some in the store and I would buy a bag and I would eat them in my car. Then I would come home and I'd eat the ice-cream that I'd bought. I would eat Cool Whip. I would then eat a box of cereal. I mean, I was bad—and it was all night that I did it. Oh, it was a sick thing. I tried to diet. This was my first inkling that I had trouble controlling and stopping the consumption of sugary, chocolaty foods. I craved them. ~Lucy

I stole, lied, snuck, and begged for the stuff. I didn't care how I got it, as long as I got it. ~Lisa

Bargaining

We swore this was the last time we'd binge-eat, that tomorrow was somehow going to be different. The bargaining side of this addictive behavior might take the form of dieting, restricting food completely, over-exercising, or grazing slowly.

Lucy spent times restricting because she thought she'd figured out how to control her food consumption. She went long periods during which she ate minimal amounts of foods—then the bingeing returned. She remembered it as a *dangerously bad situation*—very bad, because her thoughts were always about food. She bargained to not eat all day and eat one meal at night, thinking she was fine. She later learned she'd destroyed her metabolism and incurred medical issues: Her hair fell out, teeth loosened; her memory became poor—until she found a Twelve Step program to pull her out of the swamp she was drowning in.

I too bargained. I ate until I felt that the food was going to spill out of my head. The episodes were horrible but I comforted myself with the next planned diet that would begin the following day—or Monday. This idea of dieting to fix the problem excited me. It was part of my ritual—binge—diet—binge—diet to avoid life in the present.

Marilyn habitually started her day busy doing something. She'd go on and on and on through the entire day, and before she knew it 8:00 at night had arrived and she hadn't eaten since the previous night. So, a single-meal-per-day schedule justified her one long binge nightly.

Adriana banked on the theory if you ate something— enough of it—you would get sick of it. She tried that many times, and—*it didn't work.*

Awareness of Food Addiction

The awakening is marked by an initial awareness of food addiction and recall of early memories that something was wrong with our behavior. We learned as young children to eat certain foods because they made us "feel" better, but didn't realize that our drive was caused by more than desiring the taste of the food. The food could be chocolate, pastries, or potato chips, all stimulating our brain, providing a pleasurable reaction. We continued to eat these foods long after feeling full.

Lucy heard on a medical radio talk show about food addiction. She was dumbfounded when she recognized herself in the explanation. She didn't know what she had, but everything the host said on that program applied to her. She had always sought mastery over her eating—and never could gain control. She attempted to try this diet and that diet, and go this way and that way, and not eat or eat this food or that food, thinking all she needed was better self-control.

Our healing us gave answers where we once had none. We got glimpses of control over what was once out of control by abstaining from certain foods and turning to a source greater than ourselves. Prior to this awareness, retrieving foods from the garbage, off the floor, and out of a drawer, and swearing the binges must end were a daily practice. Once our eyes opened, bargaining was no longer an option. We had a hope of healing that was not present before, an answer to the early inklings something was wrong with our relationships with food.

Intense attempts to try any measure to correct our problem often led to chaos and depression. One participant was so depressed she wanted to sleep all the time, while another ran from one self-destructive behavior to the next, almost losing his job. Still others lost important relationships. A patient once told me she would rather lock herself in the bedroom with a box of brownies and the television than make love to her husband, whom she said repulsed her. Another patient ate himself to 400 pounds to avoid dating girls, for fear he would be rejected.

Life in active addiction becomes unmanageable. Thoughts of whether life is worth living become quite frequent. Maureen, a bulimic patient, learned in nursing school the exact spot to place the scalpel on her wrist—how to push and puncture the right vein to end it all. She tried twice.

We often couldn't give a name to our behaviors with food and the havoc it caused in our lives, but we knew something was very wrong.

Our intense preoccupation with food and our weight was ever present for most of us during our active bingeing, but in recovery, we learned that worrying about weight proved counterproductive; paradoxically, making recovery our central purpose resulted in weight loss. An emphasis on weight loss created a tension that often led to bingeing. One patient hopped on and off her scale like a bunny in heat three times a day hoping to find a lower reading of her weight. When she placed the emphasis on healing, it led her to a strong and spiritual transition and in time *weight loss*.

This great preoccupation with food and body shut off our spiritual connections. Controlling the intake of food and weight was a daily battle. In the next chapter, we'll examine the effects active binging created over time.

Personal Inventory Questions

1. What is your earliest memory of knowing something wasn't quite right in your relationship with food? Did you ever steal money for candy or food?

2. Have you ever had friendly chats with your Higher Source or has food replaced the super natural and become your total focus?

3. Do you recall walking to the grocery store or gas station alone as a child in order to get candy or foods?

4. Did you ever give up foods for religious purposes like Lent only to sneak them back into your life?

5. At what age did you attend your first weight loss program? Was it a good experience? Did it lead to further diets?

6. Can you relate to Charisma's experience with binge eating? What about Arthur's? Both knew early in life that something was wrong in their relationship with food.

7. Damien recalled how agitated and irritable he became after eating certain foods. What has been your experience?

8. John recalled walking across a busy street when he was quite young just to get his fill of candy. Did you do anything similar? Marilynn thought she hit the jackpot when she discovered three bags of chocolate-covered pretzels for a dollar; she ate so many she got really sick. Have you ever done something similar?

9. As a child, did you ever hide foods in your bedroom only to quietly unwrap them in the middle of the night so others wouldn't hear? Did you bargain with yourself or with God to never do this again?

10. Adriana couldn't stop at one brownie, or one candy bar. She wanted more. She discovered her need for "more" very early on. Like Lucy at birthday parties, eating slice after slice of cake until nothing was left? What about you?

Chapter 6

Effect of Active Binge Eating

Your adornment should not be an external one:
Braiding the hair, wearing gold jewelry,
Or dressing in fine clothes,
But rather the hidden character of the heart,
Expressed in the imperishable beauty
Of a gentle and calm disposition,
Which is precious in the sight of God
~1 Peter 3:3-4

All too often our emphasis is on external adornments such as hair extensions or perfect cut diamonds, clothes with name-brand labels for all to see, rather than on the internal happenings seeded in the heart. Thin, even emaciated, bodies are praised. Plastic surgery to defy aging has become the norm. The inner cloak of beauty doesn't cease with an aged or not so "perfect" body, but this truth is missed.

The young learn from television, billboards, and magazines that skinny, adorned with the newest fandangle and looking as young as one can, are in. This impressionable population often strives to become lean through starvation and other dangerous and unhealthy avenues. Tactics such as restricting, bingeing and purging, and over-exercising open up doors to eating disorders.

Like most, I too was caught up with my external image rather than the hidden character of my heart. The imperishable beauty within was a foreign concept—but once grasped, a calm and gentle disposition began to surface in me. Of course this revelation didn't happen for years as I was caught up along with the rest of society in striving for the "perfect" body through dieting, and purging by exercise. I didn't become aware of this internal struggle until well into my adult years.

As noted earlier, I knew something was wrong when I was very young, but I couldn't pinpoint what it was, especially because I was quite thin until my teenage years. Yet I was obsessed during those formative years with obtaining and eating candies and cakes, and after their consumption, I was tapped out of all energy. I didn't connect food, mood, and obsession until I began observing my grandma Ruth (whom we called Ma—and then years later Granny). She was constantly on a diet, trying desperately to get back her once svelte body.

Ma's moods swung like a pendulum from frantic to listless—from highs to lows. You never knew which grandma you'd meet up with. Sometimes she'd scream, while other times she was the warm and fuzzy grandma everyone dreams to have. But she spared her hugs with me. Growing up, I wasn't my grandmother's favorite. In fact, I annoyed the hell out of her. I was a brat and she didn't like how I got my way with everything.

Baba, my grandmother's mother, was the complete opposite of Ma. She had a calm, kind, and loving demeanor. Baba, of English descent, always dressed and with makeup on, wore lovely clothes even if she had no outing planned. She was soft spoken, hugged freely, and loved to laugh. Her home was impeccable, and her meals were made from natural ingredients. She loved blueberry pies and burnt toast—she said burnt toast made teeth white, needed to remove the blueberry stains.

My siblings gossiped that Baba also thought I was a brat, but I personally never witnessed any animosity on her part toward me—even when I misbehaved, which was most of the time. I now blame my erratic moods to sucking on sugar cubes and eating candy whenever and wherever I could. In fact, I later understood that I had a strong resemblance to my grandmother Ruth (Ma) in my metabolic chemistry and resulting behavior.

I recall one particular sweltering summer night in north Wisconsin when my siblings, Mom, Ma, and I were gathered around the television in our main summer cottage. Ma (Baba's youngest daughter) was watching the local news, and I was sprawled out on the floor next to the seven-and-a-half-foot mahogany grandfather clock with tempered beveled glass. I became mesmerized by the bronze pendulum swaying back and forth, anticipating that the gold face dial would depict the hour and signal a triple-chime movement.

The weather came on and Ma shushed me because she wanted to hear, but I kept talking to my mom over the weather forecaster. Ma stood up, came over, and slapped me, leaving her imprint and sharp sting on my face.

Shocked beyond words, I ran out of the room, yanked the entrance door open, and flew down the hill toward the lake, stubbing my bare toes on a tree stump. Then I slipped on the slate that formed the path down to the lower green cottage, where some renters I didn't know were in residence. They heard my commotion and pulled me into their home to comfort me as I wailed over my double upset. I stayed overnight, and nobody came to look for me. I was nine.

Ma, known to scream, yelled frequently at Hale, my step-grandfather; fights broke out between them regularly, and the police were called on several occasions. During one fight that comes to mind, they screamed so loudly into the night I awakened out of a deep sleep to hear glass breaking, doors slamming, and screams piercing the stillness of the night. On this singular evening, Ma whacked Hale over the head with a beer bottle.

Throughout the summers, we heard many such scenes coming out of the pink cottage to the right from our bedroom window. The cottage I ran away to the night I was slapped was referred to as the green cottage. The other two cottages didn't have a color name. They were just the back cottage and the lower cottage. I never stayed in those unless a friend's parents were renting.

My long-deceased great-grandfather Ray built all the cottages after being diagnosed with a heart condition, and told to slow down, retired from the family newspaper. Prior to his death, the four smaller cottages were rented out during the season to supplement his income. They later went to my great-grandmother Baba, but then when she died, Ma inherited the property.

Fast forward 30 years to how I learned about the connection between food and mood. At that time, Mom went to collect Granny Ruth (Ma) and Hale from their Florida home because they had become senile and unable to care for themselves. Shortly after the move back to their original hometown in Delevan, Wisconsin, which they'd left when I was 12, Hale passed away from a return bout of lung cancer. Granny was then placed in a nursing home. The first nursing home was a typical home—not much to report. But at the second nursing home, the effect of food on Granny became very clear to me.

This facility was run by white-habit Catholic nuns who were kind and loving. They immediately put a blue finch in Granny's room to sing to her every morning, and they fed her organic foods grown on the grounds. The foods were whole, not processed. Granny became sweet and, kind, the gentlest grandma anyone could ever dream of. She smiled and winked at me as she grabbed my hand while she ate. She told lovely stories of good times in her life. The transformation was magical and wonderful. She was even taken off many of her medicines. I learned that simple carbohydrates were her nemesis. I later discovered that I'm just like Ma in that if I eat simple carbohydrates or drink alcohol, I become anxious, moody, and confrontational. Granny (Ma) died at 86.

Granny's watery hazel eyes often dripped tears when she laughed, not to mention that she wet her pants at the same time. In her youthful days, she bronzed her body soaking in the sun—referring to herself as a salad when she created her concoction of suntan lotion by mixing olive oil and vinegar. She was an avid, strong, Olympic-style swimmer with a college degree in physical education who later taught swimming in Delevan at the famous Lake Lawn Resort. She was quite a beauty, according to the stories, and kept an amazing fit body. She lived a "fairy tale" life: Horses surrounded her home, and she rode the trails with vacationers and daily swam Lake Geneva in the summer months.

I'd been told Granny Ruth and Grandfather Arnold made an especially handsome couple. Grandpa Arnold sported dark, wavy hair and crisp blue eyes. Life was a fantasy, indeed, with their two daughters—my mom, Joan, and Aunt Pat. Rumor had it Grandpa Arnold knew how to "handle" Ma and kept her calm and happy—*a hidden character of the heart expressed in the imperishable beauty of a gentle and calm disposition—precious in the sight of God...* until he died suddenly while bowling on the local town league. He was 40.

After Grandpa Arnold passed away, cheated out of a love-affair marriage, Ma went out to clubs and drank alcohol and ate sweets—both of which she had a chemical reaction to—and the whirlwind of preoccupation with food and body weight began. Her adornment became an external one: A beehive hairdo twirled and plopped on top of her head, and she wore gold jewelry and dressed in fine clothes,

Ma would start and stop diets as often as her peers donned a clean pair of underwear to replace the soiled. She was sneaky—hid treats while Hale (her second husband) concealed flasks of alcohol for himself throughout their home. Ma was spiritually inhibited by active bingeing and multiple diets she couldn't adhere to. As she gained weight, she became more and more out of control with her food and mood, and she bargained to start a new diet on the coming Monday, clearly a mirror image of my own addiction. She was insecure, angry, volatile, mean, scary, and darn right annoying. I avoided her. Her problems, though, were not her fault, just as my addiction wasn't my fault—or your difficulty with food yours.

Preoccupation with Food and/or Body Weight

Granny's life-long preoccupation with food, body, and weight is the main ingredient found in disordered eating problems. Take Arthur for example, who described his spiritual recovery from food addiction as an absolute roller coaster. Even after two years of back-to-back abstinence he had a difficult time focusing on the spiritual aspect of his recovery because he was so obsessed with food and weight, and unable to let go of the diet mentality. He feared gluttony and not living lean. He was consumed by the battle of wanting to binge and yet attached to the philosophy of thinness.

Lucy, too, recalled her battle of 25 years during which time she worked in restaurants purposely to have access to an abundance of food. She methodically hid half-eaten desserts in several key spots throughout the back area of the restaurant and gobbled these down when no one was looking. Even though she had her fill throughout the evening, on the way home she hit the supermarkets that were open all night in order to buy more to eat. *"Food was calling."*

Marilyn too was caught up with her obsession with food and her body weight, and told me:

I even binged on—I don't remember if it was Slim Fast, but something like that, in the cans. You know, I was always trying to do something about my weight. I remember putting the cans in my room, in a drawer, and drinking one and finding a bug in it—because I had left it open in the drawer. I don't know what the hell I was thinking. I remember that—and I remember bingeing on the stuff. Once I stopped eating sugar, I would try to eat sugar-free things. And you know what that does to your digestion! I mean, it would tear me up—but I had some rationalization in my mind. You know, it wasn't as bad as real sugar. And then of course, the addiction to the sugar-substitute foods progressed and I said, 'Oh forget it. I can't do it.' I had lots of gas—*and the pain*; so, I went back to the sugar. But, I remember trying to stick with it.

I recollect when they came out with Whitman's, Whitman's Samplers, in sugar free. I was so excited. But I knew that was going to be a big problem because the box held a large amount. Not really, you know—but as far as my body's sensitivity to the sugar substitute, it was. So, I methodically attempted to plan what other things I could eat and spaced out the candy so that I wouldn't feel the effects [gas and bloating] to the same degree. And so, I put a lot of time and energy into that—a LOT of time and energy, okay.

Marilyn's infatuation with diet foods was not uncommon for any of us. In fact, we vacillated between diet foods, junk foods, and diet programs.

Damien recounted one time when he devoured a large pizza and part of a small pizza, and then ate the rest of the small pizza a few hours later. He admonished himself over the fact he'd eaten 16 slices of the large pizza and eight slices of the small—*possibly three days of calories.*

Charisma underwent similar experiences, noting when she started on some food, especially with sugar, flour, and wheat as ingredients, she couldn't stop. She *had* to eat the entire bag, or "... had to eat the entire whatever," often whipping up some concoction. As she loved to bake and cook, it was simple for her to just make a gooey creation.

Food served many purposes on different levels for all of us. I personally enjoyed eating alone and watching television. I felt as if I had a buddy—a friend—and I could escape from the real world and numb out.

Adriana concurred in regard to her relationship with food:

Food became my lover. I took food and I ate it in bed. It was my lover. It was safe—never left me; it was there. And I don't recall binge eating fast. I romanced the food and took my time to binge eat. I mean, it might have taken me an hour or two, but I would just continue eating. I wasn't shoveling the food down my face. Though other times I shoveled food into my face, lot of times I didn't. It was like a romance and buying the binge foods was a seduction. Food was my lover for many, many years.

Some of us leaned toward sugary foods, while others went for starchy, and it didn't matter if we were hungry or full. Take Arthur, for example; he was more partial to foods like pizzas. He obsessed over how *good* the pizza was: "...if it was a good pizza—`good' meaning if the cheese had the right level of salt in it and the crust wasn't soggy and the toppings were prepared well—had a good taste to it, was spiced properly, and the sauce had the right kind of flavor to it, I could eat a large pizza in a very short period of time." He would eat until he was full, and then as soon as he could eat more without getting sick, he would eat more of the same thing.

Sneaking and Hiding Food

People addicted to food generally sneak and hide it. One characteristic of food addiction is to plot and plan how to get specific foods, where to store them, and when to eat them. I ate in private—after sneaking to obtain the foods. Lucy hid food from her kids *so she could have it* and they wouldn't get to it. Her foods were cakes, pies, and candy.

Arthur recalled going to the candy store with his little friends and needing to slip back to the store by going a way that they didn't know. He *had to get* more candy. "...so that I had a large enough stash of sweets that I thought was sufficient." He is astounded that even back then there were things about his eating he hid.

Lucy, speaking with a sense of shame, illustrates the nature and character of one experience of sneaking and hiding food:

I remember [picking her words carefully in between bouts of nervous laughter] when the man I was living with in Jersey was down here visiting and staying with me before he moved here. While he watched television in the living room, I was in my kitchen around the corner, standing in there and eating—and I just couldn't stop. One thing I remember was feeling sick—feeling horrible—and now having to go out into the next room and act as if [getting loud and more nervous, almost as if she'd shifted back in time] ...you know. So, ah—yeah—it was a trip.

Spirituality Inhibited by Active Binging

Spiritual healing alone works if you aren't dealing with a chemical imbalance. But we suffer from a chemical imbalance, and we experienced a blockage in our spirituality when actively binge eating. We lived in a self-centered world, and yet never ended up with what satisfied us. We couldn't give of ourselves because we were immersed in addictive eating, blocking the connection to our higher consciousness. In our self-centered world, we were unable to love ourselves—*we were centered in self-hate.*

Healing requires a three-prong mindset: physical, emotional, and spiritual. How can we heal our bodies if our minds are toxic from our chemical response to certain foods? In turn, if we are emotionally bankrupt, how do we find our way spiritually? Can we spiritually connect when we are knee deep in a food binge?

I can only speak for myself and the answer is *not totally.* Yes, the binge drops me to my knees begging for relief; however, once the food partially digests I'm ready for another binge.

What comes first, cleansing from the binge or reaching out to a higher presence? Well, we can certainly try reaching out to our spiritual source, but with the physical addiction and its effects obscuring that connection, we may have to first deal with ourselves on a basic level.

An active binge edges out God. Picture, if you will, an alcoholic in an acutely addictive state trying to connect with a higher level of power *while three sheets to the wind.* He/she is not in the right state of mind to make (or remember) the God connection. The food addict too is not in the right state of mind—drunk on simple carbohydrates.

So, start the process with abstinence from sugar, flour, and wheat which prompts the physical withdrawal as the body cleanses and the mind clears and opens up opportunity to find your source.

At times, when I was loaded up with sugar, I struggled with negative images of this higher source of being, feelings of spiritual unworthiness and shame—fear of abandonment by God. Surrendering and keeping faith were difficult while I was filled with dishonesty and deception. I believed in a higher force, yet had deep spiritual struggles creating a major impediment to my ability to recover from my eating disorder. This isn't to say there weren't previous times in my life when I had felt a genuine relationship with God and a degree of a spiritual self. I still attended Sunday mass intermittently, but had lost these real connections through the course of my eating disorder.

Marilyn, a 40-year-old compulsive eater, expressed something similar: "When that [separation from the source] happens—I sort of feel like I lose that clarity about what it was like when I ate. I definitely kept myself blocked, blocked from my higher power. Vigilance is needed to maintain this program, because I don't want to lose that connection with God."

Marylyn was acutely aware of her disconnect from God when she ate trigger foods. She became blocked in her awakening. In my own quest for understanding my eating disorder, I found that others in their eating disorders replaced the higher entity with food. Food became their object of worship and their eating disorder rituals become their religious practices.

In a journal entry in August 2004, I wrote: "Binge eating destroyed my relationship with the universe. It blocked me from a loving energy and I lost all faith and trust in him. I became very angry with the Divine Source because I felt he abandoned me. Eventually, the more I ate, the Source of

Being became erased from my mind. My binge ritual became my god and my body became the devil."

Lucy was afraid to believe she could trust an enlightened source *out there* who could turn her eating disorder—a major issue in her life—into something manageable, that he would take care of her. She knew he was out there somewhere but found it hard to believe he could or would concern himself with this silly problem, since serious situations far greater than hers plagued the world.

Binge eating left me depleted of all worth, and I wrote:

I felt ugly. I felt dumb. I felt like I was dirty. I felt mean and angry. I raged. I was lost. I was vulnerable. I was scared. It was like the devil was in me—convinced me with lies that I could have some of the sweet foods that I craved. It was okay. But these were lies—all lies—telling me that I shouldn't deprive myself of these foods—that they were made for us to eat, to enjoy. – Lisa

...when it becomes a controlling battle with the food— to the point at which I'm not taking care of myself, I turn to yet another binge in order to make up for that, then it is all fear based, and has nothing to do with God and has more to do with the absence of a loving energy. – Arthur

Arthur didn't believe his binges could take away his essential nature, but he understood he could mask his essential nature—and he did. He was compelled, however, to continue growing—and found that eating properly, weighing and measuring his food, gave him comfort and security. As we were talking, he nodded toward his cupboards. "I've got scales up there and I set boundaries. I eat properly at my workplace. I actually have a cabinet with everything in it that I need in order to eat healthfully at work."

Arthur isn't perfect, and at times, he skips his scheduled meals. But he is pressing onward in his recovery with each passing month. He is abstinent from his trigger foods. He thinks that sobriety on an emotional level and sobriety from co-dependence is much more important than any sobriety from a substance alone. "The active addiction is the kind of existence that I prefer not to have, which involves rapid binge cycles—and not feeling ready to do the thing that God called me to do, and not feeling remorse because I started to do something and didn't finish it again. That's not where I want to be. I want to be where I am now."

Because I was so into the disease of eating, it just consumed my thoughts. I wish spirituality could have taken over, but it didn't. The only thing that saved me during the bingeing for the last 22 years is that I was a runner. I would go outside—in the outdoors—and I would run—and I was one with nature. I would have my headphones on with my music, because I made my own tapes that I played with all the different kinds of music. So, to me that was somewhat spirituality. But when I was in the addiction, nothing else came into my world—*the addiction was really bad.* – Lucy

Charisma is cognizant of the fact that if she isn't in a good place spiritually she isn't in a good place in recovery and will volume eat or restrict her spirituality even in abstinence. If she has eaten too much food or not enough food, it is evident to her she is missing the spiritual component. Arthur agrees. "...without spirituality—I'd say I'm more crazed and hyper and all that. I'm going to get really sloppy with my food." Charisma affirms if she isn't abstinent, maintaining a connection to spirit is difficult, and it's not worth the binge to lose that connection. She repeated firmly, "I don't want to lose my spiritual self."

We all echoed the belief that spiritual healing alone will work if you aren't dealing with a chemical imbalance, and we each suffered consequences as a result of our spirituality blocked by active binging.

Personal Inventory Questions

1. How often have you been influenced by television, billboards, magazines, or movies stars telling you to be skinny—or adorned yourself with the newest fandangle to avoid what's going on within?

2. Can you identify with a specific relative as I did with my Grandmother Ruth, who was constantly on a diet trying desperately to get back her once svelte body—or with my grandfather addicted to alcohol? Do your family members have such addictions? Can you see yourself in their behavior?

3. Arthur was always on a roller coaster with his food and so obsessed with food that he wasn't able to focus on the spiritual aspect of his recovery. He was consumed by the battle between wanting to binge and the desire for thinness. Is this you?

4. Lucy methodically hid half-eaten desserts throughout the back area of the restaurant where she worked and gobbled them down when no one was looking. Does this ring true for you at work? Do you sneak foods from your fellow workers and hide to eat them?

5. Does an active binge edge out the presence of God for you? Describe at length what this does to your psyche. Your energy.

6. When in your life did you feel as though God had abandoned you?

7. Can you relate to Charisma, who states that when she isn't in a good place spiritually, she isn't in a good place in recovery and will volume-eat with "clean" foods when abstinent—free of sugar, flour, and wheat?

8. Do you block important aspects of your life when you're in your addiction, like Lucy? She found that when in her addiction, nothing else came into her world—*the addiction was really bad.* She blocked her past experiences by numbing

out with food to avoid the emotional pain. What are you blocking?

9.   Many mood alterations result from imbalances in our neurotransmitters and other hormones that regulate behavior. Do you continue to exercise when you binge eat? Perhaps certain foods give you energy or even make you hyper. Do you over-exercise? What about chocolate, does it alter your mood—cover your pain?

10.   Have you ever experienced rapid binge cycles? How long did they last? How did you work your way out of them?

Chapter 7

Effect of Spirituality Blocked by Active Bingeing

Why did I not perish at birth?
Come forth from the womb and expire?
Or why was I not buried away like an untimely birth,
Like babes that have never seen the light,
Wherefore did the knees receive me?
Or why did I suck at the breasts?
For then I should have lain down and been tranquil;
Had I slept, I should then have been at rest.
~Job 4:11-13~

Have you ever asked why you were born? Have you ever asked why you can't stop eating? Two continuous questions I entertained were: `Why am I here?' and `Why must I eat the way I do?' *Had I slept, I should then have been at rest.* I couldn't understand why I lived a life filled with such turmoil over food and obesity, a life filled with shame.

Of course I didn't know then what I know now. I now know that I have a chemical imbalance and when I ate sugar, flour, or wheat, my imbalance was triggered and I couldn't stop eating—*then shame set in.* It wasn't my fault. *And it isn't your fault.* Certain foods acted as a drug that led to my compulsive eating, leaving me spiritually blunted while my shame soared.

Spirituality Blocked by Active Bingeing

A common thread that weaved in and out of the comments from each person represented in this book was the condition of a blocked connection to our spirit, a blocked connection to our higher source, and a blocked connection to other people as a result of our binge eating.

What causes the blocking of the active food addict's spirituality? The first that comes to mind is that the spiritual core of our being is blocked when we hang on to our sad stories. We *become* our sad stories. We identify ourselves as persons with a disease. We embrace food addiction rather than God addiction—and we feel ourselves to be hopeless victims.

Active bingeing is often described as a time of chaos with no room for spiritual growth. We use our addiction as an excuse that blocks us from living in the now. As noted earlier, shame is a constant. Relationships are lost.

We miss the opportunity to greet life because our heads are filled with frustrating and angry thoughts about how we can't stop eating and that our bodies aren't meeting society's expectations (or our own). So, we use food to elevate our moods and pull us out of a depressive funk. But a temporary high sensation is then soon followed by a crashing low.

During our periods of bingeing as our testimonies reveal, it wasn't uncommon for us to eat all day or all night when we could be alone with our stash—rather than interacting with other people. Our shame accompanied us every waking moment, only for us to temporarily forget it when we were knee deep in food again.

During active addiction, we spent every occasion trying to get back to the way we were or forward to the way we wanted to be through exercise, diet, plastic surgery, vitamins—just to find love or at least *acceptance*. We didn't realize a power greater than these failed remedies was easily available right where we were—that we could slip into spiritual alignment any time we chose. We didn't see that plain and simple truth because we were blocked by the foods and moods that blinded us like the bright morning sun—that not even sunglasses can shield us from.

A higher source exists within each of us seeking expression—yet this seed is often blocked by active bingeing—with our focus on wishing we had expired early on or hadn't even been born rather than experience one more day gnashing our teeth from loss of food control.

Anger and grief resulting from out-of-control eating can cause a sense of loss of the higher presence—a sense that God is far away. We feel that we no longer have control over the circumstances of our lives, and we feel hopeless and alone.

Family and friends don't understand us when we say something is wrong. On top of that, there's a *dis-connect* from people as well as from our Creator, our source; we feel we exist as islands. A mind filled with clutter tells us we're fat, lousy, old, and insignificant dots as persons—not very conducive to feeling worthy of the love of God (or whatever you want to call that which both made and sustains us).

Dis-ease permeates our beings and blocks us from beauty, love, God—our savior. We tire of telling everyone we're sick, and then of hearing—*no you're not—just stop eating and obsessing over food.*

Shame

People in the active phase of food addiction live with shame, worry, guilt, and self-hatred, feelings that certainly block all sense of worthiness and all spirituality. The word `shame' is believed to stem from an older word meaning *to cover.* We want to hide. We're completely alone with the self. One bite of trigger food opens the valve to non-stop eating—shame envelops us.

Marilyn threw the half-eaten cheesecake into the garbage can, cautious not to squish it while she swallowed the remaining evidence, promising to herself this would be her one last binge.

The next day Marilyn dug through the soiled garbage to retrieve the carefully wrapped leftovers, pushing away coffee grinds and the rotting vestiges of prior meals. She then wolfed down the odds and ends of the various goodies she'd hidden in the moldering trash. Soon self-disgust set in—along with self-hatred. A feeling of *nowhere to turn* rose up in her, and she felt undeserving of the good things in life, overcome with self-contempt and an urgency to dive and take cover—*she felt shamed.* In such a state, how could she connect with her spiritual essence?

Damien described his experience as like having a veil of darkness come over him, leaving him in a spiritual void where everything was black. In spite of the fact that he knowingly was courting self-destruction, he was sucked into an inability to stop eating, and he spiraled down.

Remember Jonathan, the young man who ate himself to death, discussed in my opening chapter? He was imprisoned in his body, incarcerated in his room. The bars surrounding his windows permitted no food to enter or exit, yet he continued to gain weight. At the end of his life, he weighed a thousand pounds.

How he obtained the food he ate was a secret that went to his grave with him, but Jonathan didn't stop eating, even though he knew it wasn't socially acceptable to weigh as much as four large men rolled into one person.

After each illicit bout with food, Jonathan's emotional floodgates opened, with shame launching forth immediately. He knew on a deeper level he had violated his personal, internal value system.

After the shame, then came the deluge of guilt, and his once-unyielding sense of self dissolved in an onrush of negativity. The fact that he voraciously stuffed food into his mouth, failed to either chew or taste, and lost conscious awareness of his actions, left him stripped of worth and cut off from his inborn spiritual connection.

Jonathan was paralyzed with fear at the thought that others might view him shoveling food into his mouth like a starving wild beast—that his *action(s)* would be the focus of their curiosity. How could any human being gobble down such an enormous quantity of food without even tasting it? What was the point?

The point was to take cover and remove the self from its perception of an unbearable existence by numbing himself with food—even if only for a moment. Yet the reality was the outcome—a body he couldn't hide from others. Shame was a painful feeling arising from the consciousness of gorging—done actually by his own volition. Shame allowed his body to expand to the size of a baby walrus, to make him, in his own eyes at least, unacceptable to everything shining, bright, clean, and of spiritual significance.

Why guilt after shame? Guilt allows for a feeling of responsibility or remorse for eating with the inability to stop, knowing consequences are soon to follow. Jonathan harbored a painful regret for the absence of control over his own behavior.

The shame pierced through Jonathan's very soul, which left him depleted of all appreciation of his inherent value.

Nobody knew about this young man's secret night eating because Jonathan isolated himself in his room—barricaded by tightly knit bars on the windows to prevent any food from passing through to him. Yet he always found a way to get his drug. Head hung low, feeling degraded; he once whispered to me that he wished he hadn't been born, that he wasn't worthy to be a person. *And then he died.*

Shame brews out of a physiological reaction to an addictive drug. In our case, the drug is simple carbohydrates. After we consume them, an instinctual response of shame takes over. Perhaps for us self-blame and self-contempt are a way to show we aren't altogether identified with the actions we pass judgment on. In fact, these negative emotional reactions work as a punishment for what we see as inexcusable misdeeds.

The terrible feelings are a way for us as addicts to defend against letting shame swallow us whole. Because we immediately *do* feel shame, we are less shameful. We must be punished, and so we punish ourselves, a punishment that also cuts us off from our spiritual centers. A pattern is born.

Emotional bankruptcy precedes a binge, and then results in shame, which is relieved through guilt. We are filled with self-blame and self-contempt, which leads again to unhealthful behavior with the food, and further emotional depletion. This negativity and weakness bring us back into the vicious cycle of yet another binge.

The sequence is spurred by personal humiliation, not public, until the weight starts to pile on and we become noticed. The fear is to be *"found out"* and exposed. It isn't socially acceptable to be obese, yet packing on the pounds until our clothes cut into our skin because they are tight is felt to be a deserved punishment for being out of control with our food. The penalty of exposure is justified because we have failed to be `normal.'

The shame is unbearable. If denied, it only resurfaces later on to create deeper pain and devastation. The internal, critical voice screams that we're naughty, selfish, ugly, dumb, fat, and of no value—perhaps imitating our parents or former teachers, reinforcing what we've been told—*and what we believed.*

I'd be on the night shift at the local restaurant, and like the other girls at work, I'd pile with them into a corner table, feet up on the chairs from pure exhaustion, and we'd eat. They used to laugh at me saying, `Oh what are you having?' I'd have the same thing all the time, a bowl of soup or a small plate of pasta—I'd never *really* eat.

They'd eat their cheesecake and stuff while I ate my meager ration of soup with noodles in it or pasta, never both. Then I'd leave there, planning to eat for real. And night after night, I'd run the same game—little knowing *pasta* was a trigger food and that it would trigger me *real bad.* I didn't realize. I would eat for hours and hours when I got home. Afterward, the binges left me with such guilt and shame that the next day I was a total basket case...—Lucy

Lucy wasn't alone in eating on her "best behavior" around her co-workers while she sneaked food when no one was looking. Binges often aren't in the presence of others unless they binge along with us or we feel *safe* enough to show our true selves. Lucy knew something was wrong with her actions but didn't understand where they came from.

Lucy wasn't yet aware at that point of certain foods she was physically sensitive to. She had a chemical imbalance, and when it was triggered, she ate out of control. The pasta led to a full blown binge. *The worry was intense. The guilt was intense. I hated myself. I hated the way I had to live my life. I discussed it with no one. I didn't want anybody to know that I had a problem.*

Lucy often ate the whole box of cereal, a whole gallon of ice cream—all in secret. She never did it in front of people, noting that the shame and the guilt became a part of her binge eating. The only person who knew that she binge-ate was her son and only because he lived with her. She was reminded how he shouted toward the top of the stairs in the wee hours of the night, asking, 'Are you ever going to stop eating, Mom, and go to bed?' *She felt such shame.*

Shame and guilt are poor motivating tools that often sap energy and lead to unhelpful, rigid thinking: If only we didn't eat at all. Or, we'll volume-eat this one last time and never indulge again. Our rigid thinking may work in the short term and relieve us of our mental pain, but long term, *normal*, healthful eating is never sustained from a mindset of rigid rules and regulations. Moving forward with compassion and acceptance, and an emphasis on self-forgiveness is the elixir to opening up our thinking and allowing for growth.

Food as a Drug

During my research, interviewees and patients described the experience of food addiction in the way all other addictions are described. Words such as 'sober,' 'intoxicated,' and 'substance' were brought up, while we compared the two worlds: active addiction versus spiritual recovery from the trigger foods.

Certain foods were described as drugs—even by those who were in recovery from drug addiction. On many days we were so hung over from a binge, we couldn't perform simple tasks such as answer the phone, return calls, make appointments, or show up for engagements—and all the while, we hid our addictions. Isolation protected us.

All of us reacted to certain foods as if they were drugs, creating mood alterations powerful enough to hold us in a pattern of binge eating despite our best efforts to try and break the behavior. These foods for us *are* drugs; through chemical reactions, they eventually cause a production of brain chemicals that have a drug-like effect on the body.

These brain chemicals are known as neurotransmitters. A neurotransmitter is a chemical substance that carries impulses from one nerve cell to another. They act as messages within the brain that help control the body.

If we make a beeline for crackers, pasta, bread, pretzels, or any other simple carbohydrate when experiencing anxiety, tension, or irritable moods, we are most likely looking for serotonin—a nerve chemical (neurotransmitter) that turns on when these foods are metabolized. We are self-medicating, and temporarily, we will feel calm.

Our bodies naturally make serotonin but some of us don't produce enough. Antidepressant medications such as Celexa, Cymbalta, Prozac, and Paxil, to name a few, are used to increase the serotonin. Serotonin plays a huge role in mood and appetite.

Cravings for starches and sweets can turn on and off depending on the level of serotonin, which regulates mood, sleep cycles, memory, and pain tolerance. Relatively high levels of serotonin have a calming effect that lead to a clearer mind and stable mood. Low levels of serotonin sink the mood and clarity is lost—hence, a binge to knock us out of our pain and agitation.

Dopamine and norepinephrine are neurotransmitters that also play key roles in regard to food and mood. For instance, low levels of these neurotransmitters are, like low levels of serotonin, associated with an increase in depression. Increasing dopamine and norepinephrine improves mood, alertness, mental clarity, and the ability to cope with stress. Foods higher in protein will raise the dopamine and norepinephrine levels.

Though all these hormones may have similar effects, helping with mental clarity, reducing depression and anxiety, and stabilizing mood, excessive serotonin can result in sleep disturbances, insomnia, irritability, and mental confusion. For the food addict too much in the way of simple carbohydrates will drastically increase the level of serotonin, leading to these negative effects. Eating adequate amounts of protein is critical for the food addict then to bring down the high serotonin and normalize moods.

It isn't uncommon for food addicts to fill up on pancakes laced with syrup to increase their serotonin levels and then go for a sizzling steak to pull the serotonin down, hence vacillating between highs and lows—*uppers and downers.*

Chocolate, which contains phenethylamine (PEA), a substance that stimulates the release of dopamine, also helps regulate the mood and explains chocolate cravings. Chocolate, in fact, often serves as an anodyne—a self-medication—to relieve distress or pain that we can't even put our finger on. We ignore our dark emotions and feed ourselves instead, as a balm, which eventually leads to furthering our addictions. It may be that the cravings and increased consumption are a last-ditch effort to regulate moods.

Pacing back and forth, I argue with myself about whether to go into Publix and buy a box of Entenmann's fat-free chocolate fudge brownies and a bag of baked chips—*just this one more time.* The emotional pain cuts like a knife. I simply want the bad feeling to go away—I want some relief.

What childhood pain am I covering up? Where is God? Why are brownies and chips taking me over? Was I nowhere on God's list of importance? Chocolate *is* my heroin—my drug—no difference to God—no difference to me. A drug is a drug. –Lisa

The revelation in regard to food addiction is that it isn't necessarily a psychological habit or stemming from past traumatic experiences—it's a chemical reaction. As noted above, many mood alterations result from imbalances in the neurotransmitters and other hormones that regulate behavior.

Chemical levels of emotion-altering agents such as serotonin, dopamine, and endorphins can be dramatically affected by a single meal or a change in dietary habits. Cravings for foods such as sweets, starches, caffeine, and chocolate (to name a few) originate in fundamental biological drives to improve our moods.

It isn't uncommon to see an alcoholic swap alcohol for sweet and high-fat starches along with coffee to help curb the discomfort of withdrawal and to try and improve frame of mind. This is the experience of several of the individuals who shared their stories in this book.

John learned this lesson all too well when he quit using drugs and alcohol and replaced them with simple carbohydrates and coffee laced with cream and sugar in a non-conscious effort to regulate his moods. Marilyn ignored her dark emotions and fed them with trigger foods, which lulled her anxieties but nudged her addiction out of control.

People think that drugs and alcohol are a way of life [for the addict] but for me *food* is a way of life. It's an addiction and it robs you of living a normal life because you just think of your next fix, your "fixed" food—and your thoughts are all over the place. There are supermarkets, there are doughnut shops, and there are cafés and restaurants. You have a never-ending supply of your drug. It's not illegal. You won't get arrested—you'll just go crazy. –Marilyn

Damien is acutely connected to his body and mind as a result of abstaining from sugar, flour, and wheat. On a recent trip to Russia, he ate food from a kiosk that looked like nothing but cabbage and oil and vinegar, but it had something sweet in it. Immediately after its consumption he didn't feel right, and recognized how sensitive his body was. *He felt it instantly.*

Within minutes Damien's body began to get weak—he experienced a drugged feeling he remembered *oh so well* from the days he was addicted to street drugs and alcohol. Again, he describes it, "...like this veil of darkness started to descend." His knees weakened, heat crawled up his body, and the shakes ensued. The food addict is no different than the heroin addict or the cocaine addict, or the alcoholic—or anyone with a chemical imbalance. Food addiction will steal a person's soul.

Hope

Ah, but there's hope. The first step is to exchange the addictive food for whole, natural foods free of all sugars, flours, and wheat in order to clear the mind and prepare for a transition from chaos to peace.

You ask how?

The answer is not simple nor is it an overnight fix. To start, live in the nourishment of food and the sun and the warmth of people who love you. And then, ease into spiritual practices in small bites.

Spiritual practices can be adopted and used in place of addictive foods. One such practice is prayer. Another is meditation. The beauty of prayer and meditation is that they can change your thoughts—which in turn can change your life anytime, anywhere, at any age—and it's free.

Instead of seeing your present situation as an obstacle, see it as an opportunity to open the valve and let miracle after miracle come into your life. These miracles have been right in front of you all along, yet they were blocked as you were immersed in your 'personal' sad story.

When you realize the impact of prayer and meditation introduced with a clean palate, you will immediately want to shift into a state of awe and gratitude for it, regardless of what your sad story has dictated to you your entire life.

When we lean into prayers and meditation as part of a daily healing, it can actually shush the call of food and restore the natural, physical moods of happiness and joy. This simple practice can send you into recovery by renewing your mind, body, and soul.

Personal Inventory Questions

1. Have you ever asked why you were born? Or why you can't stop eating? Or why you have a life filled with such turmoil over food and obesity, a life filled with shame? What's the answer?

2. What are your thoughts on the possibility of having a chemical imbalance, that when you eat sugar, flour, or wheat your imbalance is triggered and you can't stop eating? Can certain foods really be like drugs?

3. A common thread that seemed true for each person represented in this book was the condition of a blocked connection to spirit and a blocked connection to other people as a result of periodic or ongoing binge eating. What are your thoughts as this relates to you?

4. What do you think causes the blocking of the active food addicts' spirituality? The blocking of your spirituality? Could it be that you're hanging on to your own sad story? Have you *become* your own sad story? What are the benefits of holding on to your own sad story rather than releasing it?

5. Are you using your addiction as an excuse that blocks you from living in the now? Remember Jonathan who ate himself to death? How did his story impact your understanding of your own story?

6. How has your binge eating affected your relationships? Does it get in the way of intimacy? What are some ways you can rectify this?

7. Do you attempt to return to the way you were in your youth through exercise, diet, plastic surgery, vitamins— just to find love or at least acceptance? Is it working for you?

8. Are anger and/or grief resulting from out-of-control eating causing you a sense of loss of the Higher Presence—a sense that God is far away?

9. Sometimes family and friends don't "get" what's going on with the food addict. Does this ring true for you? Do you explain? How do you explain?

10. Have you ever thrown food into the garbage like Marilyn, only to retrieve it hours later to eat?

Part II

Realignment

Chapter 8

Journal Writing, Meditation and Prayer as Part of Daily Healing

All cravings are the mind seeking salvation
Or fulfillment in external things
And in the future as a substitute for the joy of Being
~Eckhard Tolle, The Power of Now~

The compulsive eater lives and breathes, in every waking moment, contemplating what to eat next, what has been eaten, and why that was eaten. We live for the food that perishes. Sounds silly when we actually stop to think about what we're doing. Food fests are only for a fleeting moment, leaving us guilt ridden, full of shame, and empty.

The thought of turning our attention to something greater than our limited selves, to become present in the *now* rather than numbing out with food, seems too easy to actually be part of the answer to our pain. Could journal writing, meditation, and prayer really take us to the Promised Land, provide a *food* that endures throughout eternal life? And could journal writing, meditation, and prayers connect us to the type of events and situations we might have lost or never experienced at all?

On Journal Writing

The point of journal writing is to help you process your internal disharmonies and discharge held, negative emotions as well as find particular patterns to your own binge eating as highlighted throughout this book in my own and other participants' private journal writing.

Journal writing is very personal and very intimate. It allows you to tap into your inner feelings and figure out what's going on for you in your life. Journal writing takes many forms. I, myself, especially enjoy "diary writing," which for the most part involves the unstructured, chronological recording of the extent of a person's life.

Of course, the mere fact of continuously writing entries isn't sufficient in itself to bring about deep changes in your life. To achieve a significant transformation in a personality, strong forces of energy must be generated—which is why I've added maps, weekly charts, and daily food analysis to help you structure your recovery process.

Many of my writings that you've seen in this book about my childhood and young adulthood, allowed me to tap into a spiritual energy, work through internal disharmonies, and discharge my emotions, leading me also to dig more deeply into my work as a clinical psychotherapist helping the eating disordered.

Only shortly after many significant events in my life and starting to write a personal journal did I continue on to my doctoral studies and research, where I uncovered many similar themes and patterns faced by most (if not all) food addicted persons. Those themes and patterns were only revealed to me at first from my own journal writing, interviews, research, and mapping.

You can undertake the same sort of inner probing and release, but this time the writing will all be about *you* and *your* relationship to Divine guidance, to other people, and to food. I guarantee the process will be informative and extremely self-empowering if, when writing, you maintain a mind that's open to everything and attached to nothing, so that the transformation will have room to drill deeper and take hold.

Types of Journals
A journal can be fancy leather bound book or a simple three-ring binder containing tabs that you can organize into different categories. For example, you may have a category for your daily events; one for your food, food questions, and experiences; and one for your spiritual awakenings. There are no rules. Your journal workbook is the basic instrument in which you write about your life. You will unveil gems and treasures if you simply let loose and write without guard.

Hey, this is your journal writing; divide it up the way that seems most right for you. If you fancy writing about relationships, Higher consciousness, career, and special interests—or body and health, events, dreams, and meaning of life—then that's exactly how you should pursue this. Your writing shouldn't be scripted if you want to find your inner voice and personal miracles.

On the other hand, the advantage of structuring sections in your journal avoids the risk of writing too loosely and missing an opportunity to evoke the contents of your personal life through the subconscious mind where riches await you.

Journal Writing Using a Map
When writing my dissertation before it morphed into this book, I began the process of collecting themes and patterns (from the transcribed interviews) by using a brainstorming

technique I called the "map of recovery." I turned loose and allowed my creative juices to flow naturally through my subconscious mind to avoid flat, dull, rule-oriented writing and allow original, natural, and free-form thoughts to spill across the page. I awakened a playful, childlike approach to the writing in me as collaboration between doctoral writing and child's play that flowed intuitively without critical, logical, censorship.

Once I began to record and structure the data onto my map of recovery, the themes and patterns flowed like whispers from God. I saw much that had been hidden from my view when I sifted through the transcribed data. Instead, using my map of recovery, the words spilled across the page with a magical energy, bearing treasure I most likely could have missed had I not unleashed the creative side tucked within. That enabled me to tap into the pulse of compulsive eating.

Check out my map of recovery below and create your own map to unleash your personal creative juices.

Each portion is enlarged for easier viewing, following the map.

Map of Recovery

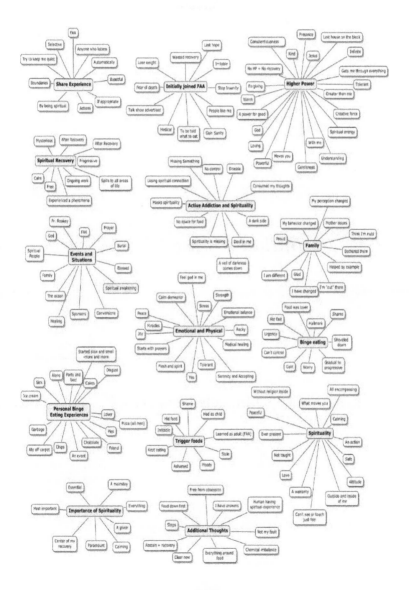

Share Experience

Initially Joined FAA

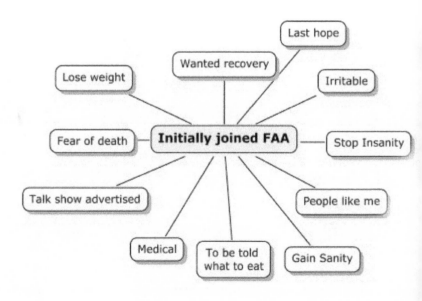

Higher Power

Spiritual Recovery

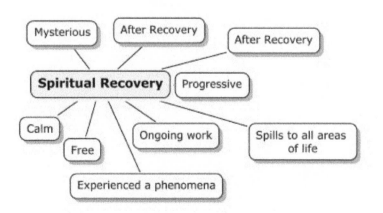

Active Addiction & Spirituality

Family

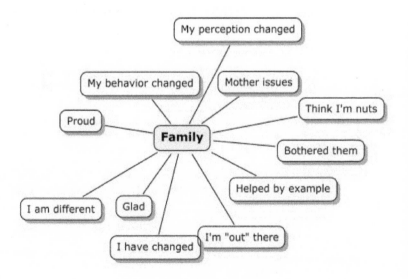

Events & Situations

Emotional & Physical

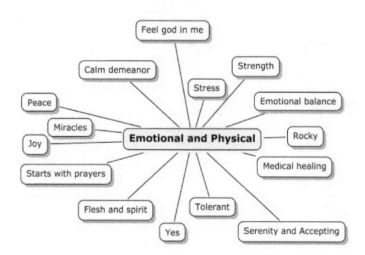

Binge Eating

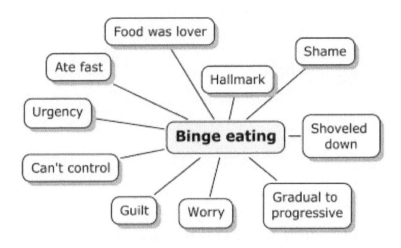

Personal Binge Eating Experiences

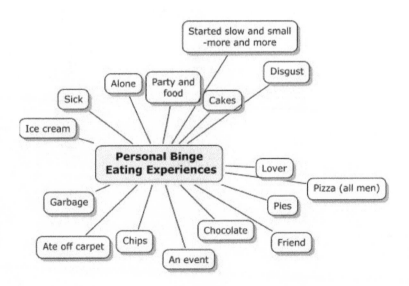

Trigger Foods

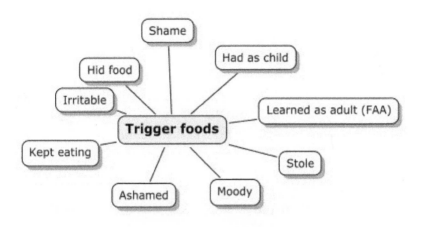

Spirituality

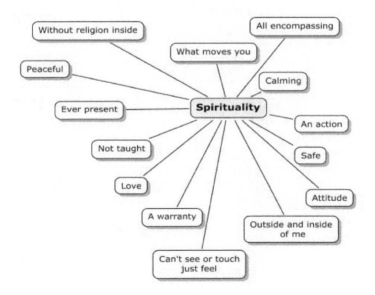

Importance of Spirituality

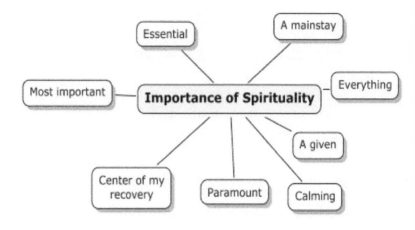

Additional Thoughts

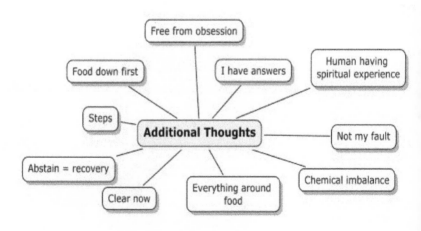

As you begin to map your recovery, themes and patterns will inevitably surface. In the course of your writing, you will become your own best critic if you allow yourself to be guided by the information ferreted out. Pleasure, satisfaction, even amazement at your personal themes and patterns are common results using mapping recovery.

On Daily Food Diary Journal

Progressing through your day while working through your food choices and spiritual recovery, in the beginning you'll find it easiest to write down what you've eaten along with feelings tied to your choices.

Provided for your convenience is a daily diary journal that will help guide you. You can create your own daily food diary journal that better fits your personality as you become more comfortable with your routine. [1]

To start, make a simple chart like the one below to write your foods (refer to **Chapter 14** for portions), and from there progress to the daily graph and work in your food along with journal time, meditation time, prayer time, exercise, successes, gratitude list, and needed changes.

Daily Servings				
Breakfast	**Lunch**	**Dinner**	**Metabolic Boost**	**Condiments**
One fruit	One protein	One protein	One fruit	Two tablespoons spice
One protein	One vegetable	One vegetable	and	Two tablespoons salsa
One dairy	One fat	One fat	One dairy	Two tablespoons yogurt
One grain		One starch	or	*Or any condiment free of sugar, flour, and wheat
One fat			One half protein	

---

[1] Note: A word of caution, before using this or any other food plan or exercise plan, be sure to check with your doctor for approval.

Daily Diary

Monday	Tuesday	Wednesday	Thursday	Friday	Saturday	Sunday
Protein	Protein	Protein	Protein	Protein	Protein	Protein
Grains	Grains	Grains	Grains	Grains	Grains	Grains
Fruits	Fruits	Fruits	Fruits	Fruits	Fruits	Fruits
Vegetables	Vegetables	Vegetables	Vegetables	Vegetables	Vegetables	Vegetables
Dairy	Dairy	Dairy	Dairy	Dairy	Dairy	Dairy
Fat	Fat	Fat	Fat	Fat	Fat	Fat
Water ---- ----	Water ---- ----	Water ---- ----	Water ---- ----	Water ---- ----	Water ---- ----	Water ---- ----
Condiments	Condiments	Condiments	Condiments	Condiments	Condiments	Condiments
Journal Time	Journal Time	Journal Time	Journal Time	Journal Time	Journal Time	Journal Time
Meditation	Meditation	Meditation	Meditation	Meditation	Meditation	Meditation
Prayer Time	Prayer Time	Prayer Time	Prayer Time	Prayer Time	Prayer Time	Prayer Time
Exercise	Exercise	Exercise	Exercise	Exercise	Exercise	Exercise
Successes	Successes	Successes	Successes	Successes	Successes	Successes
Gratitude List	Gratitude List	Gratitude List	Gratitude List	Gratitude List	Gratitude List	Gratitude List
Needed Changes	Needed Changes	Needed Changes	Needed Changes	Needed Changes	Needed Changes	Needed Changes

Prayer and Meditation as Part of Daily Healing

Compulsive eaters fully committed to their recovery understand they must engage in daily prayer and meditation as part of their healing. We human beings are spiritual. When we pray unremittingly that our addiction to certain foods will be lifted, when we meditate on daily healing, and slowly, with vigilance, eat prescribed meals, and abstain from certain foods, we can recover. Giving thanks and praise to our Divine intelligence every day continues to strengthen our recovery.

Dictionary.com defines prayer as a devout petition to God or an object of worship. It is a spiritual communion with God, whatever we happen to call that ultimate power. It is an appointed formula or sequence of words spontaneously invented on the spot to be said either in public or in private. Prayer may be heartfelt, but it can even be mechanical at first *and still be effective.*

The dictionary goes on to define meditation as a continued or extended thought—a reflection and/or contemplation—a devout religious contemplation or spiritual introspection. Often there is a blurring between meditation and prayer, vine wrapped around vine, reaching up toward the same place: serenity.

Meditation is performed in quiet—with no agenda. In meditation, we spend some time in the spaciousness of *not knowing.* Some individuals meditate by using one word to concentrate on, while others hum one note, and still others focus on something to look at, such as a cloud or flower or even a spot on the wall. Some will use a mantra, repeating it over and over again.

Meditation is the act of embracing an open and inviting clear space in the mind. It's the discovery of a corner of the mind, a quietness within the mind, a sanctuary, a resting place—*paradise in the mind,* a place of peace.

Every morning, without fail—beating the alarm—I awake to a choir of birds singing that the day has begun. I stretch and give thanks for the start of a fresh new day: *abstinent.* After lolling in bed a while longer, enjoying the sweet smell of my husband lying next to me, I move out to the garage and open the garage door to welcome the morning breeze and witness the purple/yellow hues as the sun comes up over the palm trees against the backdrop of the Atlantic Ocean.

I smile as I breathe in the delicious scent only salt air offers and begin my morning routine seated in meditation, quietly riding each breath, thinking of nothing, and embracing everything. A little while after that, I begin my eight-minute weightlifting routine, working two areas of my body—compliments of Jorge Cruise and his *8 Minutes in the Morning.* I am now connected to my breath and my body: Let the day begin.

After sipping on hot decaffeinated coffee laced with skim milk, I jump on my bike, plug into my iPhone, and absorb an inspirational podcast gifting a positive message as I pump my way up the bridge to witness a spectacular view of the ocean and Intercoastal Waterway simultaneously. I look to nature for my sustenance

As I reach the end of the beach boardwalk—riding along the ocean shoreline—I   switch to my morning rosary, going into a trancelike state and praying for patience, for my family, my patients, my students and/or whatever other concerns I send for Divine guidance. By the time I pedal back, I am invigorated and ready for anything that comes my way.

I am centered.

For me, strong spirituality replaced the intoxication that came from food. A closer relationship with the *Universe* rather than a focus on weight loss or body image led to recovery.

Constant communication with Divine love is our serenity. Our higher source is a powerful presence that is with us ceaselessly, uninterrupted. We succumb to cravings, and then beat ourselves up for our lack of "willpower," not realizing the problem isn't lack of willpower but rather lack of God power!

Our energy sinks to severe lows without this higher power. Our self-worth and self-esteem soon follow. A strong spirituality is the energy that fuels us and keeps us sane. Recovery comes about through an acceptance of a power for good that works in us in unique and personal ways.

The beauty of prayer is that it's personal. There's no right way to pray, and there's no wrong way—just your way. You can talk, sing, sit in silence, dance, cry, run, embrace nature, hug a baby, kiss a puppy, and/or watch a butterfly swirl around a daffodil—all in the name of prayer.

Prayer is powerful. Prayer can change your life anywhere, any time—alone in quiet or in the middle of a room full of people. You can be rich, poor, belong to a church, temple, synagogue, or mosque, or sit alone in a field that stretches out as far as the eye can see. Our higher source is everywhere—within us and around us.

Perhaps you are thinking, 'Why do you say prayer works? I pray and nothing good ever happens to me or for me.' If you're praying without receiving pure uplifting joy, gratitude for life, and a heartfelt happiness, you are `praying amiss.' It could be you're blocked by Little Debbie snack cakes, an overload of chocolate bars, and pints of ice cream—sunk in the mire of active food addiction. It reminds me of the saying, 'You are what you eat.' Let's take it a step further, `You are what you pray.'

This is not to encourage self-condemnation, since many of the most devout religious practitioners pray without tapping into the delight of connection to their higher source and the wonderful people who surround us.

I, myself, regularly attend mass—you could say I'm a devout Catholic. And I know all the prayers by heart and pray the rosary nearly daily. Although this conventional way of praying brings me peace, I was shocked to learn at one revealing turning point of my journey how little I truly knew about prayer.

As a clinical psychotherapist conducting hypnosis and discussing meditation, I learned by sheer accident that the power of prayer was hidden from me—disguised and yet in plain view. Other than saying the Our Father, a Hail Mary, and Glory Be to the Father—as great as these prayers are—I discovered so much more was out there for me to learn and I will share with you these findings as we go on.

Lucinda, huffing and puffing, ear buds clasped tightly in her ears—muffled sounds of Christian music escaping—came into my office drenched from pedaling her bicycle to her therapy session. Lucinda had borderline intelligence, to the point of being misdiagnosed in childhood with mental retardation. Yet, although she wasn't book smart, this patient of mine had an understanding of phenomena that far exceeded the insight of many of those in academia. She was natively intelligent, rather than intellectual.

Lucinda *knew things*. Many sessions I sat dumbfounded just listening to her speak naturally from her heart, from her spirit. Yes, she went to church and knew all the traditional prayers, but something deeper was going on inside her. Lucinda lived for the moment, not for yesterday or in fear of tomorrow. She laughed heartily and had the ability to be her authentic self—no holds barred.

Lucinda didn't have a longing for something `solid' to believe in, because she believed *knowingly*. She wasn't asking for proof or bemoaning the life she had been given. She spoke of Jesus as if he was her best friend, as if they had daily chats together. She was going home to Him soon, she would say, without any fear or sadness—though as far as I could tell Lucinda, 38 years old, was perfectly healthy and physically fit.

Lucinda lived in a small, closed-in garage made into a studio apartment. She received monthly government checks and worked a few days in a grocery store stocking shelves or carting groceries to patrons' cars. She loved her job and the little space she lived in. She saw the good in all the people she met. Lucinda lived her life as a prayer.

Although Lucinda came to me for psychotherapy, I quickly learned by working with her that psychology without prayer was really pointless. I learned, too, that she was the teacher and I was the student. Her mind was open and uncluttered with this rule and that rule. She loved freely and wholly. She lived fully and well. And she died in her sleep just as she told me she would.

Spiritual Connection to Events and Situations
Through prayer and meditation, we found our way to a spiritual connection to events and situations that were always present, but often we didn't see due to our blocked view. Miracles and healings became familiar rather than foreign.

Recovery from trigger food is characterized by spiritual connections to events and situations in daily life. Removing our *drugs* and replacing them with a *higher source* opened and connected us to a spiritual world once foreign or forgotten, or that was hazed over by our drunken stupors. With our spiritual awakening came events and situations that contained amazing happenings, medical healings, and even miracles beyond our expectations or planning.

John grieved and surrendered to the loss of a loved one on the shores of the Hudson River many years ago and shared this experience: …and I said, 'God, I don't know what prayer to recite about this, but I know that my beloved has moved on—and I need to let her go.' I knew I had to let her spirit go; I *had* to release her spirit.

It was an awakening moment when I realized if you bind somebody, they are bound to you. She was no longer here because she wasn't meant to be here, and not because of anything I had done. I had to let her go, but I wasn't certain how to do this.

I spoke to God, 'So this is what I am going to do, God. I'm going to drop this—her personal belongings—in the river, and the river is natural, and to me it represents you— and so I'm giving her to you... [There was a long pause, the only sounds that could be heard were of the fountain in the office where the interview was taking place] ...to take her home, and I release her spirit to you.'

I just sat on the bank of the river for a long time thinking, *I don't know what to do now.* And then I became aware of the fact that I didn't feel empty as I had before.

Something important had happened but I didn't know exactly what—or where to go from that point. I just looked out at the river, and I said, 'Is it finished?' And at that moment a seagull came down and kind of hovered straight in front of my me—face to face—and it was only there for I don't know—seconds—but it stopped, and flapped its wings and then it went straight up until I couldn't see it anymore.

And I realized it was finished, and I got all my stuff together and I went home. And I knew it was an ending there and I was to prepare now for a beginning.

Spiritual connection to events and situations simply appeared in our lives. We didn't seek them; they merely descended on us. Arthur heard talk of miracles, but a part of him didn't like it when people talked about healings because it "smacked of religiosity."

The descriptions of miracles that he heard from people around him weren't as believable to him as Jesus raising Lazarus. To him, it was as though they were saying, *Yeah, I had a tumor and people prayed for me, and the tumor is gone—and we praised God*, and it seemed trite—a contrived `fate'—it seemed contrived—contrived.

Arthur felt that way, until the day he saw an 11-year-old girl come out of a coma as a result of prayer, and he witnessed the astonishment of the doctors when the MRI came back negative. *There was no physical explanation for it.* Wide-eyed, he felt his perception change, and the possibility of miracles became reality.

Nothing was contrived about a little girl's eyes springing open, or her smiling and calling out, `Momma,' when only silence and distance had been predicted.

Jumping from full-blown food addiction to spiritual recovery doesn't stop ordinary life from continuing. Challenges pop up in our daily lives, which is called living.

Charisma raised her children single handedly on a shoestring budget, and knows firsthand after years of emotional abuse from an alcoholic husband, that life is unpredictable and can be difficult.

My husband and I were separated at the time and I had this darn car that simply stopped in the middle of the road, so I had to take my daughter's car, and she smokes—and her car just stunk to high heaven.

I had to take my son out to the doctor, and I was driving down the boulevard, which was full of *melalucas*, and I had the windows open. I guess anyone reading this would have to know in Florida melalucas cause this rotten-potato smell—in this car with all the smoke that I couldn't stand, and so I got all that—and I felt so miserable right then.

I just felt so abandoned.

131

And I cried. I cried and I said, *'God help me. I don't know what I am going to do here. What am I gonna to do?'* And at that very moment, the whole car filled with roses. The smell of roses, which is the Blessed Mother [tears spilled down her cheeks, and after a long pause of silence, then she said], *I just thanked him, just you know, just thanked him.*

Right then I knew—I knew that I wasn't alone, other people could abandon me but God wasn't going to do that. Spirituality is outside of me and inside of me. It is all encompassing.

It was a pleasant South Florida November, overcast morning with a cool breeze coming off the Atlantic Ocean, evidenced by the random clinking and tapping of the choir of chimes from neighbors' homes, as the sounds of another day started up.

Dogs barking, birds chirping—a mother's voice in the distance prodding her son to get a move on to avoid being late for school, and I bounded forward for a brisk walk with Sage—my 75-pound, white German Shepard.

Although a spectacular day was about to unfold, I felt sad and lethargic. Mom passed away only months before on February 7, 2002, and I longed to look into her eyes—a pool of blue—and to hear her hearty laugh just one more time.

While I was deep in prayer, barely conscious of my surroundings, a mourning dove swooped out from what felt like under my feet. I dismissed it as a *sign from above* (as I'd had numerous dove "incidents" from the day of my mom's stroke to that time), mumbling under my breath, "Just because a dove comes up out of nowhere, it isn't a sign Mom is near," until I nearly tripped a few minutes later as two doves dove past inches from my nose and Sage leaped forward and almost ripped the lead out of my hand, which left a red burn mark.

Moving on, I ignored my pain, quite annoyed with Sage, and marched on until a loud commotion ahead distracted me from any thoughts of Mom and birds. A sandy-haired boy of about three cried to get out of his stroller, all the while pointing up toward the now overcast sky.

An elderly woman, whom I presumed was his grandma, shushed him as she looked up in the direction of his little fist. Frustrated and interrupted again from my private thoughts, by instinct I looked up as well, only to see the entire roof of a home populated with doves.

Instantly a warm peace enveloped me—the dark clouds parted, and a stream of dazzling sun peeked through as the doves cooed in symphony. *This is spirit connection.*

I experienced spirituality in the house. It was there: *the presence.* I grasped the omnipresence of a higher being—just embraced it—not something you can see or touch. You just feel and sense that it's there. –Adriana

Adriana, a small-boned, simple yet strong and wise woman, with seven decades evident in clean lines spread about her strikingly beautiful face, is warm but guarded—cautious to select the right words. Adriana isn't bound by any particular religion but rather enjoys a connection to her higher source through her outdoor hiking and kayaking.

Adriana's prayers comprise an everyday type of conversation with God, and her version of meditation is aligned with the elements of the natural world: mountains, trees, animals, rivers. According to Adriana, spirit is a feeling, a presence in a room, a spiritual connection that bonds together people, events, and situations. It is an energy that is *very* peaceful and it's freely available.

One night Adriana lay in bed gripped with a feeling of abandonment. Her daughter, with a long history of drug addiction, was out there somewhere using, and Adriana could do nothing to intervene. She felt helpless and desolate—an island onto herself. Having no other recourse left, she began to converse with God, begging for relief from her inconsolable fear. As she prayed, out of nowhere, she felt a warm, peaceful energy embrace her. It felt like arms around her: a hug. *There was no one else in the house*—but she got a hug.

She felt spiritual energy in that room. *It was sooooooo intense—just unbelievable.* She felt it in the *core* of her being. She smiled as she remembered how all her worries and forlorn rumination that her daughter would be found dead in an alley somewhere were miraculously lifted.

And for a moment, while Adriana was speaking, impressions of that feeling from long ago, of the spiritual presence in the house returned, and her eyes widened and twinkled as if it were happening again. She told me, though, this feeling she'd had that time had occurred on occasion intermittently but never returned as intensely as on that night. She described this presence of a higher power as not something you can see or touch—but you *just feel it* and have the sense it's there.

John was very sick. Outside of a miracle occurring, he didn't expect he had long to live. He was at death's door with no hope of surviving:

I spent a total of six weeks in the hospital. I was very sick. I didn't know that I actually *wanted* to live anymore.

I believe my higher power gave me the chance to answer that question for myself because one day my temperature had reached 105, and they didn't know why because I'd been doing well prior to that.

The nurses put me in an ice bath. I was going in and out of comas, and at one point I could feel my spirit leave my body. I was above my body looking down. I was looking at this shriveled-up body, and I was thinking, 'That's a sickly body—that's a dying body.'

I could hear these muffled noises in the background—and it felt like—it sounded like people were dragging chains across the floor. I couldn't hear what they were saying. I was looking out and it was total darkness.

And when I say darkness I don't mean as if you turn out a light and then it's dark. It was dark like being void of life. There was *nothingness*, which is probably a better way to describe it than saying `darkness.'

But there *was* a little light. It was like a little candle light and something kept telling me, `Don't listen to the voices. Don't look into the darkness—just look at the light.'

And as I looked up into the darkness, I realized it was moving and it wasn't a solid wall of darkness. It was like fragments—and as I watched the fragments become silhouettes of people, I could hear them moaning and the dragging of the chains.

I realized what they were saying. They were calling my name. I was thinking, `I don't want to go with them.' Something kept telling me to just look at the light—*look at the light*—that's what's going to help you.

`Don't look at the darkness. Don't listen to the voices.' I kept looking at the light, kept looking into the light, and just prior to the coma I'd seen a picture of a clown on the wall and somehow this clown represented the devil to me.

It was laughing at me.

I said out loud, 'You're not going to win.' So, I looked at this light and the words came to me. I said, 'God…if it's time for me to go I am ready to go but I know I lived such a useless life and I would like a chance to do it over again if it's possible.'

And all of a sudden, a sword came up through the light and the whole room lit up, and to me that was God's spirit opening up the heavens. I knew that God had reached into my heart. He had reached into my hell and pulled me out from it. —John

Arthur's spiritual connection to events and situations is stimulated when he touches nature by working with the soil and plants, and performing other gardening tasks. Sitting in his kitchen, he described the spirituality in cutting up the back yard to put a path through the garden area and fertilizing it, and dreaming of "...*creating composts —and doing that whole return—of-the fertile-soil-back—to-the-ground thing, and watering.*"

A strong connection to natural foods and cultivating soil is *very* spiritual for Arthur.

He points to the design of the spice rack below his kitchen cabinet, and passion and pride takes over, as he expresses his yearning to learn about various cultures and what spices are used to make their foods taste a certain way. Eyes moisten as he repeats, "That is *very, very* spiritual to me."

I think that probably the highest form of spiritual connection to events and situations from my point of view is love. I think that love is the most spiritual activity that I can take part in. It is the most spiritual choice that I can make— and I see it as a choice. — Adriana

Lucy embraces her spiritual connection to events and situations as *something that begins within—within a person. It is a feeling of how you think about other people or other things. Spirit is outside the box, outside of the everyday things. Look out at the sky, the trees and inhale it in. It is a feeling other than self that brings deep comfort.*

Lucy questions if she's smart enough to know if you're born with spirituality or if it comes from life experiences or from something your parents taught or the home that you grew up in.

Lucy's mom and dad passed away in their 40s when she was an adolescent, yet her memory floods with thoughts of her father and mother as very spiritual people. They were believers in people, and without agendas or prejudice. They didn't have hate. They looked at the good in life. Unfortunately, they died very young.

Prayer and meditation using our own understanding, wherever that stands, are the seeds we plant to raise us to a higher path and sprout a strong spiritual connection. To bring us back to innocence so we may see the world with childlike wonder— and hear the birds chatter, smell sweet summer flowers in bloom, feel the rain against our skin, and see the burst of orange hues as the sun rises and sets—liberating our free-spirited self, forgotten in our active addiction.

The impact of an ever-present, strong spirituality opens us to embrace life and relieves us of our obsession with food.

This process is not simple-minded wishfulness and *fa la la we go on our merry way* but rather a spiritual journey that will unite us with our emotional, physical, and spiritual needs and their fulfillment, and deliver ultimate relief from our food addictions.

In addition to prayer and meditation, working together with patients, I have the opportunity to help them tap into their emotional, physical, and spiritual sides through self-hypnosis. Hypnosis, both self-induced and initiated by the therapist, serves as the agency of communication from that part of the brain which quiets the conscious mind and opens the subconscious mind for direction and change. Chapter 9 explores hypnosis as it connects to your Higher Source.

Personal Inventory Questions

1. Instead of seeing your present situation as an obstacle, what about seeing it as an opportunity to open the floodgates and let miracle after miracle come into your life? Are miracles possible? Journal writing can capture your miracle experiences.

2. If you pray unremittingly that your addiction to certain foods will be lifted, if you meditate on healing daily, and slowly, with vigilance, eat prescribed meals, and abstain from certain addictive foods, do you believe you can be delivered?

3. Dictionary.com defines prayer as a devout petition to God or an object of worship. It's a spiritual communion with God, whatever we happen to call that Ultimate Power. What is your personal definition of prayer?

4. Meditation is the act of embracing an open and inviting clear space in the mind. It's the discovery of a corner of the mind, quietness within the mind, a sanctuary, a resting place—*paradise in the mind*, a place of peace. Do you meditate?

5. I start each morning with a prayer followed by a short meditation before riding my bike or walking along the seashore listening on my iPhone to a podcast or daily mass to be in harmony with God. Do you have a prayer ritual? How about a meditation ritual? When can you fit in journal writing?

6. The beauty of prayer is that it's personal. Are you in constant communication with your Higher consciousness? What does it sound like? Is it a conversation, childhood prayers—or sitting in quiet to listen to His whispers?

7. Lucinda has borderline intelligence and was unable to mainstream in school due to lack of academic ability, yet she has an amazing understanding of phenomena that far exceeds the insights of those in academia. Do you have a

Lucinda angel in your life who might have taught you an invaluable lesson?

8.   What about John who lost his loved one and experienced the miracles of the dove fluttering inches from his face when he released her from the sad story of his life. With his spiritual awakening came events and situations that contained amazing happenings, medical healings, and even miracles beyond his expectations. Can you tap into your own awakenings and miracles? Why might you believe you can't?

9.   Charisma cried out to God in the stench-filled car she'd borrowed from her daughter when the car broke down. Instantly after she'd prayed, the car filled with the smell of roses. Have you ever had any similar experience as the result of prayer?

10.   We all have miracles and phenomena happening in our lives but often we're blocked from seeing or feeling the experience due to the fog created by our addictions. Prayer and meditation as part of daily healing can open the view to these phenomena. What's your experience? If you don't believe this can happen for you, why not?

Chapter 9

Self-Hypnosis as It Connects to Your Higher Source

For I am about to do something now.
See, I have already begun! Do you
not see it? I will make a pathway
through the wilderness. I will create
rivers in the dry wasteland.
~Isaiah 43:19~

Tapping into deeper emotional, physical, and spiritual levels of our being through self-hypnosis allows communication from the conscious mind to the subconscious part of the mind and vice versa —a direction and change that cuts a pathway through the wilderness. The newly flowing rivers in the dry wasteland invite previously hidden answers from deep in the recesses of the mind to emerge, and foster the healing of hurts and misinterpretations of the past. Perhaps this reintegration of long-buried injuries with the fruits of adult capabilities can offer a shortcut to recovery from food addiction—and serve as a means of releasing the obsession with food—to heal from the inside out.

My students in the introduction to psychology course I teach are fascinated by the subject of hypnosis. They can hardly wait for the discussion of the chapter on hypnosis and inevitably ask me questions about it each week prior to the week hypnosis is the topic—and make further queries during all the weeks that follow. Why such an interest? Perhaps it's the mystery that seems to surround the topic of hypnosis. The questions I'm asked after the initial one, "What is hypnosis?" are "Does it really work?" "Can anybody be hypnotized?" "Will I get lost in there?" On and on, the questions flow—and of course, one by one I tackle each inquiry.

The issues my patients raise are very similar to the ones brought by my students, except my patient's experience hypnosis firsthand specifically to release their obsessions with food, to lose weight, to quit smoking or put a stop to other addictions or to let go of a range of fears and phobias. I tell them hypnosis is definitely not a "fix all" resolution to their problem at hand but rather an excellent tool to jumpstart a recovery and often help them connect to their Higher Source by moving deeper into the subconscious mind—a springboard toward prayer and meditation.

What Is Hypnosis?

Hypnosis is a super-concentrated state of mind brought about by suggestions, which can be direct or indirect. Hypnosis produces a hypnotic state, or trance that's actually a natural phenomenon. One can tap into this relaxed state of mind through intentional self-hypnosis (the person hypnotizes himself), through induction by a therapist, or accidentally by sheer repetition of a phrase or "mantra." The hypnotic state is a "normal" altered state of consciousness, similar to, but not the same as being awake. It also is similar to but not the same as being asleep.

Below the level of our thinking, reasoning mind—otherwise known as the conscious mind, which has been "conditioned" by parents, men of cloth, teachers, experience, and so on—lies the sanctuary and/or the disturbances in the mind, of which we are, for the most part, unaware. Within this corner of the mind—below the surface—lies a world where the person stores denial, rejected memories, and highly charged emotional material. I liken this place to a murky region that interferes and blocks the conscious mind from the deeper levels of the subconscious, working as a tyrant to maintain stasis (a constant if not always happy state) in all the levels of our being.

The sweet spot of a semi, but unreasoning, consciousness beneath this cloudy sphere holds in abeyance not only our instincts and unplumbed potential endowments, but the ability to act on suggestions made to it. The first step to entering this corner of the mind—the sanctuary—requires only a willingness to explore what is housed in this space. Our everyday life is a continuous pull to the Internet, our smart phones and all the rest of the noisy, ordinary world of distraction, while we push down memories or emotional material stored and ignored in our unconscious mind.

The goal of hypnosis here is, first, to set the conscious mind with its inhibitions at rest—and to cut through the murky, personal unconscious mind—with its memories of past upsets buried there—and, second, to call upon the great subconscious mind to redirect feelings, perceptions, and actions by the use of suggestions. And it does redirect!

It's possible, without a shadow of a doubt, to redirect your thinking through the effect of suggestions to the mind by means of hypnosis.

Take Tabatha, a redheaded beauty, who strolled into my office cautiously guarded for fear hypnosis might not rid her of habitual purging of food once and for all. She'd purged since she was 13 years old, and when she came to see me was closing in on 50 years old. She had purged, at the least, five times a day for 37 uninterrupted years.

Tabatha and I met several times for psychotherapy sessions before we delved into hypnosis. She was prepared to let go of this horrendous nightmare of clinging to dirty toilet bowls in public restaurants to rid herself of her just-eaten meal while spitting up clumps of blood and experiencing anxiety attacks after a bout of dry heaves. Her eyes, sunk deep into her skull, were surrounded by the dark black bruises that often accompany purging, and she looked as if she had been in a boxing brawl. She was ready.

I recall the first time she went into a trance state and listened to suggestions—while minute-by-minute relaxation took hold, and she descended deeper and deeper—further and further from her physical body—to become fully submerged inside her mind. Her teeth unclenched and she breathed out her stress, which was replaced by a gentle breath of serenity. I saw years of a lined face smoothed, and she was restored to an indescribable radiance. From that day on, she discontinued purging, with the exception of one brief purge after a day of very bad news.

Although Tabatha's marriage was in turmoil, her finances were in ruins, and she was diagnosed with stage 4 cancer, she continued (and continues) to eat free of sugar, flour, and wheat, eat three meals and one snack spaced every four hours apart, and lives life as a prayer—even after several rounds of chemotherapy. Perhaps she might have found her way to this peaceful existence without hypnosis, but certainly hypnosis was a faster track to where she needed to be in order to live a life free of the grip of the purging monster.

143

Questions from my eager students and desperate patients continue to flow, and one by one I answer with the goal of removing fear and misunderstanding surrounding one of the oldest techniques known to mankind for changing and redirecting thoughts.

Who Can Benefit?

Anyone who wants to change the direction they're currently experiencing can benefit from hypnosis. No one is exempt from slipping into a trance with the exception of those who have severe mental illness, mental retardation, or serious brain damage and aren't able to cognitively process information.

In order for hypnosis to work in allowing Tabatha to stop her purging, her mind had to be freed from the conscious, addictive belief that purging eliminated calories and resulted in weight loss. She had to understand, instead, at a deeper level, that purging actually crippled her body, killed her metabolism, and was a slow suicide. Not only did she mentally accept the suggestion made to her in her trance, but her body accepted it and obediently ceased vomiting—since, at her stage of bulimia, throwing up occurred without her even making an effort to provoke the action.

I can cite countless examples of my eating disordered patients ceasing their eating disorder, phobias, addictions, and/or anxiety under hypnosis, attesting to the fact that, when negative blocks are removed, the subconscious functions harmoniously and independently to produce the desired results.

Questions and Answers about Hypnosis

- *How do you self-hypnotize?*

All hypnosis is self-hypnosis. One can self-hypnotize with the hypnotist or self-hypnotize listening to a CD—both teach you how to take control of your brain at a new level, and hypnotists walk you through the process. Self-hypnosis can be achieved by listening to a <u>CD</u> in the comfort of your own space without any interruption. The hypnosis induction is pre-recorded and will guide you through gentle breathing exercises followed by suggestions that fit your specific needs. Self-hypnosis is a great tool to allow you to independently learn how to enter into the hypnotic trance that will foster change. It's no different then slipping into prayer or meditation with the exception that direct changes are suggested to the subconscious mind.

- *How long does it last?*

Hypnosis generally takes 40 minutes to a few hours. Usually a person who has been hypnotized several times can slip into a trance in a matter of minutes. Once a person learns how to let go and trust her breathing, she can master self-hypnosis on her own without the direction of the hypnotist.

- *Does it work?*

Hypnosis works! Tabatha is only one of hundreds who have passed through my doors in search of changing an addiction or habit that haunted them for years. The ingredient that is a *must* is the willingness to let go and the desire to change.

- *How long has weight loss through hypnosis been around?*

Hypnosis has been around as far back as humankind itself. The induction of the hypnotic state goes as far back as the medicine men of primitive tribes who used the approach for religious and therapeutic ends. Magicians and priests of ancient civilizations were also known to practice hypnosis. People actually go in and out of trance states all the time, and have been doing so since the beginning of recorded time. More recent history acknowledges a number of well-known practitioners who induce hypnosis, such as: Father Josef Gassner (1727-1779), Frederich Anton Mesmer (1734-1815),

Jean Martin Charcot (1825-1893), Sigmund Freud (1856-1939) and Milton H. Erickson (1901-1980)—whom I try to emulate. The word hypnosis was coined in 1841.

- *How does one achieve a hypnotic state?*

A hypnotic state is achieved by way of a central focus of attention within surrounding areas of inappropriate conscious or unconscious restraint or suppression of behavior, as compulsive eating, often due to guilt or fear produced by past punishment, or sometimes considered a dispositional trait. The hypnotic state will produce an increased concentration of the mind, an increased relaxation of the body and an increased susceptibility to suggestion.

- *What happens when I am hypnotized?*

Hypnosis is the Greek word for sleep (hypnos). This is misleading because the trance state isn't sleep at all. Most of us are in a trance state quite often. When we daydream, watch television, drive a long distance in the car, we are often in a trance state.

- *What does the body do in this trance state?*

During hypnosis, whether self-induced or guided by someone else, the body is deeply relaxed, and the brain waves are at a frequency of eight to 13 cycles per second. This is the Alpha State, which is slower than the alert Beta state, but above that of sleep or even deep mediation.

- *Where will I go during hypnosis?*

Persons in hypnotic trance are fully aware of their surroundings, but their attention is intensely fixated and purposely focused on something peaceful such as experiencing a garden filled with luscious yellow daffodils, pink roses, and the swish of tall palm trees blowing in the wind with the cobalt blue sky as a backdrop while hearing the sounds of the sea nearby—wave after wave—washing onto the shoreline in order to distract from something else, such as: pain, overeating, worries, smoking etc.

- *Is hypnosis a "cure all"?*

No, hypnotherapy is not a "cure all" for the ills of the world. It is actually not a cure at all. It isn't a new art nor is it unknown to psychology and psychiatry. It is an effective method of alleviating the subject's symptoms. Although hypnosis provides great relief and change, the underlying cause of the symptoms must still be identified and then treated. This is where clinical psychotherapy can be highly beneficial.

- *What is hypnosis used for?*

Hypnosis is being used to treat the symptoms of such conditions as asthma, arthritis, Parkinson's, migraine headaches, depression, phobias, addictions, bulimia, insomnia, hypertension, nausea, gastric hyperacidity, burns, and skin disorders, and to help with weight loss and smoking cessation, and improve study habits and deal with low self-esteem. These are just some of the ways hypnosis can be implemented. The list is endless.

- *Is weight loss hypnosis approved by the American Medical Association?*

Yes, hypnosis when employed by qualified medical personnel in the treatment of certain illnesses was approved by the American Medical Association in 1958. Over the years with extensive training and certification of practitioners its use has increased in many other disciplines.

- *Could I be made to do things against my will?*

No. Hypnosis earned a bad reputation since for years it was abused in stage shows and used as a "trick" or entertainment. People are fearful that under hypnosis they will be made to do things against their will. The truth of hypnosis is that it is a method of accessing the subconscious mind. Subjects remain in complete control of themselves at all times. Presuming that the subject has a "healthy," well-meaning mind, and

147

better yet, an intelligent and wise one, it's known for a fact that no hypnotized person can *do* anything vehemently opposed to his own will and natural character.

Keep in mind that Tabatha, who was able to cease vomiting her food under a hypnosis during which I suggested to her the removal of this behavior after 37 years of uninterrupted purging, didn't actually lose the eating disorder. She continued throughout many years to periodically rely on hypnotism and self-hypnotism to direct her thinking.

- *Can anyone be hypnotized?*

No one can be hypnotized unwillingly. Hypnotic suggestibility is based on the person's willingness and trust. It is also based on freedom from fear on the subject's part. Every person can be hypnotized with the exception of infants, psychotics, mentally retarded persons and/or individuals who lack attention span, concentration and comprehension.

- *Is it possible that a subject cannot be brought out of hypnosis?*

No. All subjects are in control of their journey in hypnosis and can be brought out of hypnosis at the therapist's suggestion or on their own. Hypnosis under trained experts has definite therapeutic value, but again is not magic, and definitely the non-scientific amateur is advised against its practice. At no time in this book do I suggest or encourage in-depth analysis by any untrained individual for those who are seriously mentally or emotionally disturbed, who must seek expert help. My aim is to show how the rest of us who are leading "lives of quiet desperation" can acquire through hypnotic trance the ability to connect with their Higher Source—and with other people—and how hypnosis may be used as an additional step toward freedom from compulsive eating.

Final Thoughts

The patients I have used hypnotism with over the years weren't attending a Twelve Step program to tap into their spiritual needs as the study participants I have written about in this book were (and are). The goal with my patients is to help them toward taking full possession of themselves, finding out what they have to work with and then proceeding to work out their own salvation. Hypnotism is not the only method for activating the power of the mind. We can achieve equally dramatic results at times when the mind and emotions are fully awake during mindful and present living.

Whether using hypnosis to help connect to a Higher Source or make other connections previously discussed in former chapters such as prayer and meditation—in either situation—we must know how to look within and understand what we are looking for. No doubt the impact of the continuing awareness of a strong presence of a divine energy can influence a food addict to arrive at an all-encompassing state of health. Could the tremendous impact of this ever-present force do the work of healing for you? What is the impact of divine intervention? Read on and perhaps the answers will become somewhat clearer.

Personal Inventory Questions

1. Tapping into deeper emotional, physical, and spiritual levels of our being through self-hypnosis allows communication from the conscious mind to the subconscious part of the mind and vice versa—a direction and change that cuts a pathway through unknown territory. What's your understanding of self-hypnosis? Does it work?

2. Do you believe that within a corner of your mind—below the surface—lies a world where you store denial, rejected memories, and highly charged emotional material?

What lies beneath your conscious mind? How does it connect with food? With your Spiritual Source?

3. Are you willing to explore what is housed in your subconscious mind to find out what treasures might be stored in this sanctuary?

4. Do you believe you can call upon the subconscious mind to redirect feelings, perceptions, and actions by the use of self-suggestions? How might this work for you in relation to your food addiction and spiritual recovery? What can you hope to learn?

5. The goal of hypnosis is first to set the conscious mind with its inhibitions at rest—to cut through the murky, personal unconscious mind with its memories of past upsets buried there—and, second, to call upon the great resource of the subconscious mind to redirect feelings, perceptions, and actions by the use of suggestions. Could it be this simple? Do you think you can do this?

6. Tabatha's story was that she purged from when she was 13 years of age until seeking psychotherapy nearing the age of 50 years old and that this habit was suspended after hypnosis sessions. Did reading her story influence you? Do you think this route might work for you, too? Why not?

7. In order for hypnosis to work in allowing Tabatha to stop her purging, her mind had to be freed from the conscious, addictive belief that purging eliminated calories and resulted in weight loss. She had to understand, instead, at a deeper level, that purging actually crippled her body, killed her metabolism, and was a slow suicide. Do you accept what you're doing might be a slow suicide? Are the consequences of your actions enough to arrest the behavior?

8. How do you feel about self-hypnosis—hypnotizing yourself? Do you believe it's possible to reach that sacred inner place on your own? Do you fear being trapped within

your mind? How is hypnotic trance different than slipping into prayer or meditation?

9.   It's known for a fact that no hypnotized person can do anything vehemently opposed to his own will and natural character. All subjects are in control of their journey in hypnosis and can be brought out of hypnosis at the therapist's suggestion or on their own. Are you afraid that hypnosis can make you do things against your own will? Does this make you hesitate to try it as a therapy?

10.   If you don't have hesitations regarding hypnosis, what areas in yourself might you want to explore? What could you hope to achieve with hypnosis? How might your life change when your thinking and behavior shift in the direction you wish for?

Chapter 10

Impact of the Ever Presence of a Strong Spirituality

Make peace with silence,
and remind yourself that it is in this space
that you'll come to remember your spirit.
When you're able to transcend an aversion to silence,
you'll also transcend many other miseries.
And it is in this silence that the remembrance of God will be activated.
~Dr. Wayne W. Dyer

Could the ever presence of a Divine energy influences a food addict to an all-encompassing state of health? Could the tremendous impact of this Force do the work of healing for you—a result that you will never believe even if someone *tells* you? *Make peace with silence.* The impact of Divine intervention *will* do the work for you—a work you will never believe—even if someone *tells* you.

It is this Divine force behind recovery, a force that drives a transcendence far surpassing an addict's attachment to binge eating. The spiritual dimension presents to the individual who opens to it as a unifying field integrating the physical, mental, and emotional aspects of a person's being.

So you ask, "Well, how do I get this miraculous force behind me so I can experience the weight loss, peace of mind, freedom from food addiction and a release from my obsession with food?"

The answer is in the creative Divine spirit, which manifests anything it contemplates—*and* in your making the decision to co-create your program of recovery with your creator, who will carry you beyond your greatest wishes or imaginings.

With Divine guidance, *all things* are possible.

Without the higher energy, and if the addict doesn't participate in a program of recovery, the disease will resurface. Turning to God's ever presence in conjunction with a plan of action initiates the healing process. A program of recovery can include but need not be limited to: psychotherapy, a Twelve Step program, an `anonymous' support group, the advice of a nutritionist experienced in food addiction and a prayer group—and/or a church, synagogue, or mosque group—and the list goes on.

The spiritual dimension is the essence of self and also transcends the self. It is our closest, most direct experience of the universal life force. Food addiction is beyond our control without a higher energy to help us transcend our pain. But with the assistance of a `supernatural' hand, we can attend to our various issues and needs in order to maintain a consistent state of wellbeing free from negativity or the drive to consume addictive substances.

You are responsible for your *recovery* not your disease.

Spiritual healing *alone* works if you're not dealing with a chemical imbalance, though given *time and strong intention*, spirit can also heal a chemical imbalance. However, spirit combined with abstinence from foods that cause a chemical reaction can *much more easily* lead to spiritual healing than spirit without committed abstinence.

If you're not in peak condition mentally, physically, spiritually; if you're not "right" with your surroundings, and comfortable in your own skin, your full potential will be stunted.

Unaddressed emotional/social, physical, mental and spiritual conditions and situations will manifest themselves as speed bumps or brick walls in your ability to deal with or focus on the everyday need to eat four to five meals per day abstinent of sugar, flour and wheat. In other words, you can't handle everyday issues and occurrences or projects at hand except with great difficulty if you're clouded by a diseased, intoxicated mind.

Take Charisma, a stunning, soft-spoken woman with years of compulsive eating and years of relief from her obsession with food. She transcended into something greater than her limited experiences as she moved away from addictive foods and drew on a closer connection with her Source. Charisma oozes with the positive energy of extreme spirituality. She never fears to speak her truth regardless of the consequences.

Charisma recognized her ability to feel positive and to give and receive love because the force behind her enthusiasm was the Divine intelligence within us all. She bubbled, and her eyes twinkled as she exclaimed, "I have these wonderful feelings. I just feel God in me. I can't explain what that is, other than the peace that I talk about. It is just peacefulness."

Raised Catholic, Charisma harbored the visual of a compassionate strong, larger-than-life man called Jesus who kept her safe and secure. She identified with Jesus as a big statue that she could climb up on to sit on his lap. She compared Him to the Lincoln Memorial.

Life has not always been kind to Charisma, yet she never wallowed in her adversities. She faced many difficult times from early childhood to adulthood, which led her to Twelve Step programs like Al Anon—a place that offers support and hope for friends and families of problem drinkers—and CoDA—a fellowship for recovery from the effects of codependency. Codependence is a relationship between one individual who has an addiction (Charisma's husband, in this case) and another individual (Charisma) who becomes over-involved in the addict's life with a mission to *fix* the addict because the codependent feels responsible for the addictive person's problems.

In addition to Twelve Step affiliations, part of Charisma's transition from addictive eating to healthful eating involved her connection to her charismatic church, which adheres to a belief in the manifestations of the Holy Spirit through miracles and prophecy. Unexpected miracles came to Charisma that she attributed to the divine intervention. Often these miracles came by way of human miracle workers where she was led through divine inspiration and revelations.

Charisma stated, "I probably didn't notice the bigger difference in my moods and clarity from my dark despair until I went through a journal of step work to see certain things happened that I knew were a direct result of processing my experiences. And these changes were very spiritual."

Her Twelve Step work involved moving through a series of questions under 12 specific steps in a journal format to begin exploring personal experiences as they related to food addiction. In Twelve Step Programs, recognition and admission are the beginning steps of self-honesty and initiate a subsequent ability to find a solution.

Charisma and her mother had been estranged for many years until one day, at 57, without expectation or warning,

Charisma experienced a miraculous lightening of her heavy heart regarding her mother and a spontaneous healing of this relationship.

Charisma had held this resentment against her mother for more than four long decades. She had lived it, fed it, carried it around with her as one might a fragile porcelain doll, and it had become as much a part of her as her own breathing. This resentment nurtured Charisma's excuses for personal failures, for her co-dependence, and of course, for her food addiction. Although this occurred on a subconscious level, she was reluctant to let go of the resentment.

The unthinkable had happened: Charisma's stepfather had molested her as a child *while her mother looked on.* Her mother remained loyal to the molester rather than to her daughter and her grandchild. This choice left a deep scar in Charisma's heart. Years later, after complete silence between the two, they attended a family wedding, and as luck would have it, they sat across from each other at the reception. Charisma had entertained no thought of interacting with her mother during the party *or ever again.*

As the evening wore on, Charisma made her way to her mother's side of the room. "I did NOT intentionally get up. I was 'lifted' up and went over and hugged her." She pressed her lips to her mother's ear, inhaling her sweet perfume and without warning said, "I really love you." She astounded herself, but deep inside knew exactly where this change of heart came from. The transformation was the direct manifestation of the Holy Spirit—the ever presence of her spiritual source—in what felt like a miracle after years of distance and bitter anger toward her mom.

Although Charisma had harbored no guilt over not having a relationship with her mother, she realized for the first time that she had a bigger peace within herself after the reconciliation. Prior to that moment, Charisma had a lot of resentment about many things her mom had done since her mom repeatedly made choices that had a direct and negative impact on their lives. This pain was deeply embedded in Charisma for years.

Today, Charisma is 70 years old and her mother in her 90s. They talk, often spending quality time together.

"This was one of the biggest healings that I experienced," Charisma told me. "It was very, very spiritual, and it was a direct result of working through food addiction and a great deal of writing about my life's adversities and reaching above to my God to carry me through the tough times and the good time—all the times." She kept repeating, 'I've just got so much peace and I know it's because my body is clean. My mind can work because my body is clean."

These days, Charisma holds no resentments and rarely becomes angry. She manages any situation she faces in an appropriate, productive manner with peace and love rather than conflict and hate.

Charisma, now widowed, described her married life to a man who was "...not really a very nice person, a really troubled guy." He wasn't happy, which made it difficult for Charisma to detach from the toxicity—the poisonous atmosphere left in any space he occupied. She believes she succeeded for one reason. "I had God on my side all the time." Rather than being filled with rage and anger, she prayed for her husband. "No matter what—no matter what—no matter what, I prayed for him."

She prayed because she knew he didn't want to be the way he was, but that he knew nothing else. She employed the power of prayer.

Charisma always had a strong faith but finally it transformed into peace and clarity—through divine intervention. She stepped into peace after she gave up foods that triggered the compulsion to eat and opened herself to

157

harmony with the Divine, whereas before, receiving the many proofs of God's grace was blocked by food.

Charisma always considered herself spiritual even when she ate out of control. She described it as, "I did have spirituality, but I didn't totally give myself to it until I was able to give up the food." The clarity came when she no longer blocked spiritual alignment with food.

Charisma's intuition told her something was wrong in her relationship with food, but she couldn't grasp exactly what it was. She first came to an anonymous program "...because I was fat. That was it. I had no idea about anything." Charisma remembered that before her program she used to sit at AA meetings and listen to them and think, *God, I know just what you mean.* When she learned what her problem was, after the first Twelve Step meeting, she shouted for joy, "Oh my God, I am delivered."

Charisma's experience with food addiction held a definite binge eating component. She recalled in the fourth grade she rushed home from school and ate a quart of tomatoes on bread—*an afternoon snack before dinner was served.* Food wasn't readily available as she came from extreme poverty. She wore hand-me-down clothes, and it wasn't unusual for a big toe to pop out of a worn shoe or for her to not know when or what the next meal would be—if she could expect a next meal at all. "But we canned tomatoes. We had those. I'd just as soon have the bread though."

After pondering a moment, she blurts out, "No, now that's not the whole story. I was sexually molested by my grandfather, and he used to give me money, and I spent it all on candy—ALL on candy and food. I never came home with a penny. I had such shame about it, but that is how I soothed myself. I didn't know it at the time." Binges were interspersed with grazing. "I just ate all the time—I always was sticking something in my mouth."

When Charisma worked in sales, she ate lunches that consisted of pasta, warm bread rolls, and fried vegetables doused with an enormous serving of dressing on them. She remembered, after inhaling these large lunches, driving and having a *blackout*, a phenomenon caused by the intake of simple carbohydrates, which left her memory impaired. She had *a complete inability to recall what happened even hours before ingesting the substances.* She literally recalled nothing that occurred earlier in her day.

Charisma often dreaded going home because she knew she would eat all night. She binged and she grazed—alternating between the two. Sometimes she binged on such a vast amount of food that she vomited. Then she would flop on the couch for a sufficient amount of time to feel well enough to go right back to the refrigerator again—*stomach distended.* She lived this life the last six or eight months of being in the disease. Isolation took hold and became her norm; she seldom associated or interacted with people. Home alone *with food* was the most comfortable for her.

Charisma's husband, often gone, left her alone to sit and eat. "And that was what I did and swore tomorrow was going to be different, just as every addict does—and it was never different." Her voice slipped to a whisper, and she cleared her throat. The pain was still raw upon reflection, even though she had over 13 years clean from addictive foods.

Charisma had many food rituals. She recalled when she made a caramel concoction with brown sugar, corn syrup and butter, and put it in the freezer to cool. Of course she couldn't wait and burned her tongue, which resulted in large welts, since waiting for it to cool simply was *not* an option. She shoved in pure sugar, unable to slow down or control it while it was in the house.

Just the thought of how she ate caramel goo now sickens her. She ate until she could no longer fit food into her belly, yet she continued on until she became physically sick. She attempted to control her food addiction by having nothing in the house to tempt her, but in desperate times, she recalled, she made pudding concoctions from scratch, or ate her husband's ice cream even though she didn't like it—and had to level the ice cream in the carton in the hope her husband wouldn't notice. But she craved the sugar high she got each time.

Charisma tried to get treatment at Glen Bay, an eating disorder treatment facility, but her insurance wouldn't cover it. She was directed to an anonymous eating disorder meeting that night, though what she really wanted was to lose weight and to have somebody tell her exactly what to eat.

At this same time a member of her family on cocaine needed treatment. Charisma tried everything to get treatment for her relative, yet not for herself. As she spoke, her voice dropped down to barely a whisper, followed by a long pause and then soft sobs deep in her throat. After composing herself, she went on to state she believed she wasn't worthy of treatment, yet considered mortgaging her home to get help for someone else. It never occurred to her that she could do something similar for herself. Today, she would do whatever it took to save herself if she relapsed.

Charisma explained her Higher Power as "...a kind and loving God, not a punishing God, even though there are many restrictions in the Catholic Church." She innately knew that God loved her, no matter what. Even though some of the things that happened to her were hair-raising, she found no other explanation for how things worked except that the Divine guidance was there to care for her. She now knows he was always present, and that he was a loving, forgiving, kind and benevolent presence—only wanting good for her. No matter where she was, he loved her anyway. He waited with patience and never said, '*I told you so.*'

Although Charisma always connected to her spirituality on some level, she couldn't experience peace and clarity when she was active in her food addiction—with the exception of trickles of it when she was involved with her church. She was always active in the charismatic church and had spiritual experiences, but when she returned to her little corner to eat her food, no room remained for that spirituality. She only felt frustration and pain, asking herself, *Why I can't have some control over this...over a sandwich.*

Charisma recognized that her spiritual recovery from food addiction spread to all who were near her, often ribbing her as she turned to Higher consciousness. Her spirituality shows through without her having to wearing it on her sleeve. It just is, though she might sometimes want to shout from the rooftops. "I want people to know what God can do in their lives in recovery."

Charisma's final thoughts emphasize the importance of her putting the food down before she could work on her spirituality. "I couldn't have reached what I think God wants me to do. Hopefully, I am today what God wants me to be."

Charisma is firm in her conviction that spirituality in her life is a given: Without it, relapse would be soon to follow. Spirituality must be present, with God's acceptance of her, and her willingness to do for others. Without spirituality, her recovery is nothing. She admonishes, "Who cares how fat I am or how skinny I am, or what I eat if I don't have a good spiritual life? It's a no brainer."

Recovery Takes Precedence over Weight Loss

An essential ingredient in spiritual recovery is that recovery must take precedence over weight loss. In fact, if you turn your attention from weight loss and make recovery focus, the weight loss will soon follow, in turn.

On the other hand, if you make weight loss the focus, recovery is nearly unreachable.

When the mind chatter shifts from body weight to acceptance an internal peace and surrender surfaces. Simply put: An increased connection to God and people can release an addict's single-minded obsession with food.

Damien didn't give up his obsession with food and surrender to spiritual awakening in order to lose weight. In fact, he barely had weight to lose, and if he did, it was only a few pounds.

Damien acquiesced to recovery because of the insanity of the disease and what the disease did to him. Disheveled and eyes barely open, Damien made his way to work several minutes after a mandatory meeting was in session. It wasn't unusual for Damien to roll into work late and with food stains on his clothes from an earlier binge.

Blaming traffic, waiting for a long train at the railroad crossing, and detours due to construction were some of the excuses Damien conjured up when he was late for work. Continuous chaos, the crisis of disrupted work life and disastrous relationships were part of Damien's everyday life. It wasn't uncommon to find him slumped over his desk drooling on a pile of paperwork after an afternoon pasta lunch.

After a series of wrecked love affairs and lost jobs, Damien turned to recovery for food addiction—not for weight loss but for peace of mind.

Arthur, too, found that when he moved his attention from his body and weight, accomplishments which seemed impossible before not only became possible but even easy. He referred to this enlightenment as a "God thing."

Adriana claimed she was never able to have a mental release from the patterns of thought, only a physical release from the behavior until she *let go*, and only then did she become freed from the grip of food addiction. At first it was about the weight loss but when she surrendered to a greater source, the mental chatter quieted. She describes what occurred as "an epiphany."

Arthur binged to the point he feared he would eat himself to death as he gorged on copious amounts of food beyond normal "human" consumption:

The type of death I feared was death because of gluttony. And it was that death I feared, a death before I had completed what God wanted me to do. Death, death not of God's will, not death because it was God's time for me to go, but because I was outside of God's will and doing things that were going to cause me to die before God wanted me to die.
—Damien

Arthur went on to say he believed what Carl Jung said: *All addicts are on a spiritual quest.* This was true in Arthur's life. Although he was overweight, in the end it wasn't weight loss that drove him to recovery, but rather a spiritual quest, a search for *something* to fill his depleted soul.

Arthur had been looking in all the wrong places for spiritual continuity though many times he purposefully sought out spiritual places and spiritual people. When he reflected on his life, he always sought answers to life's question. But the intellectual answers he received were very limiting—and while indulging in the food that triggered his imbalances he couldn't hear, anyway, because the food thoughts were so loud.

Peace and Serenity

Where we once suffered chaos because of food sensitivities and compulsive eating, we now have calm. Confidence has replaced our fear.

In recovery, tranquility consciously and unconsciously becomes a central theme. To be conscious is to be aware of one's own existence, sensations, thoughts, surroundings, and so on. Unconsciousness occurs in the absence of conscious awareness or thought. Vacillating between the two while in active addiction persisted throughout our daily affairs, especially in situations that may have been challenging and disruptive. In turn, in recovery, we find ourselves having a different, more consistently conscious reaction to disruptions.

Nature brings calm and serenity that I now recognize as spiritual. I was brought up Catholic and only knew of organized religion. I understood instinctively there was something more but couldn't conceive of a higher energy that brought peace and tranquility. At first, I didn't grasp this notion. I thought my experience of chaos as I drowned in a vat of chocolate was insignificant compared to God's attention on *real* problems like murderers, drug addiction and wars.

I was wrong.

God *loves all his children regardless of their problems.* Spiritual connection is for everyone in any situation—no problem is too big or too small. As Mother Theresa says, "Pray and you will believe, believe and you will love, love and you will serve." This describes my connection. I pray to believe, am filled with love to serve and share what I know to pull others out of darkness toward the light *away from food addiction.*

My spiritual and emotional recovery happened in a gradual way. It wasn't that one day I woke up and I was in a spiritual, emotional or physical recovery. It occurred gradually, over a period of years. I just celebrated six years in recovery. The person who I am now is not the same person I was previously. In my beliefs and my morals, I'm the same person but I have a certain calmness about me—and it happened gradually. I hope it stays with me forever. Now, it's something that I work on—but I work on it kind of in an unconscious way. I don't consciously say, 'Oh now today I am gonna to do this or I am gonna to do that.' It's just something that evolves. It's something that I don't think about—it just takes place—it just happens. –Marilyn

John, like the others found personal serenity and peace when he was recuperating after a long hospital stay:

Across the street from where the hospital was, where I was convalescing, there was this sanctuary with these cloistered nuns. They spent their time praying in the Chapel of the Holy Blessed Sacrament. And I'd have to go in that neighborhood for medical treatment every week for quite a while. While I was still going to the hospital, I would see this place and I would think, someday I would like to go in there. So I went in one day, and it was as if angels were singing. I could hear them kind of singing their prayers—their spirituality—and it was just so soothing to my spirit. –John

Arthur embraced tranquility as a creative spiritual act he associated with his 12-step recovery and what was happening with him, which he liked. Peace and tranquility were present not only within himself but also in the people around him. He described it as not a *"legalistic"* religion or *"legalistic"* 12-step recovery.

In other words, Arthur remained connected with Christian-Judaic principles, on which he believed Twelve Step programs were built. At the same time, he never left the idea of one God who creatively revealed a spiritual path minute by minute. Arthur saw the difference between the ways that spiritual life was practiced in a recovery community than in the church, and following the way that he felt, he knew he needed to practice the path of spiritual inspiration.

Arthur's creative spiritual journey led him to the necessity to dig in the ground and plant some things. His garden in his back yard and the herb garden in the front of his home, coupled with his spice racks, began his tranquil spiritual journey which equaled: God, soil, nutrients and love.

In Lucy's life, as a result of an ever presence of spirituality, she found peace and serenity, which led her to a transcendental form of meditation. She learned to intertwine music, art, prayer and love to escape the outside challenges and lift her up and away from the stresses of living. She transcended like a feather in the wind to the point that job issues, a break-up of her marriage and sheer loneliness were placed on hold as a spiritual calm took over her life.

When dealing with the emptiness and sense of being overwhelmed became more than Lucy could bear, she abandoned reality—at least for a moment of respite—to later deal with situations from a more resilient, spiritual perspective.

One difficult day when spirituality was crowded out by the screams of life and Lucy physically was all tied up in knots, she twisted herself into a pretzel on the floor turning to spa music and letting it seep into every crevice of her being. She listened to soft piano and guitar melodies coupled with ocean waves splashing against the shoreline—while occasional seagulls chimed in to create an escape reducing anxiety, stress and fatigue. She shut out the world, and her body softened and she transcended to a meditative state.

I need to have that mellowness in my life. My peace and serenity are restored when I step out into my higher source's natural plane. Hiking through the mountains and forests brings me to a mellow place. ----Adriana

Arthur first found his serenity and peace in food recovery, which brought him a calm and clarity to make his spiritual education possible. Words took on more meaning, and he was able to study and understand God from different points of view. Ultimately, he was able to surrender to a power greater than he—one that he's connected to at all times.

Studying different points of spiritual mindedness, Arthur was able to overcome an avalanche of various addictions in his life. He passionately turned all his challenges over to a higher energy and released himself from the vicious hold his demons had on him. This `turning over' to his Higher Power opened up the opportunity for healthy-minded people to fill that space once occupied by his incubus.

For all of us, a new perception came into view, an awareness we embraced enthusiastically. Chapter 11 reveals how phenomena, miracles and medical healings surfaced and replaced hopelessness. Peace and constancy began to fill our hearts. We were lifted out of the slimy pit—out of the mud and mire—and planted firmly on our feet with a new song in our mouths and hearts.

In order to stay in this mindset, we continue to nurture the God within. And we know that, with God alone, all things are possible.

Personal Inventory Questions

1. Do you believe an ever presence of a divine energy can influence the food addict to an all-encompassing state of health? Could the tremendous impact of this force do the work of healing in you?

2. Have you asked yourself, how do I get this miraculous force behind me so I can experience the weight loss, peace of mind, freedom from food addiction, and a release from my obsession with food?"

3. Do you believe that with a Higher Source *all things* are possible? That turning to God's ever presence in conjunction with a plan of action can initiate the healing process? What is your plan of action?

4. Do you believe you are responsible for your own recovery? Is it the trigger food(s), or your lack of spiritual connection, or both, that prevent you from recovery? Can

your recovery take precedence over an obsession with and addiction to the idea of weight loss?

5. A program of recovery can include but need not be limited to: psychotherapy, a Twelve Step program, an `anonymous' support group, the advice of a nutritionist experienced in food addiction, and a prayer group—or a church, synagogue, or mosque group. And the list goes on. Which components from this list attract your attention?

6. If you're not in peak condition, mentally, physically, spiritually—if you're not "right" with your surroundings and comfortable in your own skin, your full potential will be stunted. Do you believe this to be true? What will you do in order to open up to your full potential?

7. What do you think about Charisma who had years of active food addiction causing havoc in her life until she turned to her Higher Source and a Twelve Step program.

8. Charisma dreaded going home because she knew she would eat all night long. She describes a *blackout*, a phenomenon caused by the intake of simple carbohydrates, which left her memory impaired. Damien also describes a fog—a veil of darkness that came over him after a food binge—and that it wasn't uncommon for him to find himself slumped over his desk drooling on a pile of paperwork after an afternoon pasta lunch. Have you ever had an experience similar to these? What was this like?

9. Do you have food rituals in which, like Charisma, you create crazy concoctions of foods when you're desperate for a "fix" and there's nothing to satisfy you in your home? As you ponder this, what feelings come to surface? Are you anxious? Sickened? Frightened? Ashamed?

10. Have you ever gone to a treatment center for your binge eating or chemical imbalance in regard to food? Have you ever thought about going, but feared the stigma or what others would say?

Chapter 11

Phenomena, Miracles, and Medical Healings

He lifted me out of the slimy pit,
Out of the mud and mire;
He set my feet on a rock
And gave me a firm place to stand.
He put a new song in my mouth,
A hymn of praise to our God.
~Psalm 40:2-3~

Often the lowest points in our life propel us into a spiritual transcendence, but we have to be "open" to it. Miracles are for all, but not all are open enough to let them in. Many are not receptive to the amazing gifts that can come directly from our Source. They don't believe such things are possible, or that they themselves are deserving.

To experience phenomena, miracles, and medical healings, we don't have to "do" anything—we just have to surrender to the possibility, and then the extraordinary surfaces and replaces despair.

As those of us reporting our process here journeyed through recovery's ups and downs, we began to find ourselves in a state of wonderment over everything and everyone we came in contact with. Peace and constancy actualized and filled our hearts. The primary connection, between us and the source of our being, materialized in a palpable way. We were lifted out of the slimy pit—out of the mud and mire—and planted firmly on our feet with a new song in our mouths and hearts. Now, we give thanks and praise daily for the multitude of phenomena, miracles, and medical healings that appear before our eyes as we go through our mundane lives.

Phenomena, Miracles, and Medical Healings

Dictionary.com defines *phenomena* as something that is impressive or extraordinary, a remarkable or exceptional occurrence. This occurrence becomes observable, when before it could not be seen even if it was present. The *miracle*, too, is an extraordinary event in the physical world that surpasses all known human or natural powers and is ascribed to a supernatural cause. Such an effect or event manifesting may be considered as a work of God—a wonder, a marvel.

Medical healings do not necessarily come by way of medicine and other common procedures doctors utilize, but rather can arise as *natural* medical healings. Not to say a medical healing can't also include medical intervention in the traditional sense: The two can be merged. But unexpected medical healings often are questioned, and considered to be hearsay, anecdotal with no scientific proof—arguably delusion or a result of quackery. Some believe that rather than a medical healing having occurred, the symptoms went into remission, or the illness or disorder followed its natural course and happened to improve on its own at the same time that spiritual appeals to a higher source may have been made.

In the context of this book, I do attribute many such healings that take place to a person turning over his or her will and life to a Divine intelligence so that the individual becomes open to receiving and manifesting healing. These types of resolution of what may be long-term difficulties are often experienced as a "knowing" of a healing taking place. In essence, we need no special training for a medical miracle to occur, nor are such phenomena difficult to understand. These spontaneous and profound healings are for anyone and everyone. You need simply believe in your own unique ability to receive and experience God's miracles.

When we open ourselves to Divine time, anything is possible—phenomena, miracles, and medical healing—all intertwined, melding one to the next, interchangeably: We can receive a revelation or material rarity we might have missed if not present in the here and now. Phenomena and miracles often go undetected until we reach this place of higher awareness—it is then we can begin to detect and manifest all we seek in our physical world—including verifiable medical healing.

One of the absolutely possible miracles of spiritual recovery from food addiction is to no longer be controlled by the binge: to no longer addictively eat high volumes of food voraciously and out of control, in isolation and believing/hoping tomorrow will be different. Those who view the world in wholly spiritual terms recognize no man is an island. We are all one, interconnected—a recognition that itself is part of the miracle for the eating disordered, who are more often than not extremely self-centered, choosing to be alone, focused on what they want to eat that they shouldn't and what they should eat that they don't.

Episodes fluctuating from bingeing to grazing and back to bingeing in an attempt to control the uncontrollable eating vanish like water evaporating in the sun: They disappear. In time, spiritual recovery shows up as a Higher Power that is superior to all our petty problems as well as all of man's self-devised `solutions.'

At the outset of recovery, the promises of spirituality become real slowly, but every *mindful* step leads to a healthier state of body, mind, and spirit. Acceptance prevails. A power for good replaces the power for bad. When we are no longer defeated by the bondage to food, a gained belief in self emerges. Emotional recovery shares space with body, mind, and spiritual recovery when food is no longer the supposed higher source. A complete recovery takes hold.

Often, before recovery, the extraordinary events in our lives went unnoticed because life (and food obsession) got in the way. Back in December of 2000, when I first entertained the idea of letting go of sugar and white flour, I had glimpses of miracles and medical healings that were to come my way. On one occasion when I flew to Chicago to help my siblings take care of our mom who'd had a severe stroke in 1998 that left her completely paralyzed on the left side of her body, I experienced a phenomena that marked the beginning of many phenomena, medical healings, and miracles for me.

Our mom was agitated and quite difficult that day, so I was grateful when she napped, just because I could get some relief from her restless demands. While she slept, I sank into the end chair close by, my legs draped over the sides, and I began to read *Man of Miracles*, written by Heather Parsons about Father Peter Rookey, a Catholic Servite priest working for Jesus, who my Aunt Mary knew about.

On page after page, I encountered the miraculous healings that took place when Father Rookey prayed. I wondered if this miracle man could help our mom find some peace, or maybe even a medical healing. To our surprise and great delight, when we called and invited him to pray over Mom, he agreed to come and visit her. So, late that afternoon, as the sun slipped away on a crisp Chicago day, we were suddenly interrupted during our caretaking duties by the sound of a car squealing and then screeching to a halt in the driveway.

Father Rookey had arrived!

He entered our home briskly swishing past us, his long black robe leaving behind a breeze and the sweet smell of oils and mints. He reminded me of a monk at first glimpse, and then on closer observation, the angel Clarence Odbody, the whimsical, endearing messenger of God in *It's a Wonderful Life*. He joked as he stumbled while moving closer to Mom that it would be hard to find his way around the room if he'd had one too many glasses of wine.

The room was, indeed, cluttered, being filled with all types of hospital paraphernalia, including a hospital bed, wheelchair, and a crane-like lift to pull our mom out of the bed when we needed to clean her bedding.

We followed Father, wide eyed and mouths agape, as we gathered around Mom's bed to hold hands and pray. First, he tended to Mom, blessing her and praying over her. Then, he carefully pulled from his right pocket a white, folded, blessed cloth containing one communion host. He gently placed the cloth below mom's chin, while administering the Eucharist on her tongue. After that, he turned to us and blessed us all with holy water, saying Satan should like the cool water as it was very hot where he lived, and then anointed each of us, blessing our foreheads with holy oil. Instantly, I felt the shift derived from the blessing when a peace I'd never known before washed over me.

After that one cold, winter afternoon in Chicago wrapped in a blanket reading about this miracle man, I was privileged to meet with him on many occasions, in many different locales. The first spring after Mom passed away, I attended one of Father Rookey's healing masses where I kneeled for most of the four-hour mass *without any discomfort.*

When the healing part of the service came, people in row after row made their way to the altar for his touch. Taking one at a time, he placed his hands on their heads and then made the sign of the cross over their foreheads, before blessing them again with a small crucifix he held in his hand. When he came to bless me, his golden-brown eyes locked onto mine, and down, down, down I went in slow motion on the hard marble floor for what seemed like hours.

A wave of heat went right through my body, from head to toe, and the sweet smell of roses seemed to fill the room. I wasn't awake, nor was I asleep. I experienced a total and utter peace that I'd never felt before or felt quite like that since. I later learned what I'd experienced was known as resting in the Holy Spirit. I also learned the smell of roses indicated the Blessed Mother was near and that the luscious smell might not have filled the room for everyone. My husband, Joe, didn't recall the floral scent, although he experienced the Holy Spirit as he locked his knees into place standing while he went into a trance and calm washed over him.

This personal encounter with my Higher Source, I acknowledged as a phenomenon, a miraculous connection with God that showed I was loved and cared for *always.*

Father Rookey's warmth, kindness, sense of humor, and transparent deep faith permanently changed my relationship with God. The miracle for me was that God is not so far away, but that he walks within each of us.

This famous healing priest from Chicago made a huge impact not only on me, but after meeting with him, Mom transformed before our very eyes into a kinder, more loving person. Warmth we hadn't seen in years materialized as she found her way back to God—which was the biggest miracle.

And to think I might have missed this grand finale had I been knee deep in junk foods.

I learned a great many things in the times I spent with Father Rookey, many of which came to me long after our time spent together as if his lessons were whispered only to reach my ears when I was ready to hear—when I, the student, was ready to learn from the teacher.

One subtle yet profound message came to me back in 2001 when we were gathered around the table preparing to eat a meal of whole grain muffins, cheese, and fresh fruit with wine. Father had blessed our mom and prayed for her before turning to the food, bowing his head in silence giving thanks to God for the food we were about to eat.

I closely observed him eat with passion and vigor, telling lovely stories about Abraham and Sarah, Daniel and the lion's den; stories of how he meditated in quiet, praying and connecting with God in preparation for healing the sick; how he didn't eat all day because his energy was needed to connect with God and the person or persons before him in need of healing.

I was awestruck because I so needed my food every four to five hours or I'd be depleted of energy. Wine would send me into a tizzy, not to mention cheese and fruit as an afternoon meal rather than vegetables and more compact protein.

As early as my memory takes me, I was a sickly child. I was anemic with low iron. I recall boxes of iron drops in the upper cupboard that were specifically for me. I was always tired and easily spiked high fevers. But I was most interested in sugary foods that gave me a lift. As I went from childhood, to adolescence, to adulthood, I was always tired and felt weakened with low blood sugar. My only out was eating more sweets, which gave me energy—at least momentarily. I wolfed down my foods to get the charge.

So watching Father Rookey delicately eat each morsel of food with such intense love was moving for me. I never ate my food with love and mindful attention. Although I couldn't eat the same foods he ate due to my food sensitivity, I now knew my manner of relating to my food was all wrong.

I began to learn that food was good, a gift from the Divine—which led to a medical healing for me. As soon as I worked the unprocessed foods into my system at regular intervals, my miracle took hold. No longer was I dizzy with weakness. No longer did my knees shake and body start to crumble from sheer exhaustion. No longer did I need daily naps at work or at home. Yes, a miracle, a phenomenon took hold—a medical healing.

Internally, I had questioned why I was saddled with an eating disorder and couldn't eat what I wanted when I wanted. A spark of truth revealed to me I needed to turn more to prayer and meditation—to sit in stillness so I could receive direction from my Higher Source—to be used as an instrument through Divine guidance in whatever fashion he needed me—and that we are all used differently.

My calling was to lead eating disordered and mood disordered persons out of their hell—to a quieter place. But how? Well, I'd have to start with myself and through meditations and prayers invite stillness into my own life, something quite foreign to me.

A myriad of meditation books line the shelves of book stores, Internet stores, and people's homes to teach people how to sit with the self. Jesus went to the mountaintop to connect with God, to hear instruction. I learned my mountaintop is anywhere my silenced mind might be. I could sit right here at my desk or in my office between patients, or out in the garage with the door open leaving a view of elegant palm trees backed by a deep blue sky and a hint of the ocean out beyond the horizon.

I don't need fancy training, books, or a guru, unless I should want to employ their services. I can find this place anywhere, anytime, through several slow, deep breaths and chanting a prayer, praying the Rosary, or repeating a calming line I'd memorized from a childhood prayer or one of the saints who'd walked before me—like the first line of St. Francis's prayer, *Lord, make me an instrument of your peace,* asking how I can be used to serve.

Prayer of Saint Francis of Assisi

Lord, make me an instrument of your peace.
Where there is hatred, let me sow love;
where there is injury, pardon;
where there is doubt, faith;
where there is despair, hope;
where there is darkness, light;
and where there is sadness, joy.
O Divine Master, grant that I may not so much seek
to be consoled as to console;
to be understood as to understand;
to be loved as to love.
For it is in giving that we receive;
it is in pardoning that we are pardoned;
and it is in dying that we are born to eternal life. Amen

What is meditation? It's the ability to achieve perfect equilibrium of the mind. It's the development of inner insights to connect to a Higher Wisdom and the present space of the Now. The ability to taste our life as a precious, continuing dynamic—changing, evolving, and transforming from moment to moment. Meditation allows us to embrace the stillness, to direct the perception of all that our lives comprise, and move into a state of awareness. It's in this sacred place that the wisdom realizations begin to surface, and all our high moments become more intense and our low moments more tolerable. Meditation is the phenomena of moving to a new sacred space within and without—to open self to miracles and medical healings.

My medical healing was not the only healing I witnessed from Father Rookey's faith-filled work. One of my nieces had a series of miscarriages, possibly directly related to her

Crohn's disease, an inflammatory condition that affects different portions of the intestinal tract in different patients. It's a disease that causes inflammation of the lining of the digestive tract, which can lead to abdominal pain, severe diarrhea, and even malnutrition.

Father Rookey placed both hands on my niece's head, and prayed over her: She now has three beautiful children. Yes, a miracle, a medical healing indeed! Although she still has Crohn's disease, as there is not a cure for it, it remains in remission and she lives a fully blessed life. Trevor, Jacqueline's husband, was filled with cancer at the same time she learned she was pregnant with their third child, certainly not a good situation for their family. They prayed and bent their hearts on a Higher Source. Today young Colton is a toddler, Jacqueline works for a high-powered corporation, and Trevor is clear of all cancer. Yes, miracle upon miracle comes when we are open to healing through the Divine.

With my newfound awareness, I can reflect back and account for miracle upon miracle laced in phenomenon I can't explain with a human answer. When I learned I was pregnant with Benjamin, I took Lamaze classes. Dr. Lamaze was influenced by Soviet childbirth practices, which involved breathing and relaxation techniques. I was determined to have a "natural" childbirth without an epidural.

During labor, I rode each contraction like a wave, breathing my way through and praying the Rosary in my head. At one point I rose above my body and watched the whole miraculous event unfold *with no pain and no drugs*. To the surprise of my doctor, I *pleased* and *thank-youed* my way through the whole twelve hours of labor. I learned firsthand I'm never alone. Yes, another miracle healing.

The Higher Power Is a Power for Good

Recognizing the Holy Spirit was a Higher Power, a Divine Source as a power for good, was one of the subtle miracles presenting in phenomena we often missed while in our food frenzy. My own Higher Power is more than a static idea of God in heaven—it is a spiritual energy that wraps around me 24/7. It is a non-judging Love energy. It is Jesus. It is the sun. It is energy. It is love. It is everything good. It is warm. It is forgiving. The mere thought of my Higher Power comforts my spirit—my soul—me. I am safe.

After exploring my own Higher Power as a power for good, I found others said things I believed, too, such as: *My Higher Power wants what's best for me. God is whole. God is good. God is kind and all embracing. God is the smile and twinkle in another's face.* The consensus is that spiritual recovery is marked by a power for good. This power for good is greater and more profound than anything we in recovery could have previously imagined.

Adriana struggled over her relationship with God in her early years. She then made food her power—her universe—to cover her pain and shame as a result of sexual abuse when she was a child. She grabbed food to bury feelings and escape from the here and now, which was unbearable and cruel. Adriana gobbled any and every food in view, so much so that her sister hid her own food for fear Adriana would find it and eat it all.

Today, Adriana has a powerful Source that replaces food. She has found a gentle God. "I don't talk about my Higher Power because I really can't describe him. I do call him, Him. At one point I called Him 'the man upstairs.' I guess the biggest revelation that comes to mind is His gentleness, love, and understanding. He is very tolerant. I have no picture of Him. I mean He has no face. There's simply this spirit. I guess spirit is the best way to describe Him. I just know He is there and I know that He is a part of my life"

Arthur lives lean, eating enough food to nourish his body without indulgence and without gluttony—a step toward being godlike—wanting to live on the right amounts of whole foods and flourish like a yellow daisy kissed by the sun, without force, without agony—existing as pure love. He points to a once wilted and neglected plant in the corner of the room and recalls how it was dead—un-revivable—and how it took ten years to revive, and now thick branches covered in luscious green foliage sprout and stretch to the ceiling as if to spring forth and touch the heavens. Arthur refers to himself as a plant. Once dying on the vine, now he thrives.

The plant reminds Arthur how the universe works. "God can take extremely small things that are essentially dead and bring life to them—so, I want to imitate God in that way." Arthur was at the point where he didn't take care of himself. He binged on foods, noting now his eating was fear based, absent of God. His greatest fear was to die an untimely death from one pizza too many. Today, like the revived plant, Arthur flourishes because God brought him back to life. It's not that God wasn't available to Arthur but rather Arthur wasn't available to God—as the Zen proverb states, "When the student is ready, the teacher will appear."

Arthur's Divine guidance is powerful and kind, wanting only wellness for him. "I say it is a fact. The overwhelming evidence that the God actually loves people, and loves me specifically is astounding. Based on my limited understanding of what humanity is, I certainly see some greatness in humanity. God, though, is an infinitely higher—as opposed to a slightly higher—power."

Like Arthur, Charisma saw God's power as gentle, loving and all forgiving—a definite power for good. She has lived through many hardships. "But in the overall picture of my life, because everybody has stuff, I realized that somehow I always find something that gets me through everything." And that something is *the Source's* infinite power and love, which spreads to all who ask and are open to receive.

Acceptance
At some point in this process of recovery we need to accept the concept of food addiction, and we need to take action to stay in physical, emotional, and spiritual recovery. This action includes daily vigilance in abstaining from toxic food, which will help foster spiritual awakening and recovery. We must understand and recognize that certain foods cause a chemical reaction leading to binge eating.

Life is hard—people are mean—and then you die transforms into an acceptance that life is not perfect or without incident; life is, indeed, filled with curve balls. This acknowledgement that food addiction exists is not a ticket to complacency or idleness, rather it promotes self-awareness and mindfulness— an always expanding holistic approach.

My demeanor today is much calmer, much more serene, much more tolerant, much more accepting, which also leads into the physical part—I don't get upset for long stretches of time. I don't get so stressed over things because of acceptance of the situation. —Adriana

After 207 days of clean eating, I hit one of life's curve balls, and I wrote the following in my diary: I am feeling waves of depression—not certain where they are coming from. I'm now finished with all of my courses for my Doctorate. All I have left are my comps and dissertation. I am grieving because I have spent so many years buried in books, research, and writing, and worry that it won't make a bit of difference. I fear when all is said and done, depression will hit me like a tornado out of nowhere—my life crumbling in its wake. I will have to face what I avoided. I turned to school months after the death of my mother to bury my sadness in the business of writing, reading, and research. Additionally, I dove into my studies after a series of miscarriages, knowing I no longer could have children—I no longer was able to fulfill my dream of more babies. I studied to no end to avoid acknowledging that my sons, Benjamin and Kris, are grown. No more parenting. No mom, no sons in need—just a pile of sadness. I am sad. I'm getting older too. I can see it in my eyes, in my face. It is very sad. Life can be sad. Before, I could dive into my food to numb these awful feelings. Oh—brownies with chocolate icing and baked chips followed by dark chocolate could pull me out of this funk. Of course, then I would end up in another funk: food addiction at its best! —Lisa

Once you become mindful of what you are negatively doing with food, you can make a choice as to whether to continue with the food addiction or not. For instance, once you become aware a bite of chocolate leads to boxes of chocolates and that what you really want is to feel safe and loved because you are lonely and alone, you can, instead, fill the emptiness by chatting with a friend, taking a walk in nature, listening to music, praying, or by doing something else that moves you away from eating food to fill the hole.

In time, I began to grasp that "overcoming" my food addiction was just as important to God as a murderer's repentance, a heroin addict's abstinence, or an alcoholic putting down the drink. And from this acceptance, my spiritual connection began and continued to progress and soar. Another miracle indeed!

Adriana learned to accept things as they are and stay in the now. She recognizes she is not in control on any given day of what others do or say, and at times when she forgets and gets caught up in the game of trying to control another, she stops, evaluates, corrects, and redirects, mindful of her own business, not the business of others—*acceptance*.

It's okay not to be in agreement with what others do, and to think that perhaps you might do it another way—but the fact remains it is *their* business.

Let go and accept whatever it is, and life becomes easier and often opens the valve to mindful living and spiritual connection, which leads to miracle awareness. Adriana transcended into acceptance by thoroughly believing that God's message to her is hers alone. She has seen that the path on this earth is her path and not a path to direct somebody else unless that person asks for help. Adriana accepted she can't live someone else's life, only her own life—a spiritual being having a human experience.

Like Adriana and me, others transcend into acceptance even when *life is hard, people are mean, and then you die* moments enter their lives:

So, if God sees spending time with me worthwhile, then it is by definition worthwhile, because what is worthwhile has been declared, and who am I to declare some other thing? So, it is what it is! (Laughs) And that God loves me is a mystery and is astounding to me. It's miraculous! That's my conception. –Arthur

Adriana knew promoting abstinence from sugar, flour, and wheat and replacing it with acceptance and spiritual healing was the right path to follow. "And then I knew sharing and aligning with God and other food addicts was where I belonged, to better understand myself and my disease. I definitely knew. It was kind of for me the last possibility. I had tried everything else. I tried everything. I didn't know about trigger foods. I didn't know about weighing and measuring. I didn't know about eating three meals a day." And she didn't have a God source to turn to in troubled times—until now.

Charisma, too, accepts with certainty she can't pick up toxic foods if she wants to maintain sanity and her devotional association with her higher source.

Chapter 12 moves into relying on partnering with a higher source rather than navigating through life solo.

Personal Inventory Questions

1. Often the lowest points in our life propel us into a spiritual transcendence, but we have to be "open" to it. To experience phenomena, miracles, and medical healings, we don't have to "do" anything—we just have to surrender, to let go, and then the extraordinary surfaces and replaces despair. Do you feel that you're open, that you can let go?

2. I describe the phenomena, miracles, and medical healings I experienced and witnessed with Father Rookey in myself and my mother, who was completely paralyzed on the left side of her body after a severe stroke in 1998. Often, out of tragedy we find blessings. What are your miracles and blessings? How have they impacted your life?

3. *Medical healings* do not necessarily come by way of medicine and other common procedures doctors utilize, but rather can arise as *natural* medical healings. Not to say a medical healing can't also include medical intervention in the traditional sense: The two can be merged. What is your experience with "natural" medical healings?

4. My Higher Power is more than a static idea of God in heaven—it's a spiritual energy that wraps around me 24/7. It's a non-judging God. It is a compassionate, caring Jesus.

It's the sun. It is energy. It is love. It's everything good. It's warm. It's forgiving. What is your Higher Power to you?

5. In the context of this book, I do attribute phenomena, miracles, and medical healing that takes place to a person turning over his or her will and life to a Divine Source so that the individual becomes open to receiving and manifesting healing. These spontaneous and profound healings are for anyone and everyone. Do you believe in your own unique ability to receive and experience God's miracle?

6. As early as my memory takes me, I was a sickly child. I was anemic with low iron. I recall boxes of iron drops in the upper cupboard that were specifically for me. I was always tired and easily spiked high fevers. But I was most interested in sugary foods that gave me a lift. As you reflect on your early childhood memories what stands out for you? Were you interested in sugary, high carbohydrate foods more than healthy foods? Were you a sickly child?

7. Mindful eating has become of great interest to eating disorder professionals in part of the "training" to become aware of eating rather than blindly scarfing down foods. As I reflected on my personal relationship with food I shared how I never ate my food with love and mindful attention. I merely wolfed my food down to get the charge and soon after was filled with remorse and guilt. So watching Father Rookey delicately eat each morsel of food with such intense love was moving for me. Have you ever eaten with mindful attention? What's the experience like to chew with conscious attention? Do you eat less and is your food a healthier choice? What's the difference in your awareness on eating binge foods versus health foods?

8. A first step to mindful eating is learning to be still within. One of the ways to reach stillness is through meditation—the ability to achieve perfect equilibrium of the

mind. What's your understanding of meditation, food, and awareness?

9.   Adriana struggled over her relationship with God in her early years. She then made food her greatest power—her universe—to cover her pain and shame as a result of sexual abuse when she was a child. Can you relate to this? Have you been burying emotions and abusive experiences with food?

10.   One of the miracles of spiritual recovery from food addiction is to no longer be controlled by the binge. To no longer addictively eat high volumes of food voraciously and out of control, in isolation and believing tomorrow will be different. Do you believe no longer being controlled by the binge is a possibility for you as well? In time, spiritual recovery shows a Higher Power that is superior to all our problems as well as all of man's self-devised "solutions." Can this be true for you too?

Chapter 12

Relying on Healing from a Higher Power

Inside of us is a place that is all-knowing,
all mighty,
which is a fragment of God.
Nourishing, healing elements within us.
There is a spark in each one of us.
~Dr. Wayne W. Dyer, Wishes Fulfilled: Mastering the Art of
Manifesting

I learned while conducting my study and while with my patients that I wasn't the only one open to experiencing miracles and phenomena, along with healings after and during cleansing from toxic foods. This is not to say these miracles and medical healings, along with phenomena, weren't happening all along—as they most surely were—however, we often missed seeing these events because we were either not open to them; not surrendered to a Higher Source to carry us while we were numbed out with food; or experiencing difficult times that kept us distracted.

John, too, after many medical healings, miracles, and phenomena, moved into a life in which prayer begins and ends each day. He starts each morning with a morning prayer:

John's Morning Prayer

God, I thank you for this day and for all of the opportunities to serve you that this day holds. May I serve you well. I pray, in your mercy, to please remove the desire from me for that which will destroy me. Please remove the desire for a drink, a drug, nicotine in any form, or sugar, or any other self-destructive behavior, thought, attitude, or feeling, any harmful sexual or eating habits.

Father, I offer myself to thee to do with me as you will. Remove from me the bondage of self, that victory over all evil may bear witness of thy love, thy power, and thy way of life to those I would help. May I do thy will always.

My Creator, I am now willing that you should have all of me: good and bad, ugly and beautiful. I pray that you now remove every defect of character that stands in the way of my usefulness to you and my fellows. Grant me peace as I go out to do your bidding. Lord, make me a channel of your peace. Where there is hatred, let me show love; where injury, pardon; where darkness, light; and where sadness ever joy.

Oh Divine Master, grant that I might not so much seek to be consoled as to console, to be loved as to love; for it is in grieving we receive, it is in pardoning that we are pardoned, it is in dying that we are born to eternal life.

John's Morning Prayer is based on *The Big Book* of Alcoholics Anonymous, and John prays in solitude using this prayer in the early morning hours as the sun peeks through the dawn.

A kind and gentle, soft-spoken, 56-year-old married man, John was brought up Catholic and comes from an Italian family. His father, an alcoholic, abandoned the family early on in John's life, leaving his mom to raise him and his siblings. John currently has five years of continuous recovery from food addiction and 30 years of recovery from drugs and alcoholism.

Among his earliest memories, John recalls going out to the penny candy store to get chips and sweets. The number of pennies he could find or steal determined how much he could buy. His eyes glaze over as he runs his tongue across his lips remembering the lush array of candies in the shop. Red rope-like licorice strings, Mary-Janes, watermelon hard candies, and little coconut candies were among his favorites. He laughs. "I don't remember much of my youth, but I sure can remember those candies. I'd binge on candy before school since we weren't allowed to have them in the classroom."

John's first glimpse of understanding food addiction came when he was 14 years old watching a popular talk show hosted by Jack Parr and listening to a guest who was a professional in the field of eating disorder treatment. John clearly remembers the guest saying, 'It's not about what you're eating, but it's about what's eating you.' Although he didn't do anything then after hearing those words, they stayed in the back of his mind that *we eat in response to something.*

Even though John believed he was aware of trigger foods early in life, a time that really stands out in his mind was the early years in recovery in Alcoholics Anonymous. He had a great deal of nerve damage, and "…a lot of tremors, a lot of insecurity, and a lot of physical and emotional things I was dealing with" as he came off alcohol.

John's sponsor, who was also in an anonymous food program, had an understanding of food recovery, saying to John, "You know, maybe part of the problem you're having is that you drink three cups of coffee at every meeting, and you put two to three spoonfuls of sugar in each cup. It's probably contributing to your shakiness. If you stop doing that, you might start to see what is you and what is the reaction to the sugar and the caffeine."

These powerful words, spoken to John, jumpstarted his awareness that he reacted to sugar and that he craved sugar for a calming high. "I was confused because a lot of the old-timers would carry candies with them and give them to the newbies to help them overcome the cravings for alcohol."

John *used* a lot of soda, cakes, and candy his first year in AA.

His sponsor's awareness of food addictions led John to get the help he needed, and through a Twelve Step food anonymous program he saw clearly that sugar was a part of his problem and didn't contribute to the solution he found in AA.

"Binge eating was always a response to my emotions. If I felt out of control, I felt that bingeing would take down the anxiety level." Being out of control sparked a fear in him of not knowing what to do with himself when he wanted to crawl out of his skin. This condition provoked him to desire something—anything—to make him feel better emotionally and to quiet the roaring lion within. He thus sought out comfort foods: potato chips and any kind of simple carbs. He ate fast and lots of whatever it was, until he went beyond his emotional distress into a new level of pain: fullness beyond his stomach capacity.

Just before John joined an anonymous program for food addiction, he ate potato chips when he watched football, starting off with a three- or four-ounce bag. Over a period of time, the size of the bag increased until it became the big family-sized bag. He rationalized that the family-sized bag was more economical. In time, football no longer brought excitement to John because his focus was on the chips, chomping and wolfing down handfuls without tasting, followed by emotional bouts of self-disgust.

Initially, John's recovery from compulsive eating was out of medical necessity—raging cholesterol—and because he felt recovery worked, based on the experiences of friends he knew in AA who were successful at conquering their food addictions. But the last straw for John was his weight. He could ignore his cholesterol, but he had trouble ignoring that the uniforms he wore to work bulged at the seams as his shirt tail wadded up and pants dipped down below the crack of his butt when he bent over. Day by day, in recovery, his food choices improved while his thoughts became more lucid, and he became aware of his body, mind, and spirit all transforming. Phenomena, miracles, and medical healings took hold throughout his healing process and continue to date.

John defines his Higher Power as spirit—something infinite—but since his ability to describe it is finite, he says, he can't completely explain. Spirituality is "…whatever moves you, whatever motivates you, and whatever helps life make sense for you." His Higher Power comes from a consciousness of God—an awareness of an omnipotent being. When he was active in his addiction, "It killed a lot of my spirituality."

John's spiritual recovery evolved over time, beginning with recovery from alcohol in upper elementary school. Over the years, he went in and out of recovery, which affected his spiritual growth. But he was about to experience phenomena, miracles, and medical healing as he reported, "I know extraordinary things throughout my life moved me—turned me—in certain directions."

One time that came to mind for John was when he had a burst appendix that was misdiagnosed and left a great deal of poison in his body so that he ended up in the hospital near death. He then went through an out-of-body experience "…where I was very clear there was a presence—my Higher Power—in the room."

Before the arrival of modern antibiotics, a burst appendix often resulted in death. In John's case, he hovered near death's door. The excruciating discomfort on the right side of his abdomen left him paralyzed with pain, nausea, vomiting, and fever. Simple, everyday tasks—to move, take deep breaths, cough and sneeze were nearly impossible, and if touched, he screamed a blood-curdling shout due to the piercing pain. When John attempted to walk, the pain would double.

Once John's appendix burst, the pain lessened but soon a high fever and abdominal swelling followed, and John's heart rate accelerated. With death imminent, the doctor operated immediately. In addition to his burst appendix, John suffered from a plethora of medical issues due to years of drinking and neglect—he fought an uphill battle every day. He was tired. "I didn't know that I actually wanted to live anymore."

Dr. Imus said he'd do everything available to medical science for John, but if John didn't want to live, nothing the doctors could do would help.

In hindsight, John recalls that he'd had many spiritual experiences throughout his life. Every time he gave up, something happened that straightened him out and inspired him with hope. His recovery from food addiction drew on prior alcohol recovery experiences that gave him strength.

Spiritual awakening is an attitude—a state of mind, an openness and a connection—a fellowship with spirit that emerges from and continues with prayer, meditation, and solitude, which in the case of John connected him to spirit and a community of like minds in a Twelve Step program. As an awakened spiritual being, he understood no man is an island; we are all interconnected in some way. He saw that he needed to learn from others who'd walked a similar path to his and now lived lives in spiritual, emotional, and physical recovery.

When John had learned about food addiction while in treatment for alcoholism more than 20 years before, he remembered thinking, "God...how do you work on all these things at once? I grieved the death of my girlfriend, while out of nowhere I all of a sudden had to grieve the loss of my grandmother." The death of his girlfriend catapulted him into grief over his grandmother—who had passed away long before, when John was very young.

John thought he was "cracking up" for mourning his grandmother because she had died years before his girlfriend had. His therapist taught him though that he hurt now for his grandma and his girlfriend "...because you used all these addictions not to feel the loss, and now you're conscious of these feelings."

After intense work on recovery from his addictions, John spent time in meditation and prayer—often out in nature at an idyllic place in the Bronx where he felt a sense of serenity. It was a time in his life when he was much tormented. One summer afternoon, he made his way to this place on the Hudson, where on the other side of the river were the Power Sage Mountains. He recounts, "Oh God, this was such a peaceful place—all these geese would run across the field, and I sat for hours on end taking it all in. During my whole first year of recovery I couldn't work due to medical problems that I had, so I would go to places like this."

Relying on God's strength within, John had the ability to handle whatever was ahead of him, but when he blocked God's energy, he fell back into the anxiety and fears from life's losses and the emotional scars that remained.

The phenomenon of John's spirituality is now not only at the center of his recovery process, but is the center of his *life*. Nothing made sense to him when he wasn't spiritually tuned in. With a soft chuckle and mischievous grin, he claims that without spirituality his job helping others becomes a worthless one. His return to school would no longer have a reason behind it, nor would anything he is doing here on earth. "What is life without a purpose—without a God source? It would add up to a lot of useless time that doesn't make any sense."

John found his purpose was to help addicts, and he earned a Master's degree in social work so God could use him as a vessel to help others. His spiritual awareness and connection birthed clarity and understanding of what it was he needed to do.

For John, spiritual connection made sense, opening his eyes and heart to miracles and medical healings. He found an appreciation for the present moment and the small things in life. Simple things such as where he lives and what he does and who he is give value and purpose to his existence now that he is spiritually in touch with himself and his Higher consciousness, and not under a cloud of active addiction. It is very evident to him that everybody has a genuine function in this world, but most people don't listen to their intuitive cores. For John, this intuition is activated by the awareness of an energy that guides, leads, and directs him in how to conduct his life.

As children, we move with a strong, clear and confident connection to our spiritual essence and instinctive knowing, though often life has a way of distracting us from it. Now, harmony with the Divine once again commands John's total attention. John listens and relates through his instincts as he tries to fulfill his reason for being here. This makes John feel good about his life: Everything seems logical. "The whole tapestry is important. When you're trying to see little pieces of it, it doesn't make sense. "

When John was at death's door from a burst appendix, he believed Divine guidance had reached into his heart—into his hell and pulled him out from it—a miracle for certain. After he was discharged from the hospital, it took him one year of convalescing to function again in a normal, everyday way. One day, shortly after his release, however, he found the courage to attend a healing service rumored to mend and make people whole spiritually and physically through a God of love and good.

John's nerves were shot from years of alcohol abuse, which left him with Parkinson-like shakes and tremors. As the nuns and priests prayed over him, though, he experienced a strong sense of a `supernatural' power.

"These were not 'normal' people," he says. "Something was going on in that church. They seemed to know just how and where to pray without much information." One of these strange people placed her hands directly on John's heart, and he thought his heart would explode as she was praying. But then an overwhelming, warm, soothing feeling spread over him. At the same time, another person praying placed his hands on John's temples, which he described like the television commercial advertising a product called Scrubbing Bubbles. The bubbles were animated and briskly scrubbed the surface of his mind like a fast drag car let out of the gate.

"It was like a scrubbing vacuum." He could hear the rumble—and feel the *scrubbing* going through his brain. Then he felt a sense of healing cleansing. Their tears washed over him as they prayed—and his own tears cascaded down his cheeks and chin, soaking his shirt as he experienced the Higher Power as a power for good.

The scrubbing bubbles made their way through him as the Holy Spirit worked to heal his wounded and withered body. Day after day, he returned to this sacred place until he experienced a physical and heart mending as his spirit lifted. "I experienced a healing I could never have gotten in the hospital because they don't heal your heart—they don't heal your spirit.

Spirituality is a state of being, rather than the practice of a particular faith or a particular belief system. Certainly for many people an initial spiritual awakening in a minimal form has likely come through the medium of some religious organization. This is a wonderful first gift from religion and its teachings—that we are spiritual in nature, and that we do in fact *all* have souls as part of our humanity. Problems arise when we try and sort out the rules and regulations that come along with organized religion. It is these restrictions that may hamper our spirituality as a state of being.

In this state of being—a consciousness and awareness of Presence, whatever one does—we share spirituality with others because we have a tranquil, peaceful mind and an ability to give selflessly without an agenda. When in an active phase of binge eating, however, we have difficulty seeing anything or anyone beyond our numb selves. And in a culture where so many celebrations and gatherings are conducted around food, it's difficult to come up for air and move out of a fog-induced state only a food addict knows so well.

John finds people tend to be more understanding if he doesn't drink because so many people don't drink today as either they have a problem with alcohol, take medication, or they don't want to drink and drive. Moreover, alcoholism is seen as an addiction; whereas, this isn't the case with food addiction. Most of society doesn't understand or accept food addiction as a real condition. Also, as John says, "Food is part of our social culture—spiritual continuity with people becomes difficult if you reject their food, since you are in a sense rejecting them."

John sees all his addictions as actually the same disease. "It's all a part of this diseased body and spirit, and every one of these addictions that I have is the same—like an octopus with each tentacle representing a spawn of `the' addiction. I'm not interested in treating myself or others for different diseases because we get lost in all of that."

At the end of the day, John turns to a closing prayer in gratitude for his sobriety—free of his obsessions with food, drink, and drugs:

John's Daily Gratitude Prayer

Lord, I thank you for the hope in my heart and the faith by which I live. I thank you for endings and new beginnings. I thank you for my jobs and my schools, and the success that you have allowed. I pray that this may continue. I thank you for the harmony in my home and in my workplace. I pray that this may continue as well. I thank you for providing for my every need: mentally, physically, spiritually, sexually, socially and emotionally, financially, nutritionally, and occupationally. I thank you for my relationships, and for what you have done and for what you have undone through Christ Jesus. I pray that I may continue sober and sane throughout the day. I thank you for tears and laughter. I thank you for the peace in my life. I thank you for the healing, not only in my own life, but in the lives of my family, friends, coworkers, neighbors, co-students and professors, fellows in recovery, all those in my life whom I love, and whom I don't love as I should.

John's prayer is one way he connects with God and the spiritual side of himself. Prayer, though, comes in many forms—through the robin's song, the cricket's click, a child's laughter, and through helping another, as well as through words and feelings of gratitude. Living life in peace and serenity is a prayer. Mere life is prayer. A God of love is our inspiration and our healing power. And prayer is our means of communication with God. The stars twinkling against a dark, clear sky is God's wink—saying he is near.

Writing *Release Your Obsession with Food*, I write as an insider, giving me authority as a person who experienced both compulsive eating and subsequent recovery. This allows me to use both my knowledge and my experience in guiding you, the reader. As a therapist, I have extensive contacts and easy access to all the latest research. I also bring to the table years of reflection alongside institutional wisdom regarding the struggle over issues of food, health, spirituality, and weight. All of these factors have shown me that, as we grow in our awareness, our connection to Divine intelligence and other people become the main ingredients needed to release the obsession from food. The last three chapters, 13, 14, and 15 will give you the essential tools to turn the corner to establish a constant connection with God through spiritual practices, sensible food choices, and tasty recipes ending with final thoughts.

Personal Inventory Questions

1. John, after many medical healings and phenomena, moved into a life in which he begins and ends every day with prayer. He starts each morning with a morning prayer. How does, or could, prayer fit into an amazing new life for you?

2. For some, saying memorized prayers feels like repeated words rather than prayer. Would personal words connect you to your Higher Source in a different way than traditional prayers? What would your personal prayer, made up of your own words sound like?

3. John's first glimpse of understanding food addiction came when he was 14 years old watching a popular talk show and listening to a professional in the field of eating disorder treatment. John clearly remembers the speaker saying, "It's

not about what you're eating, it's about what's eating you." What was your first glimpse or understanding of food addiction? What's eating you?

4. Many of us undergo serious health consequences as the result of food abuse. Initially, John's recovery from compulsive eating emerged from a medical necessity—raging cholesterol—which led him to a Twelve Step program for food addiction. Have you experienced health consequences to your food addiction? Is this going on now? What have you learned from this?

5. It's not unusual for a recovered alcoholic or drug addict, or any person recovered from other addictions to turn to a food addiction. What are your thoughts? Does one recovery lead to another addiction? Or is the addiction already buried inside the newly recovered person?

6. Do you find, like John, you binge eat as a response to your emotions? When you feel out of control, does bingeing take down your anxiety level? What does it feel like to be out of control? Does it spark fear, leaving you to not know what to do with yourself?

7. John's spiritual recovery evolved over time, beginning with his first recovery from alcohol in upper elementary school. Over the years, he went in and out of recovery, which affected his spiritual growth. Have you had a first recovery followed by relapse? How does your story compare to John's? What have you learned about yourself, recovery, and relapse?

8. John recalls that he'd had many spiritual experiences throughout his life. Every time he gave up, something happened that straightened him out and inspired him with hope. His recovery from food addiction drew on prior alcohol recovery incidents that gave him strength. Can you relate to John and recall your own personal spiritual experiences throughout your life? Under what types of circumstances did the spiritual experiences arise?

9. When John was overwhelmed by the death of his long-term girlfriend, it awoke a grieving hidden deep within, regarding his grandmother. He realized he'd buried these feelings with food and alcohol. What feelings of yours have you covered over with food?

10. As children, we move with a strong, clear, and confident connection to our spiritual essence and instinctive knowing, though often life has a way of distracting us from it. What was your early relationship with your spiritual Source? Did it change over the years? Do you find you were "naturally" closer to a spiritual essence in your earliest years of life?

Part III

Turn the Corner

Chapter 13

How to Establish a Constant Connection with God

Therefore, I tell you,
do not be anxious about your life,
what you shall eat,
nor about your body,
what you shall put on.
For life is more than food,
and the body more than clothing.
~ Matthew 6:25

Try telling an active food addict obsessed with food and the body that life is more than food, and the body more than clothing. Before, during, and after an episode of compulsive eating, the food addict is *continuously* anxious about his/her body and food—and out of sync with love and harmony.

When it's dark and gloomy, with hints of rain in the air, Sage (my fur child) begins to pace. Her ears pin straight to the back of her head and her tail just about disappears between her hind legs. Her stance is crouched—she picks each step carefully—and she's cautious, like a mouse seeking to avoid the barn owl or predacious cat.

At the first sight of lightning in the sky, Sage slips behind my modem in the computer room, *trying to escape*. She is paranoid, nervous, and out of sorts, wanting only to hide in a very dark, small space. In some sense, we food addicts, too, often dive into a tight, dark space to hide from our unfounded fears while stuffing copious amounts of food into our mouths.

Without the protective armor of our spirituality, when it is inhibited by our active bingeing, we're left in an irritable, emotional state—fearful and sad. Recovery, a gradual process, requires daily vigilance, a watchfulness that must include time for prayer, meditation, and journaling. The beliefs and morals we had prior to our spiritual recovery continue in importance, but now come packaged together with serenity and peace—and a gentler heart. We transcend the old agitation of addiction and turn into kinder, calmer, and more accepting human beings than we were prior to starting recovery.

My wish is to show you how to establish your connection with God in the hope of helping you discover a spiritual foundation within yourself that allows you to claim a peace and tranquility all your own. It would be misleading to imply I and the patients and study participants I've quoted liberally here made a complete reversal from our negative relationship with food without any struggle—and that you should too, simply by reading the words in this book. Recovery is a process that requires a certain amount of faith and trust in order to surrender and accept the healing power of our Higher Source. Remember the woman in the Bible who believed if she just touched the robe Jesus wore she'd be made whole—and, indeed, instantly she was healed. She believed *within* herself. And that can happen for *anyone* who comes to the point of deep acceptance.

When we have had all that we can bear, we will then turn with a willingness to be made whole. At this point, we will dare to surrender our old selves and turn totally and trustingly to God's healing power of love and guidance. Now the process has begun and we are being made new.

To quiet compulsive eating is no easy feat and requires taking a first baby step to receive divine inspiration—to be inspired by God. One way for us to do this is to begin walking with those embraced by a strong spiritual mind and to *catch* the wave of spiritual awareness—a hint of something greater than our limited experience of who we think we are. We can watch and learn from those who have been on the path of surrender and have tasted the healing power yielded by this inner movement. Sure, at first our surrender will create a void. And to be certain it will not fill up again with the same murky thoughts and fears that began our habituation to the food that obsessed and conquered us, we must connect to our Life Source with positive prayer.

In time, after we take this first step, the continuous drone of thoughts about our bodies and our weight will begin to quiet as we add new rituals to our daily routine such as prayer and meditation. We replace our negative, random prayer, in which we declared over and over how unhappy we were—suffering, sinful and unworthy—with positive, specific prayers of happy, healing, and blissful self-worth.

Remember—our prayers are always answered by the Creator: "As a man thinketh in his heart, so is he."~ Proverbs 23:7. What are you praying, repeating, and believing constantly?

I found solace in a simple little prayer of Saint Teresa of Avila, which launched my journey in God's direction. I repeat these words in trying times and calm washes over me, and for that moment I'm okay. And no moment could be more important than the one right now, could it?

St. Teresa of Avila's prayer

Let nothing disturb you,
Let nothing frighten you,
All things are passing away:
God never changes.
Patience obtains all things.
Whoever has God lacks nothing;
God alone suffices.

This simple little prayer is packed with a calming punch.

If we stay present—in the now—we don't have to be afraid. The tomorrows are always changing and yesterdays are gone. Everything in the world is changing all the time. But the one constant we have is God—our God—your God— any way you experience Him, whether in the form of energy, as the `universe,' and through prayer, meditation, hypnosis, affirmations, or any mean by which you can find your Source. Let go—and trust you will get where you *need* to be. Everything changes *with the exception of your Higher Source,* which takes care of your every concern—and more.

In the beginning of my recovery, I found that many days were exceptionally trying, and I often wanted to dive into a vat of chocolate, saying, "Oh, what's the use!" But in the depths of my soul I knew I had no other way out of this pure hell I'd been living for so long. So, I developed safety nets to cling to and light my way. One of my greatest discoveries was that by repeating Saint Teresa's prayer—slowly repeating the first two lines over and over: *Let nothing disturb you, let nothing frighten you*—in time, a quiet calm would come over me—a respite from my cares, if you will.

Other times I started with the first line: *Let nothing disturb you*, and then repeated the first line adding the second line, *Let nothing disturb you, let nothing frighten you*, and then I continued on to adding the third line, *Let nothing disturb you, let nothing frighten you, all things are passing away*. On and on I'd repeat the lines in this fashion to the end. This simple little exercise never failed to get me through some very hard times.

You can use any prayer, poem, or saying, repeating it over and over until you reach a state of internal calm. I have many prayers in my arsenal that I pray in this same style, one line at a time, building to a crescendo—a steady increase, linking me to God's limitless force. I don't have to do anything special, but sit in quiet and repeat a comforting prayer, and just be.

In time, I learned I had a God—a kind God, who was not about punishment, but rather about love.

In an old journal, shortly after quieting my addiction, I wrote: *God, I know you are out there and in me. I feel you. I'm open to you. I exist as a heightened spiritual being internally and externally—a perfect being. I embrace your spirit in everyday occurrences such as: the sun as it lowers and slips away behind the horizon between the ocean and the sky; the sound of rain pelting against the window promising green grass and sprouts of daffodils; a rainbow arching across the heavens, with hues of purple, blues, pinks, and yellows forming a dome above; the chatter of birds at the breaking of dawn; falling in love with my perfect mate—connecting lips—a seal of eternal love; the feel of wet, soft, luscious grass under bare feet after a summer rain—God's love envelopes me. God's love surrounds me, above me, encircling me—and dwells within me. God is everywhere and in everything.*

- As Matthew 6:25 clearly states, "Do not be anxious about your life." The instruction is to just live in the moment—the now. Don't be anxious about what you shall eat. If you eat foods that are whole, non-processed, that don't produce anxiety, you have nothing to be anxious over. If you eat balanced, small meals at regular intervals (every four to five hours), your body weight will correct itself: naturally.

Although *Release Your Obsession with Food* is not a diet book by any means (it was designed to bring you closer to *Enlightened Intelligence* and recovery from your obsession with food), Chapter 12 provides some helpful direction in making wise food choices, while Chapter 13 shares a few recipes I've enjoyed over the years. Remember, *life is more than food, the clothes you wear, or the size of your body.*

Although Saint Teresa's prayer brings me instant relief, it's our constant thoughts and words of affirmation that are *our* prayer, which will have tremendous power in our lives. *You are what you pray.* Slip into stillness and listen to God's whispers. Practice meditating on affirmations. Affirmations are positive thoughts programming the subconscious mind to attract success and improve life in the areas of importance to you. What's important first in healing a food addiction is to create a closer connection with your God, thus obtaining a sustainable relief from compulsive eating.

You can repeat some simple affirmations over and over until they meld into your subconscious, and then conscious, mind allowing you to become what you wish to be. The subconscious isn't something separate and apart from us. It's a part of the Kingdom within, and a most important part. It's not new, it's always been there, and always has been a part of you. But until now, it has been the slave to the negative thinking we want to eradicate. As you begin to better understand this positive concept and your improved way of thinking becomes more habitual the subconscious responds, and you attract and absorb love.

You get to recovery's entrance when you *let go and let God* through meditation, hypnosis, journaling, prayer, guided imagery, walking, and affirmations, or whatever form of connection that feels right to you. Pray positively and regularly through these venues every time fear grips you, and you'll become calm, serene, poised, and unafraid, trusting in God.

I found prayer by affirmation as powerful as, if not more powerful than, repeated prayers learned and cited robotically—unless used when meditating. I work with a list of affirmations. Below are a few that I find effective.

1. I am God's child. He loves me and shines his light over, though, and in me.

2. My body is perfect in every way and works well for me.

3. I am happy, and a grin comes easy to me, as does laughter.

4. Life is perfectly perfect right now.

5. Prayer runs my mind in a constant dialogue with God.

6. Angels surround me and guide me.

7. I manifest my authentic self with each breath I breathe.

8. Today is a new day, yesterday is gone, and tomorrow is not here. I am.

9. Divine intelligence is beside me in my wake and my sleep state—always present. I am never alone.

10. Nothing disturbs me. Nothing frightens me. God alone suffices.

11. My positive thoughts and visualizations are picked up in the universe for my best me.

12. Every breath connects me to my higher self.

13. I am exactly who I am supposed to be—flaws and all.

Get off the ride—the up and down weight merry-go-round and trust in yourself and in your Higher Source. Let go of the food power and adopt the God power. Stop the insanity and heal from the inside out to silence the obsession with food. Get into sync—a harmonious relationship with your power for good—and focus on your possibilities. The spiritual recovery will show up and work miracles in your life. But it's up to you. It depends on your outlook, choices of foods, and trust in something greater than yourself. If you always do what you always did, you always get what you always got. Change your destiny. Believe today not what you believed yesterday, and set the tone for tomorrow with what you believe in the faith-filled now.

No doubt as we grow in our awareness, our connection to God and other people become the main ingredients needed to release the obsession with food. Often the question is: What comes first, cleaning up our food or our relationship with God? I say pick whichever, but pick a starting point—and let the recovery begin.

My goal in writing this book was to free you from your obsession with food—so that you might step out of misery and become truly whole; hence the next chapter is reserved for a short discussion of food and recipes and the last chapter on final thoughts. I didn't want this book to become another diet book to gather dust on your bookshelf—another disappointment and letdown from the real answers you so deserve. That said, I would be doing a disservice to you by not addressing food with the goal of providing guidance to begin your life-long journey in spiritual recovery. This discussion of food is not intended as a weight loss tool though weight loss will ultimately result if your body needs a weight loss correction.

Personal Inventory Questions

1. Before, during, and after an episode of compulsive eating, the food addict is *continuously* anxious about his/her body and food—and out of sync with love and harmony. Do you believe it's possible for you that life is more than food, and the body more than clothing?

2. My wish is to show you how to establish your connection with God in the hope of helping you discover a spiritual foundation within yourself that allows you to claim a peace and tranquility all your own. When, if ever, do you recall a connection so strong with a God of your choice that you discovered a spiritual foundation within yourself, reaping peace and tranquility? If never, write how you imagine it could be.

3. Remember—our prayers are always answered by the Creator: "As a man thinketh in his heart, so is he." ~ Proverbs 23:7. What are you praying, repeating, and believing constantly?

4. Do you have a prayer you repeat that launches you into a space where calm washes over you? Have you tried repeating your prayer in sections as I do with Saint Teresa of Avila's prayer?

5. How do you feel about mindful thinking—staying present, in the now? You really never have to be afraid. Can you let go—and trust you will get where you need to be?

6. You can use any prayer, poem, or saying, repeating it over and over until you reach a state of internal calm. I have many prayers in my arsenal that I pray in this same style, one line at a time, building to a crescendo—a steady increase, linking me to God's limitless force. What's in your arsenal?

7. Affirmations are positive thoughts programming the subconscious mind to attract success and improve life in the areas of concern to you. What's of prime importance in healing a food addiction is to create a closer connection with your God, thus obtaining a sustainable relief from compulsive eating. Write ten of your own positive affirmations that feed your soul and move you toward a closer connection with your God. If you don't have any affirmations, create a few.

8. You get to recovery's entrance when you *let go and let God* through meditation, hypnosis, journaling, prayer, guided

imagery, walking, and affirmations, or whatever form of connection feels right to you. Which of these feel right for you now?

9. No doubt as we grow in our awareness, our connections to God and other people become the main ingredients needed to release the obsession with food. Often the question is: What comes first, cleaning up our food act or our relationship with God? Which do you pick and why?

10. What has been your experience meditating? Do you think this practice can bring you closer to your Higher Source and to acceptance of your dysfunctional relationship with food in order to recover?

Chapter 14

How Food Fits into Spiritual Recovery

The creation of a thousand forests is in one acorn.
Ralph Waldo Emerson, American poet, essayist.
(1803-1882)

The hot sweltering sun had begun to slip behind the clouds, promising a burst of rain and cooling of the earth. Mindy, my last patient of the day, stormed into my office, brushing back her blonde mane and wiping the sweat from her brows as she plopped onto the couch. She sank low on the cushions from the burden of carrying an additional 130 pounds of weight on her five-foot-two frame. Then she burst out, "I don't know if I can do this anymore."

And of course I responded with, "Do what, Mindy?"

"I'm frustrated and fat," she screamed. "I don't know what to eat. Can't you just tell me exactly what to eat and how much? I'm tired and discouraged. I'm filled with God's love, yet not filled with emotional stability. Shoot, I don't get how to make food choices. I ate four crispy cream doughnuts and an iced coffee laced with cream and sugar this morning because I don't know what foods are good and which ones are bad. I don't eat lunch because I'm not hungry until late in the afternoon. So I grab a quick candy bar from the vending machine to carry me over until I can get dinner on my way home. Then I stop at a drive-thru because I don't have a clue what a protein is, let alone a good carb. Help!"

I'm sure many of you reading Mindy's cry for guidance have experienced the same sentiments, not having a clue about how to string together a health-promoting meal and let go of the 'good foods versus bad foods' ideology.

Don't give up! You're closer to resolving your obsession with food than you realize. You may feel frustrated because as of yet your plan of recovery from compulsive eating is still a work in progress. But fear not. Your Higher Source works His plan for your life, so refrain from becoming weary in doing good. *The creation of a thousand forests is in one acorn.* In the proper time, you will reap your harvest—if you don't give up.

Don't *push for the forest* with a diet mentality, but rather *plant the acorn*—one meal at a time—use food as a resource to heal yourself in your recovery. When you put your focus on the *recovery*, the bonus is your weight normalizes. When you put the focus on your weight, recovery often vanishes.

Okay, so you say, "Yes, I've heard all about the wonderful miracles that come as a result of spiritual recovery, but how do I get started with the food side of the equation? What do I eat? How much can I eat? Will I have to eat this way forever? Will the weight come off? Do I weigh my body on a scale? Do I weigh my food? Do I have to write down what I eat?"

One by one I'll attempt to unravel the mysteries and answer each and every issue you're faced with as you begin this new adventure of turning your food addiction into recovery. I understand fully how weary you are. I've been there myself, at a place where I felt life wasn't fair, and I asked, "Why me? Why must I have this food addiction?" But intertwine your divine recovery with your food recovery, and you'll be well on your way. In Matthew 11:28—29, the Bible says, "Come to me, all you who are weary and burdened, and I will give you rest. Take my yoke upon you and learn from me, for I am gentle and humble in heart, and you will find rest for your soul."

And yes, you *can* recover with the right tools in place. Let me show you the way.

Food is a good thing; it's a gift from the Universe, and eating should be a pleasurable experience without guilt. In fact, a wide variety of delicious foods is available that you can enjoy as you transition from binge eating to normal eating. When you question what you can eat, the answer is simple: Any food that is real—not processed—and that's not sugar, flour, or wheat, can be eaten at four-to-five-hour intervals. This leaves you a large choice of foods to eat throughout the day.

How much you eat and what food groups for breakfast, lunch, and dinner should already be planned, which removes the uncertainty concerning what to do.

Unfortunately, we food addicts don't have a "normal" foodometer. In other words, we—for the most part—don't get the message of when our stomachs might be full or when our bodies need food and we should be hungry, which leads to our overeating or our undereating. Often we're known to skip breakfast and lunch, and then later in the afternoon, all hell breaks loose, and we binge. To offset this, you should determine breakfast, lunch, dinner, and your half-meal in advance, with portion sizes (using a food scale and measuring cups) and food groups in place.

For instance, a reasonable breakfast consists of four ounces of protein, one serving of starch (one cup of whole grain or rice or a six-ounce potato), one serving of fruit (one cup or one piece of fruit), one serving of dairy (one cup liquid, cottage cheese, or ricotta), and one serving of fat (one teaspoonful).

How you configure your breakfast is up to you. Sometimes I like to have a breakfast that closely resembles what one might consider an evening dinner. Recently I ate four ounces of steak, six ounces of broiled sweet potatoes with a teaspoon of coconut oil drizzled over the top with sea salt and cinnamon (which gave it a brown glazed look and outstanding taste)—along with one cup of fresh blueberries, eight ounces of skim milk, and a cup of hot decaffeinated coffee.

At first, you may want to commit and write down the foods you'll eat for the following day to take all guesswork out of the equation and avoid temptations from not being prepared well in advance. In time, you'll just know what to eat from the food groups that are designated for each meal, leaving you more spontaneity and freedom of choice. Make sure your refrigerator, freezer, and pantry are stocked with an abundance of fresh, clean foods for you to choose from, and you'll be set to go.

Don't you wish someone could tell you how close you are to finally resolving your weight issues and food obsession? Don't you wish someone could say, "If you just keep at it and understand why you eat, you're certain to stop binge eating?"

Or even if it would be heartbreaking, wouldn't it be nice to be told that you're wasting your time going on yet another diet, so that you could move on, try another tack, or simply eat foods that bring you, personal pleasure—and release your obsession with food, with no other aim in mind?

I've counseled thousands of patients and spoken to large groups of people over the years. Even though I might not be able to personally work with each individual I address, I can usually say something definitive about what that person's next steps should be. I also often see when their diets are simply wasting their time.

No matter what point you're at on your own food path, it's smart to periodically take stock of where you're headed and revise your eating plan as necessary. Below are some steps you can take to do just that.

Recognize Yo-Yo Dieting Isn't Working

I'm often asked how I went from overweight to normal weight after years of bouncing up and down in size. Let's be clear, I was *the* yoyo dieter of the decade from early adolescence through my thirties. My weight and my relationship with eating were constant struggles for me until I began to understand my chemical reaction to certain foods. After years of trial and error, research, clinical knowledge, weight loss, and then stability of weight, I recognized that eating whole, natural foods free of sugar, flour, and wheat restored a balanced mood for me. Eating in this simple way, I instantly became calm and centered, clearing my mind chatter. This opened my awareness of how my metabolism works, and I began the process of breaking free from yoyo dieting and building a health-positive lifestyle in regard to food.

I began to listen to my body, noticing when I was hungry, tired, irritable, and stressed. Soon, from the whispered messages I received, I started to develop a trust in my body's inner wisdom. This ability to tune in to what my body had to say didn't appear like the `poof' announcing the arrival of a magic genie. I cultivated this `knowing' through mindfulness—that is, by removing the mental clutter of everyday life and paying attention.

Of course, being able to reap the harvest of inherent wisdom as a result of paying attention to my body's messages rose from my first planting the seeds of consciousness by way of spiritual work—described at length in earlier chapters. Our first step in being able to listen to our bodies is to learn to listen to our inner spirit—and that's something *everyone* can do with practice.

Eat Three Meals Plus One Half-Meal Daily

The best way to begin your food recovery journey is to follow a simple formula of having four meals a day and breaking down each meal according to an easy structure of specific foods: fruit, protein, fat, vegetables, low-fat dairy, and whole grains. I've found, too, that at the beginning, the most workable way to do this is to commit to your food plan prior to the start of your day, rather than merely *hoping* you'll arrive at this optimal arrangement by random eating.

The process of preparation doesn't have to be taxing or time consuming. You can email yourself the next day's menu in 30 seconds. Often you won't have to even re-read your commitment or plan, as writing it down often seals the deal. In my early days of recovery, I sent my food list to a trusted mentor, who never judged or commented negatively but rather simply received my food plan, anchoring my undertaking.

Progress Not Perfection

Please know, I'm not perfect and my life isn't always filled with happiness. I get mad, frustrated, and irritable just like anybody else. The difference is I don't turn to my drug foods of the past because I realize the consequences aren't worth the indulgence. I do get mad at life when my computer crashes and I lose valuable data, or when I have to turn down a fun-filled event due to work obligations, or my husband says my mother-in-law is moving in. YIKES!!! The old me whispers, "Let's wolf down a delectable block of dark chocolate and make the world disappear."

But, no matter what life struggles present themselves, I recognize that binge eating simply isn't an option for me anymore. Nor is sugar, flour, or wheat on my food list, because I know that the devil of addiction if stirred will surface, and chaos will return with a vengeance if I ingest any of these. I compare my situation to that of an alcoholic, who can't have just a smidgeon of scotch; he must abstain completely to stay sober.

Make Room—A Higher Source Is Present

When I began to follow these specific guidelines—even when I didn't want to—my negative mind chatter quieted, and for the first time I could become still and hear God's whispers. I connected to my inner strengths, and a spiritual understanding emerged in me. I found inner peace, God, and love. Love for myself, others, and the universe evolved inside me.

Not only was I calmer, kinder, and less self-centered, but I began to perceive a bigger picture. I saw food as real and not real: God's food and man's food. I chose food of the earth, sea, and air rather than processed and boxed. I turned to God, and the "noise" in my head ceased, and the addiction flattened. These days, I eat to live rather than live to eat. Healthful foods and a refreshed faith are now my fuel to retain optimal health and weight.

Last Thoughts

At the start of this discussion, I suggested it's possible to release your obsession from food addiction when you let go of the diet mentality if someone will lead you on the journey or point you in the right direction. Follow me...

Here's a little piece of hope: If your immediate thought was `I can't live with obsessive eating any longer,' then you're a great deal closer to making peace with your food addiction than you might think, and the battle is much more one of finding a better chemical balance than you might think. Those who can't be dissuaded from a healthful, clean-eating lifestyle are a lot more likely to reach their goals, regardless of the path they originally chose.

Let's begin...

Okay, here's the part you've been patiently waiting for—the food! Addictive-free eating isn't about dieting but rather about spiritual recovery from food addiction and binge eating disorder. It's about changing your relationship with food from dysfunctional to functional. It's a lifestyle choice, not a diet. Taking a daily prescription of breakfast, lunch, dinner, and a half-meal, free of sugar, flour, and wheat, sends the proper signal to your body and ignites your ability to operate your thinking and emotions at an optimal level.

Think of your body as if it were a machine that requires "real" foods to work as fuel to burn through calories and rev up your metabolism. You wouldn't put cheap gas diluted with water into the gas tank of your car would you? Unless you wanted your car to sputter, shake, and conk out, I don't believe you would. Well, for this same reason you want "quality" foods going into your body—your temple.

By combining protein, fruit, "whole" complex carbohydrates, fats, and vegetables in balanced portions, you will create a harmony that'll satisfy your needs and fill your belly. Staying away from processed foods such as sugar and man-made carbohydrates, you'll feel better—allowing a calm to come over you.

Your body will recognize and respond with higher energy than you could ever have imagined because it's now fueled with the proper nutrients— real foods, made by God, who doesn't make junk!

Drink at least eight glasses of water a day so your body will flush out the toxins, hydrate you, quench your thirst, improve your skin, and satisfy any false sense of hunger. Often we think we're hungry when we're really thirsty.

Recovery is about getting out of the prison of dieting and quieting the lion within. The trick is to stay as close to natural foods as possible. Make every food you eat count!

Menu Ideas

· *Breakfast* always consists of fruit, a starchy "whole" carbohydrate, four ounces of lean protein, dairy, and one teaspoon of fat. EXAMPLE: half a melon, one cup cooked steel oats, two poached eggs, one cup skim milk, and one teaspoon butter.

· *Lunch* includes two cups of vegetables, four ounces of lean protein, and one teaspoon fat. EXAMPLE: two cups of steamed broccoli and mushrooms, four ounces of baked chicken breast topped with lemon and a teaspoon of butter or olive oil.

· *Dinner* consists of a starchy "whole" carbohydrate, raw vegetables, lean protein and one teaspoon of olive oil. EXAMPLE: One cup of whole grain brown rice, four ounces of sirloin steak, two cups of romaine lettuce with tomatoes and cucumbers, and one teaspoon of olive oil and vinegar.

· *Half-meal as a metabolic boost* (otherwise known in most circles as a snack) includes a fruit and dairy—and if you're dairy sensitive replace the dairy with two ounces of lean protein. EXAMPLE: one cup of Greek yogurt mixed with one cup of frozen blueberries and mangoes, adding cinnamon and ginger to taste. If you want to take this delight up a notch, freeze it for a few hours and you will have a close fit to sorbet or ice cream—but better!

- *Examples of protein:* fish, chicken, steak, lamb, eggs, hamburgers, tofu, dairy, black beans, tofu, et cetera.[2]
- *Examples of fruit:* medium apple, pear, orange, half a melon, one cup of grapes, one cup of strawberries, one large peach, one cup of fresh blueberries, et cetera.
- *Examples of dairy:* one cup of plain nonfat yogurt, one cup of plain nonfat Greek yogurt, one cup of low-fat buttermilk, one cup of skim milk, one cup of fat-free or low-fat cottage cheese (make sure it's free of sugar), et cetera.
- *Examples of fats:* one teaspoon of butter, one teaspoon of olive oil, one teaspoon of Newman's oil and vinegar, one teaspoon of coconut oil, one teaspoon of Dukes mayonnaise, et cetera
- Examples of starchy "whole" carbohydrates: six ounces of potato, six ounces of sweet potato, one cup millet, one cup peas, one cup brown rice, one cup corn, one cup cooked oatmeal, one cup cooked polenta, et cetera.

Some foods known as "gray" foods may trigger you to eat out of control. These foods include: nuts, peanut butter, chocolate, caffeine, sugar substitutes, olives, wine, cheese, alcohol, baked chips, banana, sugar-free cocoa powder, and popcorn. If you experience cravings as a result of eating these

---

[2] Men should increase their protein portion for breakfast, lunch, and dinner by two ounces.
*Drink at least eight ounces of water daily
*Dairy and protein can be interchanged
*Take one multiple vitamin per day

foods, these foods are to be avoided as you most likely are sensitive to them.

Recipes

As we all know, foods can be, and often are, over processed, which very well may contribute to cravings and out-of-control eating. My golden rule is, *Keep it simple and natural!* The food that God designed for our bodies grows from the ground, swims in the sea, flies in the air, comes off a tree, or roams on the earth. It's frightening to think that many of the packaged foods sitting on our grocery store shelves are so far removed from their natural state that they hardly qualify as food anymore. They are simply packaged, processed "stuff," put into shiny, colorful containers luring us to buy and consume, yet they no more consist of nutrition then the cardboard boxes or plastic containers they are stored in.

I'd like to share some of my favorite recipes, designed as one serving—making a complete meal—that are real foods rather than "junk" foods. I do, however, want to put a disclaimer on the "sweetener" noted in some of the recipes. Although I suggest a chemical saccharin—not considered a "natural" food—it won't trigger cravings. Hence I list this for those who use artificial sweeteners. Saccharin tablets and liquid are the only ones I know of that don't trick the brain into thinking it's real sugar. Of course the best choice is not to use any sweeteners at all and to allow your palate to clear so you can enjoy the true taste of your food.

Bread Sticks

½ cup oat-bran
2 eggs or ½ cup egg whites
1 teaspoon oil
1 teaspoon sundried tomatoes (optional)
Crushed red pepper (tiny bit)
A pinch of sea salt
Oregano, basil and/or garlic powder to taste
2 sweetener tablets (optional)
Onion flakes (optional)

Preheat cast iron pan to 400 degrees Fahrenheit. Take hot pan out of oven, spray pan with oil, and add batter. Bake in oven, turn down to 350 degrees. Bake 10 minutes
*Add veggies to complete meal
*Bread sticks can be made without the fat.
*Freeze bread sticks for a great backup meal when you're out of the house. Simply add fresh vegetables, and you're good to go.

Breakfast Muffins

I love my muffins!!! I often make at least eight servings at one time and freeze the excess. I mix up my fruits, too. I may use blueberries, pineapple, apples, or whatever fruit is in season—frequently combining one-half serving each of two different fruits.

2 eggs
1/3 cup buttermilk
½ cup steel-cut oats (or coarse yellow grits for a thicker consistency)
1 medium apple
 Pinch of sea salt
Cinnamon, nutmeg, and/or ginger to taste

Preheat the oven to 375 degrees Fahrenheit. Combine all the ingredients in a blender and blend briefly—not to too creamy a consistency. Place the ingredients in a muffin, loaf, or pie pan and bake at 375 for one hour.

Remember every oven is different so keep an eye on the muffins. I don't like mine too dry so I don't over bake. When I travel, which is often, I take them with me. They taste great and are very portable.

Breakfast Bowl: Apple and Oats
Fantastic, especially if you're on the go!

6 ounces of Silk'n Tofu
1 cup old-fashioned rolled oats (raw)
1 medium apple chopped
Dash of cinnamon
Pinch of sea salt (optional)
Touch of sweetener (optional)
2 tablespoons of plain fat-free Greek yogurt
Place in a bowl tofu, yogurt, and spices, and mix until smooth. Fold in apples and raw oats.

Breakfast Apple-Polenta-Tofu Delight
1 medium apple, chopped
    1 cup cooked corn grits in cubes (cook according to the package and pour into flat container to cool, then cut in cubes)
Liquid sweetener to taste (optional)
Pinch of sea salt (optional)
Cinnamon, ginger, and/or nutmeg to taste
6 ounces of firm tofu, cubed
1 teaspoon margarine

Brown firm tofu in pan with spices—then add and brown the remaining ingredients, corn grits and margarine. Stir until brown then add sweetener to grits. Once browned, fold in the apples and cook a few minutes—I like mine crispy so I cook this a little longer than you might. Place all ingredients in a bowl and top with two tablespoons of fat-free plain *Dannon* yogurt—the only yogurt I'm familiar with that is sugar free (or Greek yogurt if you want it thicker and creamier).

Peach Pancakes
1 large peach
½ cup raw oat bran
2 eggs
½ cup fat-free Greek yogurt
Cinnamon, sea salt, ginger, nutmeg, 2 tablespoons water, and liquid saccharin to taste

In mixing bowl, combine two raw eggs, ½ cup oat bran, cinnamon, sea salt, nutmeg, ginger, 2 tablespoons water. Mix to batter consistency. Fold in chopped peaches. Place three equal pancake shaped servings in a Mazola sprayed pan— again, the only spray I know of that is alcohol and sugar free. Brown each side. Top with ½ cup fat-free Greek yogurt.

Coleslaw
2 cups shredded cabbage
Dash of sea salt
Splash of red vinegar
Few drops of sweetener (optional)
2 tablespoons of plain fat-free yogurt
1½ teaspoons Dukes Mayonnaise (Dukes is natural and sugar free).

In a large bowl mix all ingredients together.

*To make a complete dinner meal, I add ½ cup of peas and 4 ounces of tuna, chicken, shrimp, or beef.

Black Beans and Salsa Pie

1 cup black beans
1 cup corn grits (already cooked and spread in the bottom of a round glass pie pan)
1 teaspoon of non-trans-fat Smart Balance Margarine (The only margarine I know of that is natural with no hydrogenated oils)
2 cups of salsa with a few drops of liquid sweetener to eliminate bitter taste

I like to layer the ingredients: first the cooked corn grits mixed with non-trans-fat Smart Balance Margarine, followed by the beans and then the salsa. Bake in microwave for seven minutes. It's very filling.

Breakfast Tofu Crispies

6 ounces of tofu
Cinnamon
Sea salt
Sweetener
1 cup cooked brown rice
1 cup fresh pineapple, cubed
2 tablespoons of fat-free plain *Dannon* yogurt
1 teaspoon non-trans-fat Smart Balance Margarine or coconut oil

Brown in a pan sprayed with an oil spray and 6 ounces of firm tofu. Sprinkle with: cinnamon, sea salt, and/or sweetener to taste. Lightly spray pan with oil and brown tofu with cinnamon, sea salt, and sweetener to taste. In separate bowl, place cooked warm brown rice topped with hot crispy tofu on one side and the fresh cold pineapple with 2 tablespoons of plain fat free yogurt on the other side and enjoy a totally delightful dish.

Breakfast Blueberry/Silk'n Tofu Swirl

6 ounce Silk'n Tofu (or any tofu that is creamy to blend)
1 cup frozen blueberries (fresh and/or thawed if you prefer)
1 cup cooked corn grits cubed
Cinnamon to taste
Sweetener (optional)
Pinch of sea salt
1 teaspoon of butter or non-trans-fat Smart Balance Margarine
2 tablespoons yogurt

6 ounces of *Silk'n* Tofu whipped with ½ cup of yogurt and sea salt, cinnamon, and sweetener followed by 1 cup of hot corn grits mixed with sweetener and margarine. I center the cup of warm grits on top of the yogurt and tofu mixture, and then in the same bowl place 1 cup of frozen blueberries.

Please don't confine yourself to only the recipes listed in this chapter—take the time to invent your own nutritious yet delicious meals that you can look forward to. I have a series of favorite meals in my arsenal to avoid boredom and feelings of being held captive in diet prison. I no longer want the processed foods I once adored and placed higher than my God of understanding, an all-knowing God of love and kindness. I thought I could never live without these foods, only to now find I could care less about them.

Of course it's my spiritual connection to God and people, along with the balanced eating and no sugar, flour, or wheat that removed my addiction. If I should elect to reintroduce these foods into my life, I would certainly return to a raging food addiction. But be assured, I will not do that. Nor will you, once you discover the joys and freedom of recovery.

Chapter 15 explores final thoughts on why I've written *Release Your Obsession with Food: Heal from the Inside Out.* My goal was to share my journey from active food addiction to spiritual recovery—and lead you away from compulsive eating. I hope I've accomplished this task through sharing my journey and that of my patients and the participants in my original study.

Personal Inventory Questions

1. Have you ever felt like Mindy who stormed into my office bursting out, "" I don't know what to eat? Can't you just tell me exactly what to eat and how much?" Do you, too, feel you don't know what to eat or how much?

2. Do you feel you can force your recovery with a diet mentality? How can you use food as a resource to heal yourself in your recovery?

3. Unfortunately, we food addicts don't have a "normal" foodometer. In other words, we—for the most part—don't get the message of when our stomachs might be full or when our bodies need food and we should be hungry—which leads to our overeating or our undereating. How do you feel about recording your food in a journal and weighing your food? What are the benefits? What are the pitfalls?

4. What are your favorite foods in each category: protein, fruit, dairy, fat, starch, vegetables? In your journal make a section entirely for your food choices, listing foods from each group for you to pick from daily.

5. Do you recognize a pattern of yo yo dieting throughout your life? How has it served you? Do you hang on to this destructive behavior? Why?

6. Do you experience continuous mind chatter? What is your mind chatter telling you? Mine told me things like: You are fat, disgusting, dumb, a loser, etc. What purpose does your mind chatter serve for you?

7. Do you listen to your body, noticing when you're hungry, tired, irritable, stressed, angry, and lonely? Can you turn your negative mind chatter into positive mind chatter, such as: I'm beautiful, I'm smart, my body serves me. How can turning negative chatter into positive chatter work for you? What might the benefits be?

8. Can you create recipes from your list of foods that speak to your needs and satisfaction? Do you think foods can be enjoyed and still be healthful? What healthful recipes can you create to add to your recipe section in your journal?

9. The best way to begin your food recovery journey is to follow a simple formula of having four meals a day and breaking down each meal according to an easy structure of specific foods: fruit, protein, fat, vegetables, low-fat dairy, and whole grains. What schedules can you arrange to eat three meals plus one metabolic boosting half-meal daily?

10. The goal is progress not perfection. So what can you do to lean into a better lifestyle a little at a time? Make a list of small tasks you want to accomplish with your food and in your relationship with foods. Set time tables for you to reach your goals and write down how you feel with each accomplishment.

Chapter 15

Final Thoughts

*And, behold, the angel of the Lord
came upon him, and a light shined
in the prison.
~Acts12:7~*

I awakened to the sound of the phone—ring after ring—I just wanted it to stop. I pulled the pillow over my ears and hunkered down deeper into the mattress, but it droned on and on, beckoning me to answer.

Barely aroused, I glanced at the clock, noting it was 4:00 in the morning. Then I stumbled as I made my way to the kitchen to learn who was on the other end of the phone.

I pressed the cold receiver to my ear and with great trepidation answered, "Hello."

My father's panicky voice blurted out, "It's your Mom—she had a stroke! The paramedics are here. I don't know what to do. They say they have a shot they can give her but I have to know the exact time she had her stroke. If they give her the shot too soon or too late, it'll kill her."

The room swirled as I tried to grasp what he was saying. I stammered something back, but to this day I don't know what I said in response. After we hung up, I stood dazed and paralyzed in fear for what seemed like hours, staring at the phone back in its cradle, not certain what to do.

A defining moment—my life would *never* be the same.

The dreaded call came on a Saturday morning, the eve of Easter back in 1998. Could it have been only eight hours before that I was skating with such glee with my eight-year-old son Benjamin, when we collided and tumbled to the ground only to rise laughing it off, twirling under the stars, smiling and thanking God for what a glorious life I was living? I practiced as a clinical psychotherapist and was soon to marry my prince, living in my dream house—yes, I had the perfect life. And now, Mom was faced with life or death. How quickly my world had turned upside down.

Driving bleary eyed with the tears tumbling down my cheeks, I dialed patient after patient to cancel my Saturday schedule, while trying to keep my eyes and car on the road. I was headed to the hospital four hours away to accompany my dad in what was one of the saddest and most difficult moments of our lives.

We sat in the intensive care unit, each in an individual silent prayer only interrupted by periodic, desperate conversation and sobs of disbelief. The neurologist tarnished any hope we'd mustered up when he inhumanely blurted out that she would never walk again and guaranteed she'd endure a continuing decline for the remaining days of her life.

Dad lowered his head into his hands, shaking it back and forth, mumbling, barely audible, "No, this can't be, not again," while he questioned his decision not to allow the paramedics to give mom the shot earlier that morning. He raised his head up slowly from his hands, eyes tear stained as he recounted one of *his* defining moments when *his* mom had clung to her life in intensive care nearly 50 years earlier, and he, the oldest son, needed to translate from Italian to English and back from the doctors to his family. He'd made some serious decisions then and the equally grave decisions now intertwined with those earlier ones— both terrible events playing over and over in his mind as we sat there.

His mom had died.

He'd never gotten past his guilt and grief. And now he was confronted with his wife of nearly half a century facing the end of her life as they both knew it in the same way.

Mom was obese, plus she'd picked up a cigarette habit in her fifties, didn't exercise, and favored high-fat foods—all contributing to the situation she now faced.

I pulled my chair up as close to Mom as I could, without climbing in the bed with her, and held her limp hand in mine. I'd always admired her tiny, dainty hands and feet. I watched her struggle to take one shallow breath then pause and exhale and repeat—the oxygen machine swishing in the background —her eyes closed—my mom slipping further and further away.

There I sat inhaling the nauseating smell of bleached sheets mixed with rubbing alcohol, and I pulled the spare blanket from the foot of the bed around my shoulders—teeth chattering from the cold temperature meant to ward off germs. But I pushed the discomfort out of my mind as I made a life-changing decision.

My resolution came instantly, at that moment; I vowed to bump up my mission to help eating disordered and addicted patients to recovery. For the rest of my life, I'd give of my heart and soul to find answers and direction for those in the same enchainment as my mother, who couldn't conquer obesity. I promised God then and there that I'd teach others how I'd learned to let go of my once obese body;

eat free of sugar, flour, and wheat; and lean on spiritual recovery.

I couldn't save Mom but I darn sure could share what I knew with those who still had a chance to turn their lives around.

Mom lived four more years after her stroke—completely paralyzed. Those days were very good times and very bad times all rolled into one for both her and her family. She died at 67 years old in 2002.

Now, on the eve of every Easter, I bow my head in remembrance of the early morning call all those years before—when my life turned in a new direction—a watershed moment for me. I'm not saying eating free of sugar, flour, and wheat is easy, but death or paralysis is certainly far worse.

Life is brief—live now, laugh now, and pray now.

It's time to take charge, step out of your prison, and let the light shine. Get up each morning expecting a new day filled with absolute miracles. With your first bite of real, whole food, and a prayer of gratitude to your Higher Source, all your woes can be resolved and sanity restored after the craziness of food addiction. Suddenly, the cravings are gone and the diet mentality is lifted from your shoulders. Carry on—a new life is about to take hold.

I've written **Release Your Obsession with Food: Heal from the Inside Out**, not for notoriety and fame, for my name in lights, or for recognition—but to help free you from the obsession with food. My goal was to share my journey from active food addiction to spiritual recovery—and lead you away from compulsive eating. I hope I've accomplished this task through sharing my journey and that of my patients and the participants in my original study.

As I've noted throughout my work, my mom and Ma (grandma) weren't as fortunate, and died never to know the freedom of spiritual recovery or that their defeat in the battle to lose weight wasn't their fault. My story compares two adjacent worlds: food addiction and spiritual recovery. It is my hope that this book helped you or will help you to recognize, deal with, and resolve compulsive eating—and heal from the inside out believing *anything* you want is there for the taking as long as you trust. If my journey lifted you from the pure hell of obsessive eating, I've accomplished my goal.

As referred to earlier, I'd like to think that everyone has a personal prescription on his or her own Divine Intelligence, beginning with many spiritual leaders, whether from Judaism, for instance, or through Buddhism, Sikhism, Christianity, or whatever, perhaps combined with that or another particular spiritual training. Regardless of *your* Source, you can tap into your own heart and soul using the approach that fits your belief system best, to find an authentic foundation and open the door to a much deeper, more soulful experience of life. Jesus Christ gave us the prescription:

For verily I say unto you, that whosoever shall say unto this mountain, be thou removed, and be thou cast into the sea; and shall not doubt in his heart, but shall believe that those things which he saith shall come to pass; he shall have whatsoever he saith. Therefore, I say unto you; what things soever ye desire when ye pray, believe that ye receive them, and ye shall have them.

Your father knoweth what things ye have need of, before ye ask Him.

Have the absolute faith that all things are possible to your Higher Source—a spiritual connection to Him—a selfless love. Believe it and know it within your very being, and it shall become so. Ask for your food obsession to be lifted and to have a stronger connection with spirituality and people—with no doubt in your heart—and believe that what you ask for you'll receive—and you shall have it.

This is not the end…please feel free to contact me at drlisaort@weightcontroltherapy.com. I'd love to hear from you and learn from your experiences. Also, come join me on facebook http://www.facebook.com/Dr.LisaOrtigaraCrego, Twitter https://twitter.com/Drlisaort and visit my website http://weightcontroltherapy.com/ to see what I'm doing, what I've written and where I'm speaking.

Thank you for reading Release Obsession with Food. Please post a review for the author on Amazon.

Appendices
Most Commonly Asked Questions

Why am I bingeing?
You may be suffering from food addiction and/or binge eating disorder. A binge occurs when a person consumes a large amount of food in a short period of time with little regard for any consequences.

Experts have different theories as to why a person binge eats. Some believe the drive behind it is genetic, while others see such eating as emotional in its origins. Still others define bingeing as "addictive" eating. And therapists such as me see binge eating as coming from a combination of all three factors.

Regardless of the different views, we all agree that an individual will feel guilt and shame after a binge. It's also not uncommon for a person to hide his food and binge alone— likely due to the same guilt and shame issue.

Typically, you might binge to avoid facing something that's bothering you. Additionally, perhaps you're sensitive to sugar, flour, and wheat due to a chemical imbalance (often genetic) causing you to crave more and more food, especially sweet and starchy foods—the very provisions that trigger a binge and are most addictive.

Why am I getting fatter even though I exercise?
Exercise alone doesn't necessarily lead to weight loss. You may well be eating more food than you're burning off. Then, too, perhaps you're building muscle, which weighs more than fat, and you're misreading the increase in weight on the scale as you "getting fat" when in fact you're toning—hence genuinely becoming leaner. Combining healthful eating with moderate exercise four to six days a week will usually kick up the weight loss and tone your body at the same time.

Remember to always check with your doctor before starting an exercise program.

Why am I craving sugar, flour, and wheat?

It's possible you suffer from a food addiction that leads you to desire sugar, flour, and wheat. Sugar, in fact, turns on the same receptors in the brain as the drug heroin. Some people are highly sensitive to these foods, and when these are ingested, susceptible individuals can't stop thinking about, craving, and/or eating foods in this category. The situation is quite similar to that of a person addicted to alcohol, drugs, or cigarettes.

Why can't I stop eating?

You may have trouble stopping eating because you suffer from binge eating disorder. Binge eating disorder affects millions of Americans and is more common than anorexia and bulimia combined. Eating beyond full at least two times a week for six months or longer is the hallmark symptom to diagnosing a person as binge eating disordered. If you suspect you have a problem, it's best to seek an eating disorder specialist to help you move toward recovery.

Why am I thinking about weight and weight loss all the time?

One of the criteria for diagnosing bulimia and anorexia is a fixation on weight and weight loss issues. It's possible you suffer from an eating disorder and/or food addiction. When you ingest sugar, flour, and wheat, that may create the yearning for more of these foods, as well as a fear and preoccupation with weight gain, a desire to prevent gain, and an obsession with weight loss.

Will I have an eating disorder or obesity because my family does?

Research shows that eating disorders have a strong genetic component. It's not uncommon to find a binge eater with a mother who restricted her eating or participated in extreme dieting. That said, binge eaters do often engage in periods of extreme dieting. Binge eaters are known to become numb to their feelings and surroundings as they bury themselves in an alarming amount of food. For these individuals, food moves from being a simple solution to hunger into operating as a lover, a friend, a reward for success, company, a celebration, and a filler for loneliness—as well as a "fix" for dealing with the many touchy situations life can "dish" up.

Why do I talk about food and weight all the time?

Obsessions with food and weight are basic elements found in binge eating disorder. Binge eating is marked by the consumption of a large volume of food that by "normal" standards would be considered unusually excessive. With the bingeing, come feelings of being out of control in regard to the intake of food. This creates a vicious cycle that starts with thinking about and craving foods, then binge eating of foods, which prompts remorse and shame after consumption followed by a short stint of dieting or restricting foods—only for the individual to return to the binge.

With this pattern, comes the obsession with food and weight that takes up an extreme amount of energy and thought, often blocking the person from dealing with every-day, "real" life.

Why am I hiding food?

One of the typical facets of binge eating and food addiction is that the food disordered person will hide food and retrieve it

241

later, to eat it alone. Eating in this way becomes a ritual to "fix" the sufferer's pain. Also, hiding food makes it seem as if the action isn't really occurring—a type of denial.

Furthermore, you may experience extreme shame with your bingeing and not want to be seen eating in such an out-of-control manner. Binge eating and addictive foods are eaten in an enormous volume, which might be embarrassing to you if done in front of others. Yet, a "normal" amount of food wouldn't give you the "fix" you're looking for.

Is there a cure for food addiction?

While there isn't a cure per se for food addiction, you certainly can find relief and release from obsessive eating. Working through the recovery steps listed in *Release Your Obsession with Food: Heal from the Inside Out* is an excellent starting place for you to obtain lifelong relief from this insidious disease.

How long before I see results?

Results are immediate when you begin to clear the body of toxic foods and replace them with healthful, unprocessed foods free of sugar, flour, and wheat. At first you may undergo withdrawal symptoms such as dizziness, sweating, and depressed and euphoric moods, but within 48 hours you'll experience marked improvement. Your head will clear, and focus and patience will ensue.

What are the signs that I'm a food addict?

A series of signs that may indicate you're a food addict can include:

●At some point you've wanted to stop eating and found you just couldn't, no matter how many "diet" or food plan attempts you've made.

●You think about food or your weight without interruption—most likely signs of compulsive eating.

●You find ways to "get rid of your food" such as vomiting, over-exercising, or restricting what you eat—indicating serious food issues.

●You notice you eat differently (more voraciously and ingesting a higher volume of foods) when you're alone versus with people—an indication an eating issue is at hand.

Questions I ask new patients when diagnosing their eating disorders are: Do you eat constantly or think about food constantly, and would you go to any extreme to get the foods you crave—even if it means stealing or sneaking out of the home at an unusual hour of the night, risking your safety? Do you keep telling yourself *your life will begin once you get rid of the weight?* Are you monitoring every morsel of food you eat to have control over your consumption? Do you regularly feel shame or guilt after eating? Do you promise every Monday to start your diet this time for real? Do you feel hopeless about your relationship with food? Do you crave specific foods? What foods could you never, ever give up? How do you feel about the idea of abstaining from cake, cookies, chips, or soda pop? What about carrots, celery, or tomatoes? (I didn't think you'd mind giving up the last three foods!)

How do I make a sandwich without bread?
In the beginning, you may miss your bread and flour products but once you experience the relief from obsessing over food, your focus returns, and cravings are gone; you won't notice the matter of bread anymore. The idea of eating a sandwich for lunch is a habit replaced by a new habit of eating protein (on a plate) and vegetables for lunch. I promise when you acclimate to eating unprocessed foods and experience relief, you won't miss the bread.

It seems like too much food. Do I have to eat it all?

Yes, at first it may seem like a great deal of food, but in fact calorie-wise it's most likely significantly less than what you consume when you binge eat. After a while, your body will accustom itself to regular feedings and respond with both hunger and gratitude for the clean, wholesome food.

Binge eaters typically consume more than 1,500 calories in one sitting between meals when they're not particularly hungry, and they binge at least two times a week. As a result, they're five times more likely to be obese if not severely obese, which puts them at a greater risk of obesity-related problems like heart disease, diabetes, liver disease, and colon cancer.

I'm not a breakfast person. Do I have to eat breakfast?

Yes, breakfast is the most important meal of the day. Studies show most obese persons and those suffering from eating disorders either skip breakfast altogether or fill up on sugary cereals that the body and mind don't recognize as real food. In time, your body will come to look forward to breakfast after fasting for more than eight hours during sleep. Breakfast is the perfect start to a healthful day of eating. It sets the tone for the rest of your day of eating natural foods.

How can I travel eating this way?

In the early days of your recovery eating, you can bring all your foods with you. Toting your foods along is the easiest way to avoid falling into a negative food trap. Temptations from old-time favorites can lure a person during long weekend getaways and vacations. Be armed and ready with a wide variety of prepared meals, and you'll take the guesswork out of your travel-food agenda.

Many department stores sell freezer tote bags, making it convenient to store your food for at least several hours. Some places also sell plug-in freezer bags that hold your food frozen for days. During your hotel stay, request a refrigerator and microwave in your hotel room to store and heat your food. Once you're settled, locate the nearest grocery so you can replenish the good foods you'll need while you're away.

How can I eat out at a restaurant?
I find avoiding the menu allows my decision making to be quite easy. I usually order fish, chicken, or steak and instruct the waiter that I want no sauces, marinades, or meat tenderizers (most of which are loaded down with sugar and/or flour). I ask for salad with oil and vinegar on the side to control how much fat is used on my salad. Most restaurants serve either sweet potato or regular potato. Ask for butter on the side. I personally don't use a food scale in public (to avoid curious onlookers), but don't eat more than a fist's worth of protein or of potato.

How do I bypass temptation when someone is eating cake?
Eat your planned meal before attending a party or when cake is served. Save your metabolic boost (fruit and protein) for the same time the cake is offered. You may even want to leave the event or the room where cake is being eaten— sometimes "out of sight" leads to "out of mind." Why make such a big deal of a bite of cake? You know why.

How can I avoid falling into the trap of compulsive eating, especially on holidays and birthdays?
The best way to handle celebrations and parties is to know which situations trigger your cravings and avoid them if possible. Drink water throughout the day to ensure you're

rehydrating and avoiding false hunger. Exercise to keep your endorphins up and bypass depressed moods. Practice relaxation therapy including deep breathing exercises or meditation. Redirect your thinking (think about something other than eating), or distract yourself until the compulsion to eat passes. Don't slide backward. Move forward.

How do I avoid feeling deprived?

Instead of thinking about the foods you can't have, rather think about the foods that you're allowed. You'll discover a wide variety of foods to choose from and enjoy. Get creative and you'll find many alternatives to what you were eating. Change your thoughts and you'll change your life. Switch your fixation to other pleasures in life as well—watch a fashion-design show on TV, listen to music and dance to the tunes, watch a movie, read a book.

How can I stop eating?

To stop eating, you need a plan and an understanding of why you binge eat in the first place. Find a certified eating disorder specialist in your area who has experience with treating food addiction and who can help you with your issues. Also, you may want to check out any Twelve Step program that discusses food addiction. Perhaps having a sponsor and reaching out to other addicts in recovery will speed up your process.

Most important, when you change what foods you put in your body, up to 70 percent of your problem with food addiction will disappear. Add your Higher Source to the equation, and voila, the situation becomes solvable. When you decrease the burden of addicting/junk foods, you open the vault to Divine Source and your connection to other people. Often the eating disordered person isolates herself (himself) from others, and the recovered mentor and friends bring people and Source back into her (his) life.

How does my Higher Source factor into releasing my addiction to food?

The first step to releasing binge eating is to surrender to a Higher Source and to admit your food addiction is unmanageable on your own. Often people get stuck regarding bringing God into their recoveries due to a past (mis)understanding caused by strict religious teachings about God as a scary, mean energy or being.

The God or energy you turn to is one of your own making—a God of love and kindness. Reaching out to a Higher Energy Source releases you from the pressure of handling this massive disease on your own. To think we can survive on our own without a connection to our Creator feeds the addiction.

Is there a difference between binge eating disorder and food addiction?

Often you will find binge eating disorder intertwined with food addiction because, technically speaking, both could be viewed to mean the same thing. On closer look, binge eating disorder is continuous and emotion-based eating while food addiction can be controlled by removing the chemical triggers (sugar, flour, and wheat). A binge eater is not necessarily a food addict, but all food addicts binge eat. To correct food addiction, which includes binge eating, eat every four hours: first a balanced breakfast, a lunch, and a dinner, then a snack (as a metabolic boost), and you'll tame the lion within. When you do that, you'll most likely find that you don't think about food all the time because you're getting plenty to eat.

How do I handle people who think I'm imagining this disease?

Does it really matter what others think? The only thing that matters is that *you* understand your disease and how to treat it. You'll get tons of comments from those who believe you should just eat less and use your willpower. Well, with addictions, there's no such thing as willpower. When the food addict demon rears its ugly head we are pummeled by defeat. Mind your end of the street and let go of what others think because it's a battle not worth fighting. Again, it doesn't matter what others think, it only matters what you think.

What about doctors? Will they understand my condition?

Times are changing. More and more doctors accept that food addiction is real and it must be treated to prevent a host of diseases (heart, diabetes, joint problems, *et cetera*). In my early days of practice, I rarely had referrals from medical doctors with the exception of psychiatrists. Today, I'm called daily as a result of referrals. Times have changed, indeed! Physicians are slowly but surely being educated.

What is the best way to treat my addiction?

There is no single perfect way to treat your addiction. If you believe your addiction is jeopardizing the quality and functionality of your life and causing you a range of problems, seek medical assistance along with psychotherapy from a trained eating disorder professional; consider a Twelve Step anonymous program for food addiction; and consult a trained nutritionist (http://www.iaedp.com/).

The Dissertation
Background of the Study

My actual study began as a doctoral inquiry into the spiritual journey as experienced by eight individuals working a Twelve Step program who had achieved long-term abstinence. Once I began revising my dissertation, it morphed into *Release Your Obsession with Food: Heal from the Inside Out.* I added patient experiences as well, to enhance and drive home points I'd made in the first form of my thesis.

The explorations with the original eight participants (including me) delved into each person's viewpoint and observation of his or her compulsive eating issues and probed the experience of taking on the Source as a focus rather than, or in addition to, food. My intention was to highlight each individual's insights into this process as the person lived such a progression and commented on it. Along with those participants I reference in the body of the book, I also researched and investigated my own evolution in releasing my obsession with food and reestablishing the primacy of God in its place.

The patients and people discussed in *Release Your Obsession with Food...* range from individuals in their mid-teens to someone more than 70 years of age. All those mentioned in the book have been associated with either Twelve Step groups, psychotherapy, or both. In accordance with Twelve Step protocol and patient confidentiality, names have been changed to keep each person anonymous, while the name of the exact group has been omitted.

Although a great amount of weight was lost by most discussed in this book as a result of "clean eating," and many were at one point extremely overweight, some of the people I mention never had a weight issue at all. In either case, all binge-ate to their detriment in some area of health and/or life. And regardless whether overweight or not, each experienced a subsequent shift from lethargy and fuzzy thinking to clear thinking, energy, and improved moods.

Mood refers to a prevailing emotional state over time. One mood often seen in a clinical setting, dysphoria, is a state of mind characterized by shifting unpleasant feelings such as anxiety, depression, or unease. Binge eating is associated with a wide range of psychological problems such as negative self-esteem, impaired social functioning, and other types of day-to-day distress that result in dysphoria.

The word "addiction" isn't included in the most recent version of the *Diagnostic and Statistical Manual of Mental Disorders* (2000). "Substance dependence" may be the closest in capturing the essence of what has traditionally been labeled addiction (Walters, 1996) with reference to all the diagnoses set forth in the *DSM-IV-TR*. To be clear, a diagnosis of substance dependence encompasses: "…a maladaptive pattern of substance use manifested by recurrent and significant adverse consequences related to the repeated use of specific substances, which includes: withdrawal, tolerance, preoccupation with the substance; heavier or more frequent ingestion of the substance than intended; involvement in activities designed to procure the substance; reduction in important social, occupational, or recreational activities; and disregard for persistent physical or psychological problems caused by the use of the substance." (*DSM-IV*, 2000, pp.198 - 199).

In performing my research, I pondered if emotional and mental stability and their lack were directly related to spiritual and/or religious beliefs or simply to trigger foods in and of themselves. I learned the relationship was a combination of both.

Eating without resorting to sugar, flour, or wheat shifted the person's thought processes and physiological cravings from binge eating to *normal* eating, opening up the invitation to a spiritual connection. This is not to say each binge eater didn't *believe* while actively binge eating, but it is to say the connection with the Source was clouded.

Before I released my own obsession with food, I was haunted by specific foods and gorged on large quantities of food in a short period of time regardless of the negative physical, emotional, mental, spiritual, or social consequences.

An abundance of anecdotal evidence suggests engaging in spiritual practice may lead to a spiritual transformation as well as an overall improved wellbeing. In addition, more and more literature is providing objective evidence of positive effects of spiritual practices. In fact, all of us involved in my study expressed that releasing our suffering to our Higher Source led to profound and deep awareness's of the self and a closer spiritual understanding of our pain.

Although stories of the physical and emotional components of food addiction are woven throughout this book, it was the spiritual recovery that actually drove my investigation. With that said, a brief discussion of the physical and emotional aspects seems called for.

The negative physical effects on the person in an active food addiction stage are generally twofold. First, a *physical intolerance* to foods means that, along with possible symptoms such as nausea, headache, shakiness, and so on, an accompanying negative emotional and mental response may result from ingesting these substances. The physical effect of active food addiction also points to the possibility of an active addict becoming overweight or obese.

For participants in the study I describe, physical recovery from food addiction began immediately as a result of changing their types of food intake, and those of us who were overweight or underweight returned in relatively short order to a normal weight for our body sizes and bone structures. In time, after abstaining from trigger foods (sugar, flour, and wheat), our recoveries took precedence over the focus on our bodies and weight, and instead our attentions turned toward prayer, meditation, and working a Twelve Step program and/or therapy of some sort. In time, we all reached a spiritual place of peace and serenity, not at every moment of our lives, certainly, but for a preponderance of our waking hours. Those emotional imbalances that did arise would dissipate reasonably quickly, as for those normally mentally and emotionally robust.

Some of the subjects I've written about in this book had several years of unbroken success with release of their obsessions with food, while some of those I discuss continue to struggle. I, along with all others cited, self-reported my experience related to my obsession with food and compulsive eating. The group reported on in the actual dissertation lived in complete abstinence from the consumption of trigger foods (such as sugar, flour, and wheat), along with any major mood-altering substances for a period of at least six months. The resulting release from our obsessions with food continued to the time of the interviews and to the best of my knowledge is ongoing. Our relief from compulsive eating has ranged to more than 13 plus years.

Intent in Study Design
I purposely chose a small group of individuals for the dissertation study in order to capture a rich understanding of the lived experience of the food addict in spiritual recovery. While this could have an effect on whether we may generalize from the findings, my aim was really to understand the unique events undergone by the participants. My intention wasn't to present data that can be replicated or that can be generalized across a population.

The goal here was to reduce the risk of losing this richness of personal observations to a large volume of data. Had I chosen a greater number of participants, I would have chanced losing important themes and patterns that might be found. My objective was also to allow readers to feel each of our experiences as being as real as I could present, with the hope that a similar place of peace and tranquility would be discoverable by others.

Each human experience is unique onto each individual, and capturing the lived memoir can only add new information or another perspective to already existing facts and figures.

Each of us who participated in the actual dissertation study (not those whose patient stories I've added here) was independently encouraged to speak freely and candidly about the topic question, the guided questions, and/or other relevant topics. In addition, I collected journals, diaries, prayers, and personal stories from those who wished to express their feelings on paper in order to add additional meaning to their revelations. We all utilized journaling both as a way to self-reflect and as a means by which data was collected and recorded.

Treatment Models
In the field of psychotherapy, not a great deal of enthusiasm exists for treatment of eating disorders through spiritual influences, yet it is my experience that addressing the spiritual issues of patients with their eating disorders (and other disorders or life challenges!) often results in a more successful treatment. In order for spiritual recovery from food addiction to be considered a key component to psychotherapy, I believe a shift in the attitudes of psychotherapists is essential.

Spirituality and food addiction have to be recognized as the flip sides of each other. I'm willing to note that this idea might be a foreign concept to the patient. However, the therapist can assist the patient in identifying and exploring spiritual recovery from food addiction as an added benefit to help facilitate growth and change, much in the same way that other issues are brought into the light in a dynamic therapy and tested for their power in effecting healing.

I know many people in all parts of the world who are very successful in their food addiction recoveries due to engaging in Twelve Step groups. Moreover, many eating-disordered persons gain relief by means of psychotherapy treatment. To satisfy the end-goal of my dissertation, I included only subjects who participated in a Twelve Step program. For the purpose of this book, however, and to add to the richness of the information I would offer readers, I chose a few patients from my private practice who may or may not have attended Twelve Step groups and blended their experiences in this narrative, also changing their names to protect their anonymity or chance of recognition.

From years of working closely with the eating-disorder population, I recognize recovery is very difficult to attain on one's own without therapeutic intervention and/or a strong support group comprised of other food addicts. I hope that the valuable information that emerged from this study will be used in various ways in working with patients who suffer from the difficult trials of food addiction.

Given that obesity is on the rise and is often connected to binge eating—which is an element of food addiction—it's critical in developing treatment models to appreciate the actual phases of food addiction. This understanding will allow us to have a better feel for the qualities and textures of this disease. My study explored the individuals' perceptions of their spiritual emptiness as it connected to their struggles to rein in out-of-control eating through a series of unsuccessful strategies. In all cases, as their problems worsened, these sufferers were left riddled with guilt, shame, and conflict.

Children are gravely affected by obesity and attention deficits as a result of poor food choices. My work opened up questions regarding children who feel something is terribly wrong in their relationships with food and their preoccupations with food and/or body weight. Educating children and parents in a clinical setting might provide a step toward preventing a lifelong struggle with addictive eating.

Purpose of the Study

The initial purpose of my study was to explore the internal spiritual experience of food addicts actively implementing a Twelve Step program. As time wore on, I realized that the tones and shadings from my having gathered actual patient's experiences with compulsive eating over the past 20 years of private practice added a dimension that reinforced and complemented the data I'd gained from the original study. My mission was to have a better understanding of food addiction and to identify the essential themes and meanings of the participants' experiences, hoping for the advancement of treatment and prevention.

My investigation aimed to uncover some of the ways food addiction impacts the spiritual, emotional, and physical realities shared by me and others, as explored through our reflection, examination, sifting, and clarification of the phenomena. I think of recovery as it relates to a three-legged stool. Together, each leg represents the foundation of healing: spiritual, emotional, and physical. An individual who ignores one of the legs of this foundation is at risk of weakening the support of the healing process.

Personal Motivation

The research question. *What is the experience of spiritual recovery from food addiction?* had been a preoccupation of mine since the age of 13, when the personal experience of food addiction became evident to me. Although I didn't know at the time that this disease had a name, I knew the obsessive-compulsion in the realm of weight and food wasn't normal. Once an underweight little girl, I soon became 100 pounds heavier, and the compulsion to eat specific trigger foods flurried out of my control.

I spent uninterrupted hours, binge eating more than 1,500 calories in one sitting between meals when I wasn't particularly hungry, and I binged more days in the week than not. I always ate my food quickly in isolation, followed by the negative chatter in my mind abusing me—shame inevitably taking hold. I was worthless. And in reality I was in big trouble. I had an undetected eating disorder!

As far as eating disorders go, anorexia and bulimia no doubt get the most media attention. But it turns out that binge eating is the most common. In my 20-plus years working in a clinician capacity with eating disorders, I've found that binge eating disorder occurs in 80 percent of my patients, whereas anorexia and bulimia occur in 25 percent and 30 percent, respectively.

What's really worrisome, in addition to the excess weight that often follows binge eating, this obesity is associated with, or is a precursor to a deluge of serious diseases, including type 2 diabetes, cardiovascular disease, stroke, and certain cancers (Fairburn & Brownell, 2002).

Although deeply frightening, this news doesn't scare the food addict out of his or her pathology. All that those in active addiction can think about is the coming binge—not the consequences. As noted elsewhere in this book, my own mom passed away prematurely because of chronic obesity.

She was only 67. She suffered a massive stroke at the age of 62, a few weeks short of her 63rd birthday. I believe her top weight was well over 375 pounds. She stood five foot four inches. Her saga gave rise to my own developing story. My life was starting to shadow her life in many ways. And because of this sad state of affairs, I arrived at the topic of my dissertation.

Our stories of food addiction shared in this book are just the tip of an iceberg of stories that need to be told, souls who need to be healed, and bodies that must be restored to optimal health as our Divine Source intended. As a result of my compulsive eating, it was inevitable I'd be at risk of severe obesity, which put me at a greater risk of obesity-related problems such as heart disease, diabetes, liver disease, and possible colon cancer—with the enormous amounts of foods passing through my digestive tract, not intended to process foods at such a drastic rate. As I neared 235 pounds on my five-foot, six-inch frame, I knew I was in deep trouble in every respect.

Today, my weight ranges between 133 and 137 pounds. I went from dire obesity to a weight considered normal for my height. My motivation for starting the dissertation was to bring hope to the many that fight this insidious disease every breathing moment of their lives.

Discovery

The aim of my exploration was discovery, with recovery for self and others in the spiritual, emotional, and physical realm as the ultimate goal. Because the arena being researched was the daily struggles of the food addict, I felt it necessary to individualize each lived experience. For this reason, I believed the method of collecting and analyzing the data had to be qualitative in order to avoid the study being too far removed from what the respondents had undergone and risk losing the human shadings of their sets of circumstances.

The "heuristic" approach, or one based in understanding from a more human, intuitive point of view, seemed best suited for my research, as it offered me a means of collecting and analyzing my own process along with those of each person studied for this project—and at the same time minimizing the interruption of that individual progression.

I thus gathered the descriptions of various aspects of the typical course of a food addiction disease from first-person accounts through formal and informal conversations and interviews. Most important, I felt, was that I, too, had a personal experience with and an intense interest in the experience studied, and that the seven other persons in the study also shared a passion for detailing and understanding the development of spiritual recovery.

The research question was built from determination and a readiness to discover a fundamental truth.

My quest led to an understanding about human existence and behavior. It was a personal opportunity to explain the lived process of spiritual recovery and added the most insight possible into understanding phenomena related to the disease of food addiction.

The intent of this investigation was to immerse myself in the journey of spiritual awakening via the lived experience of recovering from compulsive eating disorders. One of the key ingredients of my study was that I (along with the other participants) had personally gone through the realms of occurrences under study and brought intense interest and ardent involvement to the topic. As Moustakas and Douglass (1985) state, "In its purest form, heuristics is a passionate and discerning personal involvement in problem solving, an effort to know the essence of some aspect of life through the internal pathways of the self." (p. 39)

My goal has been to awaken and inspire others so that they may respect and make a connection with their own personal questions and problems in this area. My wish here is for you, too, to tap into your own private questions and concerns that arise from your daily struggle with food and spirituality.

Despite tape recorders, the informal, conversational atmosphere I established encouraged dialogue consistent with the rhythm and flow of talk in search for meaning. My interviews with participants elaborated each person's lived understanding of his/her own spiritual recovery: how the effort affected personal behaviors, and what struggles, if any, the food addict experienced internally. I suggested that each of us keep a journal prior to the interview as a way to reflect on the inquiry and a way to collect meaningful data.

I avoided sharing my personal accounts with the interviewees in order to ward off any influence on their responses, and to stay on task, which was to obtain and clarify their stories. Having participants remain fully present and open to their experiences throughout the interviews was a continuous challenge for me. The interviews lasted from 48 minutes to two hours.

Once I left each interview, I immediately rested quietly with the new information, taking pertinent notes. I personally transcribed each interview in its entirety before conducting the next interview, so that I could remain one with the material and focus on what a specific person told me in an individual rather than collective and confusing way.

Recovery

The basic foundation of recovery is abstaining on a physical level from all mood-altering substances. Abstinence leads not only to the beginning healing stages, but also to a total recovery from food addiction. Not eating any trigger foods whatsoever is a critical starting point to an individual's healing from food addiction, but recovery doesn't stop there at all. The spiritual and emotional components are keys as well.

Think of recovery as it relates to a three-legged stool. Together, each leg represents the foundation of healing: spiritual, emotional, and physical. An individual who ignores one of the legs of this foundation is at risk of weakening the support of the healing process. A strong recovery from food addiction stands on all three legs of this course of recuperation as it connects to each person's mental and social psyche, which is ever changing as each individual makes his way in a very personal journey through recovery.

I chose a Twelve Step program to begin my own recovery journey because it was the only approach I knew of that tapped into the spiritual and emotional and somewhat physical aspects of food addiction—with the focus on recovery not weight, a focus that somehow miraculously led to substantial weight loss. To be clear, prior to my entering the Twelve Step program, I'd previously lost nearly a hundred pounds through Weight Watchers, a company where I'd worked for 13 years.

Back then, in losing those one-hundred pounds, I'd white-knuckled my way through, between dieting and bingeing, but eventually began to regain weight, to the point of adding back 35 pounds. I was lacking my connection with the Creative Source and an emotional reconstruction; I strictly relied on diet mentality. The Twelve Step arena was a place for this shrink to hang her hat anonymously and find the help that I so desperately needed!

A Personal Thought

For many decades I made daily entries in journals of my life and included stories that ranged from details of my bouts of binge eating to incidents involving my spiritual recovery. The opportunity to explore the experience from a personal perspective while conducting this study from a professional perspective has given me a richer understanding of the recovery process. My own spirituality and recovery from addictive eating has enhanced new ways of accepting my means of living in my world and of understanding that this *is* my life—living vigilant, ever awake and alert, abstaining from trigger foods, in constant search of spiritual growth.

The interview process is no doubt a high point in the work I've done that founded the dissertation and breathed life into *Release Your Obsession with Food: Heal from the Inside Out.* I had an instant bond with all of the interviewees and I identified with their intimate and personal trials from pre-recovery to spiritual recovery. In addition, adding my patient experience from a twenty-year-span resource pool enhanced my understanding and connection to recovery from the obsession with food.

While I worked on the initial gathering and digestion of information for the dissertation—and ultimately, *Release Your Obsession with Food,* I took several long weekend retreats in the sleepy little town of Madeira Beach, Florida and stayed at my family beach house—filled with childhood memories of losses and new beginnings, tears and laughter, binges and diets. I took long walks along the seashore, steeped in self-reflection over what I'd discovered from my research and from re-reading personal accounts of the various stages of my eating disorder, both in full bloom and in recovery.

The full nature, essence, and meaning of what I pondered brought me to a new understanding of spiritual recovery from food addiction. No longer do I frantically reach for addictive foods, eating beyond "normal" human consumption. I view myself through a new lens entirely, eating scheduled, portioned meals four times a day, enabling a shift from self-absorption about what I ate or will eat to authenticity, self-efficacy, and wellbeing. I discovered beneath the thick folds of my addiction, a free-spirited person embracing life on all fronts and living my best life possible.

Please feel free to contact me at drlisaort@weightcontroltherapy.com. I'd love to hear from you and learn from your experiences. Also, come join me on facebook http://www.facebook.com/Dr.LisaOrtigaraCrego, Twitter https://twitter.com/Drlisaort and visit my website to see what I'm doing, what I've written and where I'm speaking.

Acknowledgements

The completion of a work such as a dissertation turned book is never the product of a single person alone, but rests on the merit of many contributors. I express my deepest gratitude and appreciation to my husband and best friend Joseph Vincent Crego, who tirelessly supports my dreams and continues to be the wind beneath my wings in all my endeavors. I am filled with love and appreciation for both my sons Benjamin and Kris Crego, who remained my constant cheerleaders from day one, even if it meant foregoing the computer when they were younger. I also acknowledge my father Benjamin Ortigara for his support with daily e-mails encouraging me to march forward, no matter what. Although my mom Joan Ortigara is no longer with us on the physical plane, I acknowledge her faith in me and feel her *presence* throughout this journey. A special hug goes to my sister Michelle Boucek whose unwavered aid never ceased. I also acknowledge my best friend Yvonne Farr Olson (she died way before her time) who believed in me long before I ever believed in myself. And no book can sing without a great editor—thank you Miki Hayden you are a miracle worker…and an amazing friend.

My heartfelt gratitude belongs to all the anonymous interviewees who agreed to be part of this project, which would not have been possible without the willingness of each and every person who openly and honestly shared their personal experiences with me. I thank all of you for placing your trust in me and opening your hearts.

Last, thank you patients for all you continue to teach me. I dedicate this book to you and all who suffer from an obsession with food.

Bibliography

Allison, D.B., Fontaine, K.R., Manson, J. E., Stevens, J., & VanItallie, T. B. (1999).
Annual deaths attributable to obesity in the United States. *Journal of the American Medical Association, 282,* 1530-1538.

American Association of Pastoral Counselors. (2006). *American association of pastoral counselors and the Samaritan institute report.* Retrieved on January 15, 2006
http://www.aapc.org/survey.htm

American Obesity Association. (2002). *What is obesity?* Retrieved on November 11, 2005, http://www.obesity.org/

American Psychiatric Association. (2000). *Diagnostic and statistical manual of mental disorder* (DSM-IV-TR: 4th ed.). Washington DC: Author.

American Psychiatric Association. (1994). *Diagnostic and statistical manual of mental disorders* (4th ed.). Washington DC: Author.

Anderson, D. A. & Paulosky, C.A. (2004). Psychological assessment of eating disorders and related features, In Thompson, K. (Ed). *Handbook of Eating Disorders and Obesity, 6* (2), 112-129. New York: John Wiley & Sons, Inc.

Andrew J.G., Gold, M., Yijun, L. (2004). Interaction of satiety and reward response to food Stimulation. *Journal of Addictive Diseases, 23* (3), 23-37.

Becker, A.E., Keel, P., Anderson-Fye, E.P., & Thomas, J.J. (2004). Genes and/or jeans? Genetic and socio-cultural contributions to risk for eating disorders. *Hawthorn Press, Inc., 23, 3-7.*

Bensley, D.A. (1998). *Critical thinking in psychology: A unified skills approach.* Pacific Grove, CA: Brooks and Cole Publishing Company.

Berkus, V. (2003). America's compulsion: Food addiction. *Counselor: The Magazine for Addiction Professionals, 4* (3), 51-57.

Bowden, J. (1998). Recovery from alcoholism: A spiritual journey. *Issues in Mental Health Nursing, 19* (1), 337-352.

Brantlinger, E., Jimenez, R., Klingner, J., Pugach, M., & Richardson, V. (2005). Qualitative studies in special education. *Exceptional Children, 71*(2), 195-207.

Brown, S. (1985). *Treating the alcoholic: A developmental model of recovery.* New York: John Wiley & Sons.

Bullitt-Jonas, M. (2000). *Holy hunger.* New York: Vintage Books, a Division of Random House, Inc.

Bunnell, D. (2004). The "new" eating disorder. *A Professional Journal of the Renfrew Center Foundation Perspective.*

Camic, P.M., Rhodes, J.E., & Yardley, L. (Eds.) (2003). *Qualitative research in psychology: Expanding perspectives in methodology and design.*

Washington, DC: American Psychological Association.

Carroll, B. (2001). A phenomenological exploration of the nature of spirituality and spiritual care. *Mortality, 6* (1), 81-98.

Chapkis, K. L. (2002). An heuristic investigation of the body image experience of spiritual feminists. *Dissertation Abstract International, 63 (10), 4879B* (UMI No.3068732)

Choudhuri, D., Glausser, A., & Peregoy, J. (2004). Guidelines for writing a qualitative manuscript. *The Journal of Counseling & Development, 82* (4), 443-447.

Claire, W. (1999). Gender, adolescence and the management of diabetes. *Journal of Advanced Nursing, 30* (5), 1160-1166.

Compulsion. (n.d.). *Dictionary.com Unabridged (v 1.1).* Retrieved January 16, 2008, from Dictionary.com website: http://dictionary.reference.com/browse/compulsion

Cox, B. (1995). Belief versus faith. *American Psychologist, 50* (7), 541.

Craig, E. (1978). The heart of the teacher: An heuristic study of the Inner world of teaching. (Doctoral dissertation Boston University, 1978). *Dissertation Abstracts International, 38*, 7222A.

Creswell, J.W. & Miller, D.L (2000). Determining validity in qualitative inquiry. *Theory into Practice,* 39 (3), 124-131.

Cummins, S., Parham, E.S., & Strain, G. W. (2002). Weight management: Position of the American Dietetics Association. *Journal of the American Dietetics Association, 102*, 1145-1155.

Cushman, W.H., & Rosenberg, D.J. (1991). *Human factors in product design.* Amsterdam:Elsevier.

Davis N. L., Clance, P. R. & Gallis, A. T., (1999). Treatment approaches for obese and overweight African American women: A consideration of cultural dimensions. *Psychotherapy: Theory, Research, Practice, Training, 36* (1), 27-35

Dyer, W. (2012). *Wishes fulfilled: Mastering the art of manifestation.* Indiana: Hay House Publishers

Dyer, W. (2007). *Change your thoughts—Change your life.* Indiana: Hay House Publishers

Dyer, W. (1992). *Real magic: Creating miracles in everyday life.* New York, NY: Harper Collins Publishers

Dilthey, W. (1985). *Poetry and experience. Selected works* (Vol. V). Princeton, NJ: Princeton University Press.

Douglass, B. G., & Moustakas, C. (1985). Heuristic Inquiry: The internal search to know. *The Journal of Humanistic Psychology, 25*, 39-55.

Eating Disorder Referral and Information Center (2003). Retrieved on February 15, 2004, from http://www.edreferral.com/

Ericson Phyllis (1996). "Journey of the soul…The emerging self" …from dis-ease to discovery." *Dissertation Abstracts International, 58 (8),* 4579B (UMI No. 9542654).

Fade, S. (2003). Communicating and judging the quality of qualitative research: The need for new language. *The British Diabetic Association, Ltd, 16,* 139-149.

Fairburn, C., & Brownell, K. (2002). *Eating disorders and obesity.* New York: Guilford Press.

Fairburn, C. G. & Wilson, G. T. (1993). Binge eating: Definition and classification, In C. G. Fairburn & Wilson (Eds.). *Binge eating: Nature, assessment and treatment,* 3-14. New York: Guilford Press.

First, M.B. & Tasman, A. (2004). *DSM-IV-TR Mental disorders: Diagnosis, etiology & treatment.* New York: John Wiley & Sons, Ltd.

Flegal, K.M., Carroll, M.D., Odgen, C.L., & Johnson, C. L. (2002). Prevalence and trends in obesity among, U.S. adults, 1999-2000. *Journal of the American Medical Association, 288,* 1723-1727.

Food Addicts Anonymous (2005). Retrieved on October 17, 2005: http://www.foodaddictsanonymous.org/

Food Addicts Anonymous World Services (2001). *Food addicts anonymous: The twelve- steps and twelve traditions to recovery* (4th ed.). West Palm Beach, FL: Author

Food Addicts Anonymous World Services (2002). *Food addicts anonymous.* West Palm Beach, FL: Author.

Food Addicts Anonymous (2005). Retrieved on October 17, 2005: http://www.foodaddictsanonymous.org/

Garner, D., & Garfinkel, P. (1997). *Handbook of treatment for eating disorders* (2nd ed.). New York: Guilford Press.

Gibran, K. (2010). *The prophet.* Printed in the USA

Gilo, C. M., Shiffman, S. & Wing, R. (1989). Relapse crises and coping among dieters. *Journal of consulting and Clinical Psychology, 57* (4), 488-495.

Gold, M. (2004). Eating disorders, overeating, and pathological attachment to food. *Journal of Addictive Diseases, 23* (3), 1-3.

Greeno, C., Wing, R. & Shiffman, S. (2000). Binge antecedents in obese women with and without binge eating disorder. *Journal of Consulting and Clinical Psychology, 68* (1), 95-102.

Guba, E.G. & Lincoln, Y.S. (1989) *Fourth generation evaluation.* Newbury Park, CA: Sage.

Haddock, K. & Dill, P. (2000). The effects of food and mood and behavior: Implications for the addictions model of obesity and eating disorders. *Hawthorne Press Inc., 15* (1), 17-47.

Hardman, R.K., Berrett, M. E., Richards, P.S. (2003). Spirituality and ten false beliefs and pursuits of women with eating disorders: Implications for Counselors. *Counseling and Values, 48* (1), 67-78.

Hiles, D. (2002). Narrative and heuristic approaches to transpersonal research and practice. CCPE, London.

Jaffe, M.L. (1998). *Adolescence.* New York: John Wiley & Sons Inc. Johnson, C.L., Sansone, R.A. (1993). Integrating the Twelve Step approach with traditional psychotherapy for the treatment of eating disorders. *International*

Journal of Eating Disorders, 14 (2), 121-134 Jones, S. L. (1994). A constructive relationship for religion with the science and profession of psychology: Perhaps the boldest model yet. *American Psychologist,* 49, 184-189.

Jourard, S. (1971). *The transparent self.* New York: D. Van Nostrand Co. Kalra, S. P. & Kalra, P. S. (2004). Overlapping and interactive pathways regulating appetite and craving. *Haworth Press Inc., 23* (3), 5-21.

Kathrine, A. (1996). *Anatomy of a food addiction: The brain chemistry of overeating.* Carlsbad, CA: Gurze Books.

Kidd, S. (2002). The role of qualitative research in psychological Journals. *Psychological Methods,* 7 (1), 126-138.

Kleiner, K.D., Gold, M., Frost-Pineda, K., Lenz-Brunsman, B., Perri, M., & Jacobs, W. (2004). Body mass index and alcohol use. *The Haworth Press, 23* (3), 105-118.

Kuffel, F. (2004). *Passing for Thin: Losing half my weight and finding myself.* New York: Broadway Books: A Division of Random House, Inc.

Leedy, P. D. & Omrod, J. E. (2004). *Practical research: Planning and design* (8th ed). Upper Saddle River, NJ: Merrill Prentice Hall.

Lilenfeld, L. R., Kaye, W. H., Greeno, C. G., Merikangas, K. R., Plotnicov, K. & Pollice, C. (1998). A controlled family study of anorexia nervosa and bulimia nervosa: Psychiatric disorders in first-degree relatives and effects of proband comorbidity. *Archives of General Psychiatry, 55,* 603-610.

Marcus, M. (1997). Adapting treatment for patients with binge eating disorder. In Garner, D.M. & Garfinkle P.E. (Eds.), *Handbook of treatment for eating disorders,* (484- 493). New York: Guilford Press.

Marcus, M. (1993). Binge eating in obesity. In C.G. Fairburn & G.T. Wilson (Eds.), *Binge eating: Nature, assessment, and treatment* (pp. 77-96). New York: Guilford Press.

Marlatt, G. A., & Gordon, J. R. (1985). *Relapse prevention: maintenance strategies in the treatment of addictive behaviors.* New York: Guilford Press.

Mitchell, J.E., Specker, S. Edmonson, K. (1997). Management of substance abuse and dependence. In Garner, D.M. & Garfinkle P.E. (Eds.), *Handbook of treatment for eating disorders,*(415-423). New York: Guilford Press.

Moustakas, C. (1990). *Heuristic research: Design, methodology, and applications.* Newbury Park, CA: Sage Publications.

National Center for Health Statistics. (2002). Prevalence of overweight among children and adolescents: United States, 1999-2000. Retrieved on October 16, 2005: http://www.cdc.gov/nchs/fastats/overwt.htm

National Institute of Mental Health. (2002). *Eating disorders. National Institute of Mental Health Publications.* Retrieved on October 16, 2005: http://www.nimh.nih.gov/publicat/eatingdisorder.cfm
Orford, J. (1985). *Excessive appetites: A psychological view of addictions.* New York: John Wiley.

Overeaters Anonymous (2004). Retrieved on October 17, 2005: http://www.overeatersanonymous.org/

Owens (P.G.) Women's experience of binge eating disorder. *Dissertation Abstracts International, 64 (9),* 2792 (A). (UMI No. 3103339).

Parham, E.S. (1996). Compulsive eating: Applying a medical addiction model. In Vanltalle, T.B. & Simopoulos, A.P. (Eds), *Obesity: New directions in assessment and management.* Philadelphia, PA: The Charles Press Publications.

Patton, M.Q. (1997). *Utilization-focused evaluation: The new century text* (3rd ed.). Thousand Oaks, CA: Sage.

Patton, M. Q. (2002). *Qualitative evaluation and research methods* (3rd ed.). Newbury Park, CA: Sage.

Peeke, P. (2012). *The hunger fix: The three-stage detox and recovery plan for over eating and food addiction.* New York, NY: Rodale Press, Inc.

Polanyi, M. (1966). *The tacit dimension.* Garden City, NY: Doubleday.

Polanyi, M. (1962). *Personal knowledge.* Chicago: University of Chicago Press.

Pressfield, S. (2002*). The war of art: Break through the blocks and win your inner creative battles.* New York, NY: Warner Books, Inc.

Progoff, I. (1975). *At a journal workshop.* New York: Dialogue House Library.

Ranson, K., McGue, M. Iacono, W. (2003). Disordered eating and substance use in an epidemiologic. *Psychology of Addictive Behaviors, 17 (3),* 193-202.

Ratliffe, C.A. (1997). The experience of gaining control over compulsive eating: An heuristic investigation. *Dissertation Abstracts International, 58 (2),* 987B (UMI No. 9721712).

Rennie, D., Watson, K., & Monteiro, A. (2002). The rise of qualitative research in psychology. *Canadian Psychology, 43* (3), 179-189.

Robson, C. (2002). *Real-world research: A resource for social scientists and practitioner- researchers* (2nd ed.). Cambridge, MA: Blackwell.

Rogers, P., Bristol, U., & Smit, H. (2000). Food craving and food "addiction": A critical review of the evidence from a psychosocial perspective. *Pharmacology, Biochemistry & Behavior, 66 (1),* 3-14.

Schonberg, L.E. (1998). The experience of recovering from an eating disorder while parenting. *Masters Abstracts International, 37* (1), 369 (UMI No. 1391846).

Shank, G. (2002). *Qualitative research: A personal skills approach.* Upper Saddle River, NJ: Pearson Education.

Sheppard, K. (2000). *From the first bite: A complete guide to recovery from food addiction.* Deerfield Beach, FL: Health Communications Inc.

Sheppard, K. (1993). *Food addiction: The body knows.* Deerfield Beach, Fl. Health Communications Inc.

St. King, J.A. (1999). What is the experience of being in an obsessive relationship with a specific food? *Dissertation Abstracts International, 60 (2),* 844B (UMI No. 9919751).

Stoltz, S. (1984). Recovering from foodaholism. *Journal for Specialists in Group Work, 9* (1), 51-61.

Tashakkori, A. & Teddlie, C. (1998). *Mixed methodology.* London: Sage Publications.

Taylor Smith, F., Hardman, R.K., Richards, P.S., & Fischer, L. (2003). Intrinsic religiousness and spiritual well-being as predictors of treatment outcome among women with eating disorders. *Eating Disorders, 11* (1), 15-26.

Thornton, L. (2005). The model of whole person healing: Creating and sustaining a healing environment. *Holistic Nurse Practitioner, 19* (3), 106-115.

Thompson, K. (2004). *Handbook eating disorders and obesity.* New York: John Wiley & Sons, Inc.

Tolle, E. (2004). *The Power of now: A guide to spiritual enlightenment.* Vancouver, B.C., Canada: Namaste Publishing University of South Florida College of Medicine and Academy for Eating Disorders. (2003). Recognizing the connection: Eating disorders and Obesity. *Health Learning Systems, 1* (2), 1-8.

Vieten, C., Amorok, T., & Schlitz, M. (2005). Many paths, one mountain: A cross-traditional model of spiritual

transformation. *Institute of Noetic Science.* Retrieved on September 13, 2005:
http://www.metanexus.net/conference2005/pdf/vieten.pdf

Wadden, T., Brownell, K., & Foster, G. (2002). Obesity: Responding to the global epidemic. *Journal of Consulting and Clinical Psychology,* 70 (3), 510-525.

Walsh-Bowers (2002). Constructing qualitative knowledge in psychology: students and faculty negotiate the social context of inquiry. *Canadian Psychology, 43* (3), 163-178.

Walters, G. (1996). Addiction and identity: Exploring the possibility of a relationship. *Psychology of Addiction Behaviors, 10* (1), 9-17.

Wang, G.J., Volkow, N.D Thanos, P.K., Fowler J.S. (2004). Similarity between obesity and drug addiction as assessed by neurofunctional imaging:A concept review. *Journal of Addictive Diseases, 23* (2), 39-53.

Wayman, L.M., Gaydos, H. L. (2005). Self-transcending through suffering. *Journal of Hospice & Palliative Nursing, 7* (5), 263-270.

Weiss, B. & Weiss, A. (2012). *Miracles happen: The transformational healing.* New York, NY: Harper Collins Publishers

Wilson, G.T. (1993). Binge eating and addictive disorder. *In C.G. Fairburn & G.T. Wilson (Eds.) Binge eating: Nature, assessment and treatment.* New York: Guilford Press.

Wilson, G.T. (1995). Psychological treatment of binge eating and bulimia nervosa. *Journal of Mental Health, 4* (5), 451-458.

Wilson, G.T. (1999). Eating disorders and addiction. *Drugs & Society, 15* (2), 87-101.

Wilson, G.T., Fairburn, C., Agras, W., Walsh, B., & Kraemer, H. (2002). Cognitive-behavioral therapy for bulimia nervosa: Time course and mechanisms of change. *Journal of Consulting and Clinical Psychology, 70* (2), 267-274.

Wilson, T., Vitousek, K., & Loeb, K. (2000). Stepped care treatment for eating disorders. *Journal of Clinical Psychology, 68* (4), 564-572.

Wolfe, W. L., & Maisto, S. A. (2000). The relationship between eating disorders and substance use: Moving beyond co-prevalence research. *Clinical Psychology Review, 20,* 617-631.

Wonderlich, S. A., & Mitchell, J. E. (1997). Eating disorders and comorbidity: Empirical, conceptual, and clinical implications. *Psychopharmacology Bulletin, 33,* 381-390.

Woodside D.B., Field L.L., Garfinkel, P.E., Heinmaa, M. (1998). Specificity of eating disorders diagnosis in families of probands with anorexia nervosa and bulimia nervosa. *Comprehensive Psychiatry, 39,* 261-64.

Wurtman, J. & Frusztajer, N. (2006). *The serotonin power diet: Eat carbs—Nature's own appetite—to stop emotional overeating and halt antidepressant-associated weight gain.* New York, NY: Rodale Inc.

Dr. Lisa Ortigara Crego

About the Author

Dr. Ortigara Crego a clinical psychotherapist, addiction psychologist and Visiting Professor in private practice worked in the field of eating disorders for well over two and a half decades. She earned a doctorate in addiction psychology, a master's degree in social work with the emphasis on mental health, and is certified as an eating disorder specialist, masters certified addiction professional and licensed national Board Certified Clinical Hypnotherapist. She worked in the weight loss industry for well over two decades. She speaks around the country on recovery from compulsive eating utilizing spiritual and mind healing. Dr. Lisa contributed several chapters in Sage publications and runs a blog which is found at Weightcontroltherapy.com.

Professional membership organization affiliations: The National Association of Social Workers, the National Board for Certified Clinical Hypnotherapists, the International Association of Eating Disorder Professionals, and the American Psychological Association.

Notes

CPSIA information can be obtained
at www.ICGtesting.com
Printed in the USA
LVHW011341261118
598272LV00002B/105/P